Older people's mental health today:
a handbook

Edited by Toby Williamson

Mental **Health** Foundation

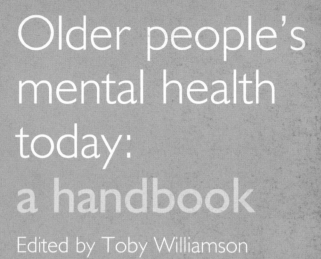

OLM-Pavilion

Contents

eople's
health

ook

illiamson

WITHDRAWN

Mental **Health** Foundation

OLM-Pavilion

Older People's Mental Health Today: A handbook

© OLM-Pavilion/Mental Health Foundation 2009

The authors have asserted their right in accordance with the *Copyright, Designs and Patents Act 1988* to be identified as the authors of this work.

Published by:
OLM-Pavilion
Richmond House
Richmond Road
Brighton
BN2 3RL
Tel: 01273 623222
Fax: 01273 625526
Email: info@pavpub.com

First published 2009.

A catalogue record for this book is available from the British Library.

ISBN: 978 1 84196 247 4

OLM-Pavilion is the leading training and development provider and publisher in the health, social care and allied fields, providing a range of innovative training solutions underpinned by sound research and professional values. We aim to put our customers first, through excellent customer service and good value.

Editor: Toby Williamson
Production editor: Kerry Boettcher
Artwork: Hayley Coleman
Cover design, page layout and typesetting: Emma Garbutt
Printing: Ashford Press

Contributors

Ruth Bartlett is a senior lecturer in dementia studies at the University of Bradford. She is co-ordinator of the BSc in Dementia Studies and teaches on the Msc in Dementia Studies. She has a professional background in mental health nursing, and worked with people with dementia in a range of acute and social care settings. Ruth gained a BA (Hons) in Politics and MA in Cultural Politics at the University of East Anglia and a PhD in Sociology at Oxford Brookes University. Her doctorate explored meanings of social exclusion in relation to people with dementia in care homes and she has publications on personal experiences of social exclusion/inclusion and the concept of citizenship. Ruth was recently awarded a First Grant by the UK Economic and Social Research Council to explore the campaign activities of people with dementia.

Lesley Carter trained as a registered nurse in the 1970s specialising in acute and forensic psychiatry and later care of the elderly. Lesley has held various operational, management and director roles. As lead nurse for West Sussex, Lesley focused on improving training and standards of care across mental health. During this time, Lesley also was a visiting lecturer in nursing at Brighton University. In 2005, Lesley moved to the Department of Health, initially working at the London Development Centre, where she undertook a project with the King's Fund. Lesley later extended her work within the Care Services Improvement Partnership, moving her focus from operational delivery to supporting policy development and translating that policy into manageable pieces that could be better delivered to organisations. Lesley has written a number of articles and tools to support policy implementation. Currently, Lesley is seconded into the Department of Health working with the regional deputy director and the public health team, leading the regional implementation of the National Dementia Strategy and as a resource to further promote the spread of dignity in care across the capital.

David Crepaz-Keay is head of patient and public involvement for the Mental Health Foundation, that undertakes research, develops services, designs training, influences policy and raises public awareness to help people survive, recover from and prevent mental distress. He is leading the development, delivery and evaluation of 60 self-management courses for people with a severe psychiatric diagnosis across Wales. Prior to this, he was chief executive of Mental Health Media, an organisation that challenges discrimination and exclusion of people with a psychiatric label. David is an eloquent and passionate campaigner against discrimination on the grounds of mental health history. With over 25 years of involvement, first as a user of mental health services, and later as a campaigner, writer and lecturer, he is also a strong advocate of service user voices being included in mental health service planning and delivery. David was a commissioner for the Commission Patient and Public Involvement in Health (CPPIH) (January 2003–August 2007). The Commission was created to give the public a voice in decisions that affect their health. He was a founder member of the newly established English national survivor user network (NSUN). David is a former civil servant, who wrote economic models at HM Treasury and is currently undertaking a doctorate in promoting effective mental health service user involvement at Middlesex University.

Jane Gilliard is a qualified social worker who has worked with and for people with dementia for over 20 years. She established Dementia Voice, the dementia services development centre for the south west and was its director from 1997 to 2005. She was the chair of the National Network of

Dementia Services Development Centres and has been involved in many key national working groups in dementia care. Jane was a member of the working group that developed the National Dementia Strategy, and is now the National Programme Manager for supporting the implementation of the Strategy. Jane is a visiting professor at the University of the West of England, Bristol.

Mary Godfrey is a senior research fellow at Leeds Institute of Health Sciences within the University of Leeds. Her interests include prevention, the experience of ageing, illness, recovery, mental health and well-being in later life. Her work spans research in partnership with older people on quality of life and unmet needs, and the organisation, delivery and outcomes, of services across health and social care. Her published work includes, *Building a Good Life for Older People in Local Communities* based on participatory research with older people around quality of life and its translation into service strategies (Joseph Rowntree Foundation, 2004); *Depression and Older People: Toward securing well-being in later life* (Policy Press, 2005); and *Prevention and Service Provision: Mental health problems in later life* (www. mhilli.org) for the Inquiry into Later Life Mental Health. Current and recently completed research includes an evaluation of intermediate care, a comparative study of reimbursement and delayed discharge policy, implementation and outcomes for older people in England and Scotland, and an evaluation of Leeds Partnership for Older People's Pilot (POPP) focused on service innovations for older people with mental health problems.

Lisa Haywood provides a unique approach to mental health issues, which has evolved from 20 years of executive and non-executive work at senior level combined with her own personal experience. Among other achievements she ran a charity for six years, doubling the income and increasing staff and volunteers by a third. She was vice chair of national Mind for 12 years, chairing their policies committee, which provided an overview of the parliamentary, legal and policy work. From 2005 to the present as the senior consultant with Haywood Consultancy, her work has broadened out to include interim and project management; supervision and coaching of chief executives and senior trustees in such diverse organisations as Age Concern, Mind and Greenpeace; and service reviews. She has been a Mental Health Act Tribunal member since 2006. Everything she does is coloured by her deep commitment to the participation of service users with an emphasis on self-direction and personal autonomy. She has a particular strength in the development of service user involvement structures in both statutory and voluntary organisations and clients have included the Royal College of Psychiatrists, Haringey Primary Care Trust and the National Survivor User Network.

Philip Hurst works for Age Concern England and Help the Aged in a role that combines influencing national health policy with interpreting policy on health services as it relates to older people. Key priorities in mental health have included arguing for a clearer understanding of age equality in both policy and practice, campaigning for improvements in the diagnosis and treatment of depression in older people, and contributing to the work of the special interest group on older people in the programme to improve access to psychological therapies. Philip was a member of the secretariat for the Independent UK Inquiry into Mental Health and Well-being in Later Life and served on the external reference group for the development of the National Dementia Strategy.

Catherine Jackson was editor of the monthly magazine *Mental Health Today* from its launch in 2000 to 2008. She co-edited the companion Pavilion handbooks *Mental Health Today* and *Child and Adolescent Mental Health Today*. She is currently managing editor of *Bereavement Care* journal and a consultant editor, researcher and journalist.

Drew Lindon is the policy and development manager for The Princess Royal Trust for Carers. Drew is their national lead on mental health and substance misuse issues, developing strategy and partnerships nationally in these areas, and has written for a range of press publications in the past. He works closely with The Princess Royal Trust for Carers' network of independent carers centres, The Royal College of Psychiatrists, and The Mental Health Foundation amongst other organisations. Drew is also a member of the All Party Parliamentary Group on Mental Health. In addition, Drew has worked extensively with carers for people with mental health problems in local settings, managing the Mental Health Carers Project at Hammersmith and Fulham Carers Centre from late 2004 to mid 2007. Drew has always had a keen interest in mental health and the support of both service users and carers. This was further encouraged by his experiences volunteering for York Nightline, as well as his work for the North and East Yorkshire and Northern Lincolnshire Strategic Health Authority. Drew lives and works in London.

Jill Manthorpe is professor of social work and director of the Social Care Workforce Research Unit at King's College London. She has particular interest in support for older people from social care and other sources. She has completed research into dementia services and services for older people, as well as work on mental capacity and decision-making, elder abuse, individual budgets, inter-professional care and strategies for older people from minority ethnic groups. Current work includes studies of the diagnosis processes related to dementia, international workers in social care, support workers, self-directed support, and adult safeguarding developments related to the Mental Capacity Act (2005). She was a member of the NICE clinical guidelines dementia group and of the programme board for the Department of Health's *No Secrets* review. She has published widely on social work, dementia care and adult safeguarding and risk.

Andrew McCulloch has been chief executive of the Mental Health Foundation for six years. Prior to his appointment, Andrew was director of policy at The Sainsbury Centre for Mental Health for six years, where he established a reputation as a leading authority on mental health policy. He was formerly a senior civil servant in the Department of Health for 16 years and was responsible for mental health and learning disabilities policy from 1992 to 1996. He has spoken and published widely on mental health issues. Andrew's other experience has included being a school governor, the non-executive director of an NHS trust, and the chair of mental health media. He has chaired or served on a range of national advisory committees and is mental health adviser to the National Endowment for Science, Technology and the Arts. He has a PhD in Psychology from the University of Southampton and has a special interest in life span developmental psychology and adjustment to later life. He has sought to draw attention to the importance of social change in an individual's psychological adjustment in old age.

Alisoun Milne has worked at the University of Kent for over 12 years. She is currently a senior lecturer at the Tizard Centre in the University of Kent's School of Social Policy, Sociology and Social Research. Prior to this, she was a research fellow at the Personal Social Services Research Unit and has an extensive background in social work and social work management. Her key research interests are mental health in later life, older carers, carers of people with dementia, and early diagnosis of dementia. Recent research projects include, GP attitudes to early diagnosis of dementia, a review of dementia screening instruments, a study of barriers to employment for carers, and an evaluation of an intermediate care service for people with dementia. Alisoun regularly contributes to the development of training and guidance materials, for example, the Social Care Institute for Excellence e-learning resource *An Introduction to Mental Health of Older People*. She is a member of a number of national and local advisory groups – including the South East Dementia Collaborative Oversight Group, and has published widely for academic and practitioner audiences.

Jane Minter is head of corporate policy and strategy at Housing 21, which is a major, specialist, not for profit, provider of housing, care, support and dementia services for older people. She was previously seconded to the Department of Health promoting the role of housing in health and care for older people. She has worked for Housing Associations' Charitable Trust, the National Housing Federation and Age Concern England in the field of older people's housing. She began her career working in the Citizen's Advice Bureau Service in South London. She was a board member of the Elderly Accommodation Counsel until recently and was on the board of the Age Concern sponsored UK Inquiry into Mental Health in Later Life, which reported last year. She is a member of the Communities and Local Government and Department of Health Housing for Older People Development Group, working to see the strategy for housing in an ageing society implemented.

Bridget Penhale is currently reader in gerontology at the University of Sheffield. She has a first degree in Psychology, and has been qualified as a social worker since 1981. Bridget has specialised in work with older people since 1983, and has worked in urban, rural and city areas in addition to hospitals. After a successful career as a social worker and manager spanning 15 years, she took up an academic post at the University of Hull in 1996, moving to Sheffield in 2004. She is past chair of the British Association of Social Workers Community Care Sub-Committee, and former vice-chair of Action on Elder Abuse. She is currently chair of the Hull Domestic Violence Forum. Bridget also participated in a number of projects with the Social Services Inspectorate of the Department of Health concerning elder abuse, the discharge of frail elderly people from hospital, and older people with dementia living in the community. Bridget is a board member of the International Network for the Prevention of Elder Abuse (INPEA). She has also published material on decision-making and mentally incapacitated adults, and extensively on elder abuse. Her research interests include elder abuse, adult protection, domestic violence, mental health of older people, bereavement in later life, health related social work and intergenerational relationships. She was the principal investigator of the recently completed Department of Health funded research project on adult protection (2004–2007) and provided project management to the UK study on elder abuse. Bridget is also currently involved in a number of other research projects on elder abuse and adult protection, including acting as academic co-ordinator for the RIPfA Change Project on Adult Protection. She is recognised nationally for her work on adult protection and internationally for her work on elder abuse.

Aparna Prasanna is currently training to be an old age psychiatrist in the UK. Born in India, she completed medical school gaining distinctions from Mysore University in 2001. Early on in her career in psychiatry, she became interested in the mental health of older people. She became a member of the Royal College of Psychiatrists in 2005. The assessment and management of distress in dementia has formed her core interest. Her other research interests have been in mental capacity and illness perception in dementia. Outside of work, she cherishes her time with her young family.

Kapila Ranasinghe was born in Sri Lanka and attended the University of Peradeniya. After completing primary medical training, Kapila sat for the postgraduate MD examination and then for the MD psychiatry. He was awarded the board certification as a consultant psychiatrist by the Postgraduate Institute of Medicine, University of Colombo in May 2005. After completing the training in Sri Lanka, Kapila was offered further training by the Royal College of Psychiatrists through the consultant assisted sponsorship scheme. Kapila trained as a specialist registrar in old age psychiatry with the Greenwich community mental health team, Oxleas NHS Trust and at the Southbrook Community Mental Health Centre, South London and Maudsley NHS Trust. Although very few postgraduate doctors return to their country of origin after completing training in the UK, Kapila returned to Sri Lanka to develop psychiatric services there. In October 2006 Kapila assumed duties as an acting consultant psychiatrist at the Angoda hospital. This is one of the biggest psychiatric facilities in south east Asia. Kapila started a plan with other consultant colleagues to improve the quality of care at the hospital. Kapila has also been conducting training programmes in old age psychiatry throughout Sri Lanka in collaboration with the Sri Lanka Alzheimer's Foundation. Kapila is a regular contributor to several journals and publications including regular weekly articles in the national women's newspaper *Rajina*. The articles are targeted at reducing the stigma associated with psychiatric illnesses and imparting knowledge to the general public. He also conducts TV and radio programmes with a view to improving the knowledge of psychiatric service users, their families and general public.

Lynne Read began her career in the NHS back in 1981. She started as an outpatient clerk. Following a six-month period working as a health care assistant, Lynne went on to train as an RMN and qualified in 1988. Throughout her career she has worked primarily in older people's mental health services in a series of senior clinical and management roles. Lynne was recently appointed clinical lead for Ealing older people's mental health service at West London Mental Health NHS Trust.

Kevin Sole is assistant operations director for acute and primary care services at North East London NHS Foundation Trust and the London Borough of Barking and Dagenham.

Adrian Treloar is consultant in old age psychiatry at Oxleas NHS Trust and visiting senior lecturer at the Institute of Psychiatry, London. In addition to being in charge of Medical Education for Oxleas NHSF Trust from 1999 to 2007, he produced research and helped to write national guidance on the ethics of covert administration of medicines. He has developed considerable expertise in the management of dementia through to death at home, and has lectured nationally and internationally on the palliative care of dementia, as well as delirium and the management of Parkinson's disease. He has pioneered advanced care of dementia at home, enabling several dozen patients to live at home until their death, and has both researched and developed understanding of how this can be achieved. He is currently working with the National Council for Palliative Care as a member of their cross cutting dementia working group. He co-authored their publication *Exploring the Palliative needs of Dementia*.

Jo Warner is a senior lecturer in social work at the University of Kent, having previously held lectureships in health and social care at The Open University and in applied social studies at Oxford. She has a background as a practitioner in community development and social work. Her main research interests include sociological approaches to risk, mental health and social welfare. Her work to date has focused on the way social work practice is constituted in relation to risk work and the impact of cultures of inquiry, fear and blame on professional practice, in general. More recently, she has begun exploring the risk-related concepts of stigma, vulnerability and trust, and how people negotiate 'everyday' risk and insecurity. She is guest editor (with Dr Elaine Sharland) of a forthcoming special issue of the *British Journal of Social Work* on risk and social work in 2010. Selected recent publications include: (2006) inquiry reports as active texts and their function in relation to professional practice in mental health. *Health, Risk and Society*, Vol. 8, No. 3, pp. 223–237; Warner J & Gabe J (2008) Risk, mental disorder and social work practice: a gendered landscape. *British Journal of Social Work* **38** (1) 117–134.

Toby Williamson works for the Mental Health Foundation, where he is currently responsible for the Foundation's older people's mental health programme. He has also been head of policy at the Foundation and managed its programme of research and development on adult mental health issues, with a strong focus on service user involvement. While working for the Foundation Toby was seconded to work in government to support the implementation of the Mental Capacity Act – as head of policy he co-chaired the Making Decisions Alliance, which successfully campaigned in support of the Act. Prior to working at the Foundation Toby worked in adult mental health services where he was involved in setting up, working in, and managing a variety of services in both statutory and non-statutory organisations for people with severe and enduring mental health problems living in the community. He has published a variety on older people's mental health, team working, user involvement, and attitudes and values, and has also designed and delivered training for multidisciplinary mental health teams based in the community. He has both personal and family experience of mental health difficulties, including dementia. For better or for worse, Toby has never acquired a formal mental health qualification although he does have a professional lorry driver's licence – but prefers cycling as a way of looking after his mental health.

Introduction

Toby Williamson

'Old age isn't so bad when you consider the alternative.' (Maurice Chevalier)

Introduction

We are all growing older. We also all have mental health, in the same way that we all have physical health. One in four of us will experience a problem with our mental health and this figure increases as people grow older, particularly beyond the age of 65. But mental health problems are not an inevitable part of growing old and many older people enjoy good mental health and well-being.

This handbook is for staff who work with older people in health and social care services, including the voluntary, independent, and housing sectors, who want to know more about mental health issues. It will also be of interest to students and anyone else who wants greater understanding of older people's mental health.

Each chapter is written by an expert in the field, including practitioners, academics, policy experts, people from the voluntary and housing sectors, and people who have used mental health services. **Part 1** looks at what keeps older people mentally well and healthy, together with relevant policies and legislation. **Part 2** looks at the different types of mental health problems and conditions that older people may experience, together with the types of services and care that are available.

Older people, mental health, and mental health problems

We are living in an ageing society. In the UK there are 10 million people over the age of 65 and this is set to increase by 50% over the next 10 years. The so-called 'baby boomers' who were born after World War II when the birth rate increased significantly are growing into their 60s. Many can expect to live much longer than their parents because of improvements in personal health, housing, health and social care services, and because of living in a more peaceful and prosperous society. They will also continue to be active contributors to society. But most will experience some deterioration in their physical health as they grow older and well over 25% of people over the age of 65 will experience a mental health problem like depression, or condition like dementia. This figure increases significantly as people get older. Many will require support and assistance to manage their physical and mental health. How this will be provided for growing numbers of people and who will pay for it remains unclear. Ensuring that an ageing population can continue to contribute by providing the right kind of support is as big a challenge for 21st century society as that posed by climate change. This handbook examines these issues, both from a 'whole population' perspective as well as looking at their impact in relation to older people who experience mental health problems and the services that they need.

Mental health and mental health problems

When discussing mental health for people of any age, language is important because people's understanding and use of words can change depending upon who they are and the context in which they are being used.

This handbook draws a clear distinction between 'mental health' and 'mental health problems'. It is only in the last 10 years or so that there has been significant attention paid to the concept of 'mental health' or 'mental well-being' as distinct from mental health 'problems', 'illness' or 'conditions'. This will be discussed in more detail but what is important is that good mental health or emotional well-being is not simply an absence of mental health problems, but a positive state of being for a person. This involves a combination of internal and external factors that enable the person to function in society, to their own satisfaction and broadly speaking, the satisfaction of others. **Part 1** of this book explores the mental health and well-being of older people in much more detail.

Mental health 'problems' on the other hand refer to the range of specific difficulties that people may experience with their mental health, over and above the usual range of human emotions that include sadness and anger as a normal reaction to an event or situation. Depression and anxiety are mental health problems that are commonly experienced by older people, although by no means are they an inevitable part of ageing. More serious problems, which many prefer to call mental illnesses, such as schizophrenia and bipolar disorder are much less common among older people but are still significant. The authors in **part 2** where these are discussed use different terms but there is a general recognition that whether one prefers 'problem' or 'illness' the mental health difficulties experienced by older people are the result of a combination of biological, psychological, emotional, individual, social and environmental factors and they may all need to be addressed to resolve the difficulties successfully.

Dementia, however, does not lend itself well to being described as a problem or illness. People who have been diagnosed with dementia, their families, and staff who work with them generally use the term 'disease' or 'condition'. Dementia is different from mental health problems such as depression or schizophrenia because it is organic, results in steady mental and physical deterioration, and currently the progression is largely untreatable. A term such as 'condition' seems very appropriate in that sense.

Unfortunately, 'mental health' has often been used or interpreted to mean 'mental illness' or 'mental health problems', and the term 'mental' is a somewhat tainted word, frequently used pejoratively. Sadly, stigma and discrimination against people with mental health problems of all ages is still commonplace. Additionally, for all older people, irrespective of whether they have a mental health problem or condition or have experienced one in the past, they are also likely to have experienced prejudice or discrimination concerning an issue common to all – their age.

Age – definitions, differences and discrimination

Defining 'old' is increasingly complex – pensionable age is currently still set at 60 for women and 65 for men, though over the next 10 years it will increase for women born after 1950 to 65. From 2024 it will increase for both men and women to 68. Government has also recently indicated that it will consider an end to the default retirement age altogether (Department for Work and Pensions, 2009). Many mental health services for older people continue to use the threshold of 65 to separate older people's services from services for younger adults. However, a range of high profile older people's organisations, such as Saga and Age Concern/Help the Aged define it as beginning at 50 in terms of eligibility to use their services. There are also variations between what local authorities use in terms of eligibility for their older people's services. Because we are living longer, distinctions have also been drawn between 'young old' (65–75), 'old old' (75–85), and the 'very old' (85+). And of course, older people themselves will vary enormously in how they choose to define themselves in respect of how old they feel, sometimes irrespective of their chronological age. The process of ageing is addressed in **part 1** also.

Having age thresholds in mental health services certainly creates a sense of separation and some would argue may have prevented older people getting access to the full range of services that are available to adults under the age of 65. However, having age thresholds for services can also help in how services are planned, and reflect some of the changes people experience as they grow older. Perhaps most importantly, the age threshold can also help protect older people's access to services, which otherwise they may not be offered or received because of the effect of ageism and age discrimination in the provision of health and social care services (Mental Health Foundation, 2009).

Society, individuals, personalisation and choice

Recent policies and services that relate to older people's mental health have partly grown out of a growing awareness of our ageing society, with both the numbers of older people and life expectancy increasing significantly as the baby boomer generation grows into their 60s. Their expectations and demands of health and social care are likely to be quite different from their parents' generation (Williamson, 2008). People over the age of 65 are also an increasingly complex demographic group with growing visible diversity in terms of race and ethnicity, sexual orientation, household compositions, lifestyle and beliefs, as a result of the changes that occurred in British society from the end of World War II onwards (Leach et al, 2008).

The effects of demographic change have also been reflected in the values and policies affecting health and social care, including mental health services, which have emerged over recent years. Terms such as 'choice and control', 'empowerment', 'personalisation', and 'recovery' have become commonplace and are good indications of the way health and social care is developing to meet changing expectations. 'Patient', 'client', even 'service user' are being replaced by 'consumer' or 'customer' of care. There is a much greater focus on public mental health – promoting good mental health and well-being for all – rather than just concentrating on illnesses and problems. A growing awareness of health inequalities, and the impact that wider socio-economic inequalities have on people's health is taking place. In the age of the internet the saying that 'doctor knows best' or 'just grin and bear it' do not reflect the enormous increase in access that people have to information about health and welfare issues, and possible solutions to mental health problems and conditions. The perspective of older people, and carers, together with the implications of concepts such as 'personalisation' and 'recovery' can be found in **part 2**.

Nevertheless, these changes come also with their challenges. It may prove difficult for many in the current cohort of the so-called 'old old' and 'very old' to adjust to these changes, particularly with the emphasis on personal choice and control over the services they receive, unless they are provided with significant support. Whether the increased diversity of service providers, including the voluntary and private sector together with informal sources of support such as family carers and other mental health service users, can meet increasing need at a time when resources for services are likely to be diminishing also remains to be seen. And tackling complex issues such as social exclusion among older people (especially those with mental health problems), and the inter-relationship between health inequalities and socio-economic inequalities, in order to secure population-wide improvements in older people's mental health is truly a major challenge (Friedli, 2009). This handbook provides a range of perspectives on the practical impact of these challenges and how they might be tackled.

A rapidly changing landscape

We also live in a fast moving world. The planning for this book took place in the spring and summer of 2008, prior to the 'credit crunch' and the onset of perhaps the worst recession in a generation. The impact of that recession on older people's mental health (as well as the rest of the population) is likely to prove enormous and for most, not a positive experience. It will also have a substantial impact on health and social care services including mental health services with, almost inevitably, significant cuts in resources over the coming years. This handbook does not directly address this but readers should have it in their minds (if not their experience) when considering the various issues covered in the different chapters.

The last 12 months have also seen very significant developments in health and social care policy and practice that have important bearing on older people and mental health care. These include the following (not all apply across the UK but governments in Scotland, Wales and Northern Ireland are developing new policies and services to address many of these issues):

- a new strategy for older people for the whole of the UK (Department for Work and Pensions, 2009)
- publishing an equality bill in 2009 (that if passed by Parliament, will ban discrimination in the provision of goods and services including health and social care, on the basis of age, across the UK)
- an end of life care strategy for England (Department of Health, 2008a)
- a public consultation to review the *No Secrets* guidance for safeguarding vulnerable adults (Department of Health, 2008b)
- guidance issued by the National Institute for Health and Clinical Excellence (NICE) on mental well-being and older people (NICE, 2008)
- a national dementia strategy for England (Department of Health, 2009a)
- *New Horizons* – a new strategy for mental health in England, which includes the mental health of older people (Department of Health, 2009b)
- a National Health Service Constitution (Department of Health, 2009c)
- the establishment in 2009 of the Care Quality Commission (CQC) – a new regulation and monitoring body for health and social care services and people detained under the Mental Health Act in England
- a national study of older people's mental health services by the Healthcare Commission, now part of the CQC (Healthcare Commission, 2009)
- undertaking a national review of age discrimination in health and social care
- a green paper on the options for the future of funding for adult social care in England (HM Government, 2009)
- new safeguards in 2009 for people who lack mental capacity who need to be detained in care homes and hospitals, and new regulations allowing people who may lack mental capacity to receive personal budgets and direct payments.

Conclusion

The rate of change and activity currently taking place at both an individual and societal level, which has a bearing on older people's mental health is enormous. What the future holds is difficult to predict but this handbook will give the reader a firm grip on the past and present, and enable them to apply the knowledge and understanding in whatever way they engage with older people's mental health in the future.

Acknowledgements

I would like to thank all the authors for their contributions, together with Kerry Boettcher at OLM-Pavilion, Catherine Jackson for assisting with developing the outline for the book, and Kathryn Hill, Mark Peterson and Laura Parker at the Mental Health Foundation.

References

Department of Health (2008a) *End of Life Care Strategy – Promoting high quality care for all adults at the end of life*. London: Department of Health.

Department of Health (2008b) *Safeguarding Adults: a consultation on the review of the 'No Secrets' guidance*. London: Department of Health.

Department of Health (2009a) *Living Well with Dementia: A national dementia strategy*. London: Department of Health.

Department of Health (2009b) *New Horizons*. London: Department of Health.

Department of Health (2009c) *The National Health Service Constitution*. London: Department of Health.

Department for Work and Pensions (2009) *Building a Society for all Ages*. London: Department for Work and Pensions.

Friedli L (2009) *Mental Health, Resilience and Inequalities*. Denmark: World Health Organization.

Healthcare Commission (2009) *Equality in Later Life*. London: Healthcare Commission.

HM Government (2009) *Shaping the Future of Care Together*. London: TSO.

Leach R, Phillipson C, Biggs S & Money A (2008) Sociological perspectives on the baby boomers: an exploration of social change. *Quality in Ageing* **9** 4 19–26.

Mental Health Foundation (2009) *All Things Being Equal*. London: Mental Health Foundation.

NICE (2008) *Mental Wellbeing and Older People*. Quick reference guide. London: National Institute for Health and Clinical Excellence.

Williamson T (2008) From the 60s to their sixties. Baby boomers – challenges and choices for public mental health. *Journal of Public Mental Health* **7** (1) 4–8.

Part 1:
Mental health
and well-being
of older people

Chapter 1

Old age and mental health in the context of the life span: what are the key issues in the 21st century?

Andrew McCulloch

There are as many myths about ageing as there are about mental health and mental ill health. The fact is that older people are exactly that – people who have grown older. They are people with a personal history or biography that includes biological (eg. genetics, food intake), psychological (eg. resilience) and social (eg. inequity and poverty) factors. They are people who have experienced some of the best and worst that life can bring and have responded in their own way. They may have acquired wisdom, or dysfunctional beliefs and behaviour patterns, and often both. They may or may not have experienced mental ill health during their life.

This is the key context in which mental health and old age must be viewed. To put it another way, the presence of mental health and/or mental illness in old age will be the result of a dynamic interaction between a whole range of factors throughout a person's life course. Nothing is inevitable about ageing except eventual death (and perhaps taxes!), and mental ill health is certainly not an inevitable result of ageing. In fact, many older people experience improved life satisfaction and an amelioration of past psychiatric symptoms if they have been living with mental illness.

This chapter will attempt to prepare some of the ground for the rest of this book by addressing the following questions.
i.   What is ageing?
ii. What is mental health?
iii. What is the relationship between the two?
iv. What are the life course factors that can impact on mental health in old age?
v.   What are the key issues for the 21st century?

The changing context of ageing

The length of people's lives and the context in which we age changed drastically during the 20th century and this may have both positive and negative effects on mental health (Williamson, 2008). Many people are now living for 30 years after retirement, some in good health for much of this time.

We are also seeing the baby boomer generation entering old age with a very different set of attitudes and assumptions about ageing – for many, the meaning of ageing has changed and people do not see themselves as old just because they are retired.

Ageing and life span development

Ageing has long been the subject of scientific study and the sciences of gerontology and life span developmental psychology are highly relevant to our understanding of mental health in late life. There are some excellent textbooks that set out these approaches in more detail (eg. Schaie & Willis, 1996, Birren & Schaie, 2001) as well as some classic studies of how individuals change and develop across life (eg. Levinson et al, 1978). This information and understanding is very much under-utilised in the mental health sector, perhaps because it leads us away from simplistic interpretations of mental health and mental illness in late life, or indeed at other life stages. Integrating life span perspectives with time-bound or cross-sectional ones is difficult, although at the individual level a good family doctor or psychotherapist will of course attempt this on a daily basis.

There are various ways in which ageing and life span development have been considered. These reflect the different understandings of ageing and the ageing process that we need to have in order to understand mental health and late life.

(a) Chronological age is important because it determines the bureaucratic and service response an individual receives but also, fundamentally, because it determines which cohort of individuals you belong to and therefore what social, cultural and historical experiences you have during your life (Coleman & McCulloch, 1985; 1990) and this impacts on your adjustment to old age. For example, people who lived through the second world war reported a profound impact on their lifetime attitudes and coping styles both positive and negative.

(b) Biological age is the extent to which your body and the different body systems and organs, critically, for our purposes, the brain, have aged. Of course not all biological ageing is negative – as our raw information processing and memory skills decline our strategic judgement can improve because different pathways and processing capabilities are opened up. Also not all individuals experience the same declines in IQ scores, for example, with age. Ageing is the result of an interaction between genetically programmed physical ageing (senescence) and lifetime history and environment. Normal senescence is quite different to dementia or other organic brain diseases and the nature of the memory loss is different.

(c) Psychological age is the extent to which we feel old and acquire 'age appropriate' behaviours. There is an interaction with biology – for example, the masculinisation of women and feminisation of men with age (eg. men become more supportive and group/community-minded and have improved emotional intelligence in mid-life) is clearly partly biological in origin. But 'you are only as old as you feel' has a good degree of truth. Many people also feel that they must adopt age appropriate behaviour but these norms are often internalised or self-generated rather than directly imposed by wider society.

(d) Social age is partly bound by chronological age, however, there is clearly a choice on the part of society and in government policy about how we treat older people and a choice by older people about how they organise themselves. Age discrimination is a negative effect of socially determined responses to both perceived and chronological age and is not a normal response to older people in all societies as older people have often been revered for their wisdom or even just for their survival skills.

Our understanding of life span change and development reflects these complexities and has fallen into several different 'schools of thought' or approaches some of which are as follows.

(i) **Psychodynamic** (ie. originating from the thought of Freud) work on ageing has been very important in shaping our thinking especially Erikson's classic work (Erikson, 1965). Erikson proposed a theory of the life cycle in which we face eight challenges during eight life stages. In mid-life we face the challenge of 'generativity versus stagnation' – what we can produce and leave for future generations – and in old age that of 'integrity versus despair' – can we acquire some wisdom and perspective on life or do we sink into depression? The idea of the mid-life crisis comes from this school of thought. There is some scientific evidence to support some of Erikson's views although he is essentially blending clinical and other observation with his personal philosophy.

(ii) **Developmental/cognitive**. This is the idea that human development continues after childhood and adolescence and is influenced by the great developmental psychologists like Paiget and Vygotsky who focused mainly on child development. Kohlberg, for example, has proposed a theory of moral development where we acquire new moral understandings as we change and develop through life (Kohlberg & Kramer, 1969). This is important as adult development is about cognition, emotion and life events – in other words bringing thinking and feeling together and moving forwards is seen as crucial to development and, of course, this also underpins good mental health. In fact, there is a close relationship between notions of positive development in adulthood and old age and good mental health. To some extent Kohlberg's idea that we can acquire a more integrated and strategic moral understanding with age is compatible with Erikson's ideas. Whitbourne's cognitive life span model of identity formation is also highly relevant to our understanding of mental health and old age. He suggested that once a person's core identity is formed in childhood the superficial aspects of identity (how you present yourself to the world) are generated as a result of your thinking about your life span as a whole. He generated the concepts of life story (our own perceived biography) and scenario (expectations about the future). Clearly a person's thinking about both of these aspects of their life could have a critical impact on mental health and especially depression (which can involve a negative life story and negative scenario) (Whitbourne, 1986 – there is a good summary in Schaie & Willis, 1996).

(iii) **The psychology of ageing in a social context**. There has been a lot of work looking at issues of retirement and also how the individual adjusts to old age. 'Disengagement theory' suggested that it is normal for individuals to gradually divest themselves of social roles and responsibilities and implied that this was healthy. This has been gradually superseded by 'continuity theory' that suggests that people adjust best by retaining previously valued activities, roles and attitudes, or modifying them. There has been a lot of related applied work that shows, for example, that flexible retirement is a superior model to fixed date retirement.

(iv) **Experimental psychology**. There has also been a lot of work on how information processing, intelligence and personality change with age, some of it very detailed. As stated above, while many deficits may occur as part of the ageing process, some should be viewed as functional – eg. long-term memory does not decline in the same way as short-term memory, and whereas reasoning speed in tests declines, strategic reasoning powers and judgement may improve or be maintained.

(v) A life course public health perspective. There is also a significant public health literature that looks at the accumulation of life events and the advantages and disadvantages that accrue to the individual that can change physical and mental health outcomes. These studies show how social benefits (eg. education) or insults (eg. unemployment, poverty) have a massive effect on health outcomes in old age (Blane, 2005). They also point to how key transitions in life, which include retirement and changes in family roles (eg. empty nest and grandparenting), can affect health and can be handled at both an individual and social level in more or less healthy ways.

Critically, the various strands of the literature tell us that:

- there are well understood psychological changes with age
- they are not all negative or senescent in nature
- there is still a lot of psychological 'work' to be done in old age that can result in rewarding and well-adjusted old age
- older people have much to offer, but similarly if they are deprived or suffer too many 'insults' such as bereavement and physical ill health they will be vulnerable.

At a practice level there is an overwhelming message that we need to be person-centred in seeking to understand individual biography, stories, cultures and needs.

Mental health and mental illness

The nature of mental health and mental illness is explained in more detail in another of the Pavilion mental health handbooks (McCulloch, 2006). Essentially, mental health is the core resource that enables us to function – it relates both to thinking and feeling so it includes both happiness/contentment or positive feelings of life satisfaction, but also the positive thinking and skills that allow us to take action, maintain relationships and value ourselves. Mental illness is not the opposite of mental health and increasingly there is consensus that a two dimensional model of mental health and mental illness is required (see **table 1** and also Friedli, 2008). This can accommodate the fact that there are a lot of people with quite poor mental health who do not have a psychiatric diagnosis and conversely there are people with a diagnosis, even one of a severe disorder, who are in 'remission' or whose diagnosis does not impinge much on their life, and who generally enjoy good mental health.

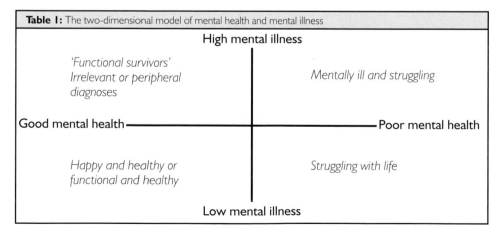

Table 1: The two-dimensional model of mental health and mental illness

High mental illness

'Functional survivors'
Irrelevant or peripheral
diagnoses

Mentally ill and struggling

Good mental health ——————————————— Poor mental health

Happy and healthy or
functional and healthy

Struggling with life

Low mental illness

In terms of old age, for example, you could have the first stages of dementia while still enjoying generally good mental health, but equally you might have the first stages of dementia coupled with depression and poor functioning. This would depend on personal characteristics and possibly the nature of services, information and early intervention you received.

Mental health and old age

Good mental health in old age will bring many benefits.

- It enables us to enjoy old age and also to cope with bereavement, physical illness and other insults that old age often brings.
- It enables older people to continue to make their contribution both economically (see for example Age Concern & Mental Health Foundation, 2006) and, for example, as grandparents or socially.
- It is fundamental to delivering a good old age and 'good death' that we all aspire to.
- It may reduce care costs by helping prevent mental illness or limit the impact of mental illness, including organic brain disease.
- It will help reduce the impact of physical illness, for example, by reducing the prevalence or impact of heart disease and type II diabetes (Hyman, 2001).

Generally speaking, we understand the roots of good mental health in old age and how good life experiences, healthy lifestyles, meaningful activities and relationships, and positive ageing can contribute to a mentally healthy old age. We also understand the specific factors that are of special importance in old age that include mobility, physical health, social networks, opportunities for meaningful activity and so on (Age Concern & Mental Health Foundation, 2006). Little, however, is being done by society to promote good mental health in old age, either by addressing issues that may impact earlier in people's lives or by targeting mental health promotion initiatives directly at older people. If we successfully promote good mental health in old age we will increase people's functionality generally, while also, potentially, limiting the impact of certain mental illnesses such as depression. On the other hand, individual interventions to reduce specific mental illness that are not embedded in an overall public health approach are unlikely to have much impact on their own. **Diagram 1** summarises some of the factors that can have a lifetime impact on mental health in old age.

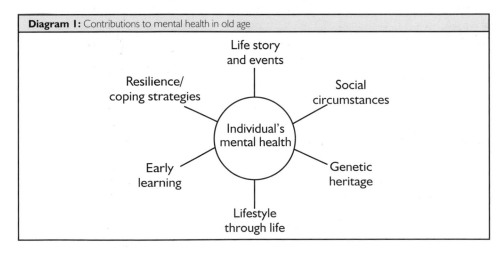

Diagram 1: Contributions to mental health in old age

Life story and events

Resilience/ coping strategies

Social circumstances

Individual's mental health

Early learning

Genetic heritage

Lifestyle through life

Old age and mental illness

As already stated, many forms of mental illness are either rarer in old age or tend to ameliorate with age (eg. schizophrenia and manic depressive illness) albeit people with mental health problems often have poor physical health and tend to live shorter lives (Jenkins et al, 2002).

However, dementia and depression are two key illnesses that are both more common in old age and are of strategic importance in health, social and economic terms (Age Concern & Mental Health Foundation, 2006, Age Concern, 2007). Depression is the most common mental health problem in old age affecting 13–15% of all older people at a clinically diagnosable level and 40–80% of older people in care homes.

There is increasing awareness of this issue but depression in old age is still under-diagnosed and under-treated relative to depression in adulthood. Too often, professionals take a fatalistic attitude to depression in older age or struggle with issues such as differentiating normal bereavement processes from depression. In addition, when therapy is offered it is usually just antidepressants, whereas a range of treatments is required depending on levels of severity including psychotherapy, social network interventions, exercise, diet and even alternative therapies or pet therapy.

While depression in old age has similar features to that which occurs earlier in life, negative thoughts may often focus on the ageing process including physical limitations, negative assessments of what has been achieved during the person's life and bereavement. This is where thinking like Whitbourne's – outlined above – can help us understand the different nature of depression in old age. Sometimes depression in old age can be a despair or ennui about life where the individual sees their life story as generally negative and their future as hopeless. Psychotherapy and other interventions need therefore to pay attention to the particular needs of old people to gain value from the past as well as the future. There is a need as always for self-acceptance but also in later life a life review that results in an understanding of the person's unique strengths and lifetime contribution as well as a realistic assessment of shortcomings. In many cases the specific vulnerability to depression in an older person will relate both to an earlier episode of depression during adult life, to specific life events, or indeed to problems experienced in childhood and adolescence: depression will not be simply age-related.

There is also increasing understanding of dementia, which consists of a family of organic brain disorders, the two most common of which are Alzheimer's disease and multi-infarct dementia (also known as vascular dementia). While they have different causes it is likely that there are genetic and lifestyle components, and there may also be links with other physical and mental illnesses in some cases, as well as links with traumas such as head injury. Dementia is not a random accident but also has lifespan correlates and risk factors that are being increasingly understood. There is also increased risk for people with some learning disabilities. Because of demographic change this group of illnesses will be the most important disease group in terms of economic consequences and demands on the health and social care system in the first half of this century (McCrone et al, 2008).

Approximately 1% of people between 60 and 65 have dementia, 5% of people over 65 and 10–20% of people over 80. Understanding of dementia in general health and social care services, and also in adult mental health services, is poor and early diagnosis is rare, yet early diagnosis is key to supporting early intervention, decision-making and making best use of the remaining time for individuals and their loved ones. Government is consulting on a draft dementia strategy at the time of writing, which has a key focus on this issue (Department of Health, 2008).

Whether an older person has dementia, depression or some other mental disorder, the issues referred to above will be key to supporting them in a person-centred way. Too often we hear of bad practice in which older people are treated without dignity or respect or an understanding of who they are. Good services and responses, by contrast, take a person-centred approach allowing opportunities for reflection, reminiscence, and thinking about what has been achieved in the past as well as opening up opportunities for new social networks and recovery, or at least greater dignity and self-determination, almost whatever the circumstances.

Mental health and old age – what are the key issues?

Table 2 lists some of the key strategic issues we must face in terms of mental health and old age, and **table 3** lists some of the key issues in respect of intervention. To a large extent they are interrelated. We need to recognise that if we are to improve the mental health of older generations we must intervene at a social level – for example, to provide adequate pensions, housing and reduce crime – and at service level – to introduce mental health promotion and vastly improve primary and secondary mental health care for older people. This agenda is one of the greatest challenges we face in the 21st century sitting alongside population, energy and climate change issues. But it has not yet been fully recognised as such.

Table 2: Key strategic issues in mental health and old age	
Mental health promotion/public mental health	Mental health services
People living longer	Treatment advances likely
Debt and poverty (people on long-term welfare benefits – impending recession?)	New models of care delivery
Loss of social networks, fragmentation	Workforce issues
Availability of housing	Costs and who pays
Social change and modernisation	Evidence needed
Diversity and diverse groups	Dementia dominates debate
Rising expectations	Dangers of medicalisation
Transport	Joining up mental and physical health (applies to public health too)
Age discrimination	Problems associated with the existing organisational divide between MH services for older people and younger people
Retirement patterns	
Evidence and interventions needed	
Community cohesion	
Spirituality	
Fear of crime	
Increase in people with substance and alcohol misuse problems	
Greater and more complex demands on carers	
More mistrust of professionals/services – service users seeking own treatments/remedies via the internet	

In terms of the overarching strategic issues we need to ask ourselves the following questions.

- What is changing about our society that may affect older people's mental health both positively (eg. improved communications) or adversely (eg. fragmentation of families) and is there anything that can be done about it?
- What is changing about the new cohort of older people that will impact on their mental health and mental health services (eg. rising expectations in baby boomers, increased diversity)?
- What structural issues are key to the public mental health of older people where there are policy interventions (eg. transport, access, poverty)?
- How can we address the very real age discrimination experienced by older people?
- How can we offer a role and a 'safe place' in our society for older people?

Such questions are key to the mental health of older people as a whole but are issues for the whole of government and the whole of society. Intervening may be costly but so will be not intervening – these are political choices.

Table 3: Key delivery issues in mental health and old age

Mental health promotion and illness prevention	Mental health service delivery
Relationships including social network interventions and intergenerational contact schemes	Access to relevant therapies including psychotherapy
Diet eg. nutritional standards for care homes	Medication management
Exercise including bespoke exercise interventions for older people	Intermediate care
Mental activity, mind gyms, memory gyms	Staff training in primary and secondary care
Cognitive/attributional style (= the way you think) covering self-help, group work and psychotherapy (crossover with services)	Using older staff to work with older people
Debt counselling and financial capability	Keeping people out of hospital or care homes
Volunteering and work opportunities	Person-centred, continuous, care
Specific antidiscrimination activities	Lifestyle analysis and coaching/support to make improvements to health
Greater potential use of IT – more IT 'savviness' among service users	Greater use of IT
	Personalisation/individual health care budgets
	More focus around self-help, self-management approaches

From a health and social care perspective there is also a range of key issues to be considered in terms of moving forwards with mental health promotion and improved mental health service delivery and I have summarised some of these in **table 3**, and many of these issues will come up throughout this book.

Conclusion

To a large extent we seem to have lost our respect for older people and lost a sense of their contribution and how different their lives have been. We have also done little in services to apply the rich understandings of old age that the science and literature have given us. An old person's mental health status is not an accident but a result of influences they have experienced throughout life and what they have made of their life. It would be a tragedy for future generations if we did not start to rectify these critical shortcomings in our society and our services.

Acknowledgements

I should like to thank Toby Williamson and Isabella Goldie at the Mental Health Foundation for their helpful comments, and Professor Peter Coleman for sharing his thoughts with me on these issues over the years.

References

Age Concern & Mental Health Foundation (2006) *Promoting Mental Health and Well-being in Late Life*. London: Age Concern (jointly with the Mental Health Foundation).

Age Concern (2007) *Improving Services and Support for Older People with Mental Health Problems*. London: Age Concern.

Blane D (2005) The life course, the social gradient and health. In: M Marmot & R Wilkinson (Eds) *Social Determinants of Health* (2nd ed) pp54–77. Oxford: Oxford University Press.

Birren JE & Schaie KW (2001) *Handbook of the Psychology of Aging*. Orlando: Academic Press.

Coleman P & McCulloch A (1985) The study of psychosocial change in late life: some conceptual and methodological issues. In: JMP Munnichs *et al. Life Span and Change in a Gerontological Perspective*. London and New York: Academic Press.

Coleman P & McCulloch A (1990) Social change, values and social support: exploratory studies into adjustment in late life. *Journal of Aging Studies* **4** (4) 321–332.

Department of Health (2008) *Transforming the Quality of Dementia Care*. London: Department of Health.

Erikson E (1965) *Childhood and Society*. London: The Hogarth Press.

Friedli L (2008) *Mental Health, Resilience and Inequalities*. Copenhagen and London: WHO Europe and the Mental Health Foundation.

Hyman SE (2001) Mental health in an aging population. *American Journal of Geriatric Psychiatry* **9** (4) 330–339.

Jenkins R, McCulloch A, Friedli L & Parker C (2002) *Developing a National Mental Health Policy*. Maudsley monograph. Hove: The Psychology Press.

Kohlberg L & Kramer R (1969) Continuities and discontinuities in childhood and adult moral development. *Human Development* **12** 93–120.

Levinson DJ *et al* (1978) *The Seasons of a Man's Life*. New York: Ballantine.

McCrone P, Dhanasiri S, Patel A, Knapp M & Lawton-Smith S (2008) *Paying the Price*. London: King's Fund.

McCulloch A (2006) Understanding mental health and mental illness. In: Jackson C & Hill K (Eds) *Mental Health Today: A handbook*. Brighton: Pavilion.

Schaie KW & Willis SL (1996) *Adult Development and Aging*. New York: Harper Collins.

Whitbourne SK (1986) *Adult Development*. New York: Springer-Verlag.

Williamson T (2008) From the 60s to their sixties: baby boomers – challenges and choices for public mental health. *Journal of Public Mental Health* **7** (1) 4–8.

Chapter 2
Mental health and well-being in later life: definitions and determinants

Alisoun Milne

Introduction

There is a widely held view that old age is inevitably a period of physical and mental decline. In fact, only a minority of older people experience severe or serious mental illness and much can be done to ameliorate both risks and symptoms of the key mental disorders associated with later life (Office for National Statistics, 2004). The focus of this chapter is mental health rather than mental illness; the links that mental health has with quality of life and overall well-being; the risks to mental health that ageing presents; and the role of the wider socio-cultural context in alleviating, or deepening, mental health vulnerabilities. It is underpinned by an overarching appreciation of the role of lifelong, and/or age related, inequalities in understanding mental health risk.

Mental health and well-being in later life

Good mental health is as important in older age as it is at any other time of life. Everyone has mental health needs, whether or not they have a diagnosis of mental illness. Our mental health influences how we think and feel about ourselves and others, and our ability to communicate and to manage change. It is central to health and well-being and has a significant impact on quality of life. Importantly, mental health is routinely identified by older people themselves as pivotal to 'ageing well' (Bowling, 2005). The research literature consistently identifies that, having a role, good social relationships with family, friends and neighbours, an adequate income, being physically fit, and living in a supportive neighbourhood, are promoting of mental health (Age Concern England, 2003; Health Scotland, 2004). The issues that older people identify as undermining of mental health are deteriorating physical health, loss of independence, loneliness, fear of death, living in poor housing and neighbourhood, and decreased income (Victor, 2005). The negative impact of losses – that tend to accumulate in later life – and physical illness are key risk factors for developing mental health problems, particularly depression (Godfrey & Denby, 2004). How well an older person adjusts to late life challenges is a key factor in determining ongoing mental health. Those older people who are able to adapt well tend to fare better (Robinson *et al*, 2005).

Despite its common usage, a coherent and widely adopted definition of 'mental health' remains elusive. The World Health Organization (2003) defines it as, '*a state of well-being whereby individuals recognise their abilities, are able to cope with the normal stresses of daily life and make a contribution to their families and communities'*. Research with older people suggests that mental health is characterised by the following dimensions: a sense of well-being, the ability to make and sustain relationships, and the ability to meet the challenges and circumstances that later life brings. Of particular importance is an older person's continuing capacity to experience enjoyment and adjust to new, and sometimes difficult challenges (Mentality, 2004). The Mental Health Foundation views good mental health as the ability to: develop emotionally, creatively, intellectually and spiritually; initiate, develop and sustain mutually satisfying personal relationships; face problems, resolve them and learn from them; be confident and assertive; be aware of others and empathise with them; use and enjoy solitude; play and have fun; laugh, both at themselves and at the world (Mental Health Foundation, 2003). Mental health appears to be closely bound up with self-perception. How older people view their mental and physical health is as important as any objective assessment of illness or reduced ability. How a person feels s/he is coping with daily life is as, or more, significant a barometer of 'well-being' than an objective assessment of the number or type of health problems they have or their 'capacity to cope' (Bowling, 2005; Victor *et al*, 2009).

There is considerable synergy between those issues which contribute to good mental health and those that promote 'quality of life', a construct that is now widely used in research with older people (Bowling, 2005; Livingstone *et al*, 2008). Quality of life is a multi-dimensional concept encompassing emotional, social, psychological, and health related, domains; broadly it encapsulates 'how good' a person's life is overall (Thompson & Kingston, 2004). Recent work by Bowling identified the following dimensions as the 'building blocks' or drivers of quality of life:

> *'Having an optimistic outlook and psychological well-being, especially in relation to making downward rather than unrealistic upward social comparisons; having good health and physical functioning; having good social relationships, preventing loneliness and feeling helped and supported; maintaining social roles, especially a large number of social activities, including voluntary work and having individual interests; living in a neighbourhood with good community facilities and services, including access to affordable transport, and feeling safe in one's neighbourhood; having an adequate income; and maintaining a sense of independence and control over one's life'* (2005: 221).

As can be seen from this distillation, quality of life is a dynamic and multi-level construct reflecting macro (societal), meso (community), and micro (family and individual) influences, and is a collection of objective and subjective dimensions that interact together (Lawton, 1991). That there are theoretical distinctions between the liveability of the environment – social capital, the individual – personal capacities and psychological capital, the external utility of life and inner appreciation of life, adds to its complexity (Veenhoven, 2000). Of particular relevance to this chapter is the concept of psychological capital or well-being, which itself subsumes the dimensions of 'mental health', 'life satisfaction', and 'self-efficacy'. Self-efficacy has been evidenced as a particularly important factor in the promotion of mental health; in particular it contributes directly to enhancing an older person's ability to adapt to the challenges that ageing often brings (Baltes & Baltes, 1990). This dovetails with emerging evidence about 'resilience', which has been identified as one of the key explanatory factors in the so-called 'disability paradox' – that many people with chronic conditions consistently rate their own quality of life highly (Albrecht & Devlieger, 1999). This includes people with Alzheimer's disease (Livingstone *et al*, 2008). The concept of 'quality of life' not only allows for the possibility of a good life quality despite adversity but focuses on assets rather than deficits. It also accommodates a life course perspective, which recognises that a person's reserves in later life reflects a lifetime's accumulation, and/or depletion, of resources and skills (Grundy, 2001). This is one of the criticisms levelled at health-focused models of quality of life, which tend to prioritise physical health domains over those related to resilience, self-efficacy and social or psychological well-being (Covinsky et al, 1999).

Similar criticisms have been made of 'successful ageing', a concept closely theoretically and conceptually aligned to that of quality of life. The literature tends to define 'successful ageing' as disease driven – the avoidance of physical or cognitive impairment – neglecting the possibility of positive adaptation or compensation (Depp & Jeste, 2006). While research supports the contention that 'good health' is highly prized by older people, it is not the only element that matters, nor is 'being in poor health' the same as 'perceived health' (Office for National Statistics, 2004). Further, evidence suggests that it is the loss of control and independence associated with physical and/or mental health that undermines quality of life rather than the illness per se (Bond & Corner, 2004). Despite the distinctions researchers make, recent work with older people suggests that 'successful ageing' may be conflated in the minds of ordinary citizens with notions of quality of life. In a 2003 study by Reed et al, successful ageing was viewed as incorporating the following: being able to adapt to continuous physical change; engaging in relationships; maintaining independence; having enough money to participate; fulfilling desires and personal objectives; and taking part in meaningful activity. This underscores the need for researchers to, '…move beyond "professional centrism" (Stastny & Amering, 1997) and ensure their models and measurement instruments are grounded in lay perspectives' (Bowling, 2005: 42).

As can be seen, there is considerable common ground between the constructs of mental health, quality of life, and successful ageing. While mental health may be viewed as a narrower construct than its 'parent' frameworks it is important to recognise that it is as much a product of quality of life or successful ageing as it is a component. Whatever differences there may be around definitions in all three areas, in relation to mental health there is broad agreement that it is an equally important part of quality of life as physical health and it is intrinsically bound up with a range of dimensions that both directly and indirectly impact upon it (Age Concern England, 2007). That many older people struggle to separate out those elements of life that contribute to 'good mental health' as distinct from 'good quality of life' is a notable feature of research in this field and one that suggests work on understanding the determinants of mental health in later life is the next step on the path to improving it.

Determinants of mental health

In order to explore the determinants of mental ill health in later life it is useful to conceptualise risks to, and protective factors around mental health, as being located in three broad spheres – macro level societal factors, meso level community or environmental issues and micro level family or individual resources. Appreciating how vulnerable, or not, an older person is to mental ill health requires the adoption of a life course approach – that is a perspective that takes account of an individual's past experiences and lifelong socio-cultural context. Further, building up a coherent understanding of those factors that increase, or decrease, an older person's vulnerability to mental illness will help in the development of strategies to prevent mental ill health and promote mental health. A number of risks can be located in the wider demographic context where we begin our task of unravelling the multiplicity of issues and influences.

Demographic and bio-psychological variables

Old age itself may be a risk factor for, at least depression and dementia, rates of both increase in later life. Explanations for vulnerability to depression appear to lie, at least in part, in increased risk of physical ill health, reduced opportunities for social participation and loss of relatives and friends to death (Age Concern & Mental Health Foundation, 2006; Victor *et al*, 2009). These factors are explored in more detail below. For dementia, it is a well established fact that the risk of Alzheimer's disease increases substantially with age; whereas only 5% of people aged over 65 are affected, this figure rises to 25% of those aged 85 years and over (House of Commons Committee of Public Accounts, 2008). Rates of vascular dementia also increase as do severity of symptoms. Overall, two-thirds (68%) of all people with dementia are aged 80 and over (Alzheimer's Society, 2007). Nearly double the number of women suffer from dementia than men. Both the higher mortality rate among men and the higher age-specific dementia prevalence in women contribute to the preponderance of women among the 'oldest-old' with dementia.

Twice as many women also suffer from depression in later life than men, although this is a life course trend rather than one specific to old age. That a high proportion of the very old – those aged 85 years and over – are women and that 40% of this age group suffer from at least one episode of 'case level' depression is a particular demographic risk for women (Age Concern England, 2007). Risk factors have, in fact, been little explored although life course disadvantage has been cited as part of the explanation (Milne & Williams, 2000). Higher levels of disability, which are commonly linked to very old age, are more likely to affect women, as they predominate statistically. That older women are much more likely to be widowed is also a factor; depression is much more common among those who have never married, are divorced or widowed. There is, additionally, evidence that older men have a higher mortality risk than older women linked to depression, men aged 75 and over had the highest suicide rates of all men until a decade ago (Beeston, 2006).

Black and minority elders appear to be at increased risk of emotional or psychological problems, although there is very limited hard data on the extent of mental ill health in minority populations. It has been argued that this is as a consequence of the combined impact of the daily stresses that affect all older people, their minority status, and the nature of their post-migration experiences (Godfrey & Denby, 2004; Milne & Chryssanthopoulou, 2005). It is notable that over the next 20 years, the number of older people – and hence the overall number of people with dementia – will rise especially quickly in several minority ethnic groups as first generation migrants reach the age where the risk of dementia is considerably raised (Alzheimer's Society, 2007).

A number of specific bio-psychological factors also play a role in deepening the risk of mental ill health in later life. In relationship to the dementias, in about half of all cases of fronto-temporal dementia, there is a family history of the illness. Although it is a numerically rare type of dementia, it incorporates Pick's disease, frontal lobe degeneration, and dementia associated with motor neurone disease. All are caused by damage to the frontal lobe and/or the temporal parts of the brain. Where there is a family link the course of the disease usually follows a specific pattern; some of these inherited forms have been linked to abnormalities on chromosomes 3 and 17. There is a specific risk of dementia to a minority of people with Parkinson's disease; people with Huntington's chorea are at high risk of developing a dementia-type illness in the later stages of the condition (Jacoby *et al*, 2008). There are also well-established links between the increase in the number and severity of physical illnesses more common in later life and depression.

Delirium – acute confusion – is a relatively common disorder among older people. It is marked by sudden onset of confusion, disorientation and memory problems. The cause is most often physical in nature, including urinary and other infections, and dehydration. Delirium develops in up to 50% of older people who have had operations, and half of all cases of delirium develop after admission to a general hospital (Anderson, 2005). Most older people who suffer from symptoms of anxiety develop these earlier in life and have grown old with the disorder. This may also be the case for older people with depression; some research suggests that a significant predictor of late life depression is previous episodes (Henderson et al, 1997). There is, additionally, no reason to suppose that traumatic childhood experiences that place adults at risk of depression do not continue to influence mental health in older age. We know, for example, that women who have been abused in childhood are four times as likely to develop major depression in adulthood, a pattern that may well continue into mid and later life (World Health Organization, 2001; Mental Health Foundation, 2007).

Socio-economic situation

Living in poverty, particularly over the longer term provokes stress, worry, fear of not being able to make ends meet and loss of control over life; it is a specific risk factor for isolation, loneliness, depression and social exclusion (Godfrey & Denby, 2004; Victor et al, 2009). Being poor impairs an older person's capacity to make choices, undermines independence and reduces opportunities to take part in social and other activities (Age Concern England, 2004). For example, impoverished older people are less likely to own a car; this severely compromises their ability to live independently particularly in rural areas (Milne et al, 2007).

Nearly two million older people in the UK live in poverty; two-thirds of pensioners rely on state pensions and benefits for at least half of their income. Older women, long-term carers and older people from minority ethnic groups are at particular risk of living in chronic poverty (Godfrey et al, 2005). For women, this is primarily a consequence of life course issues, limited access to occupational pension schemes, time out to raise children and/or care for elderly relatives combined with pay inequalities endured throughout their working lives (Milne & Williams, 2000). Current policies, which are downgrading the role of the state pension and emphasising private pension arrangements, are likely to reinforce such inequalities and create 'two nations' in old age (Victor, 2005). Older people living on low incomes are also disproportionately more likely to occupy inadequate housing, experience fuel poverty and live in environments that can feel unsafe such as run down housing estates (Office of the Deputy Prime Minister, 2006; Social Exclusion Unit, 2006).

Conversely, having access to a reasonable income, particularly an occupational pension, is evidenced as having a positive impact on mental health and well-being (Age Concern & the Mental Health Foundation, 2006). It provides a degree of comfort and the means to take advantage of opportunities, make choices and participate in enjoyable activities, such as going out for a meal, that promote inclusion. This has a direct and positive effect on levels of anxiety and stress. Older people with money also tend to live in nicer neighbourhoods, feel safer and are less exposed to crime and environmental decay. Money can also cushion the impact of loss; the negative impact of a disability, for example, can be mediated, to some degree, by access to aids and adaptations, private treatment or alternative therapy, private care at home and/or access to private transport.

Losses

Losses accumulate in later life, especially in very old age. Despite increases in life expectancy, 26% of people aged 50 to 64 in Britain report a long-term illness or disability – this increases to 74% of people aged 85+; rates are higher for women overall. The main causes are musculoskeletal illness and cardiovascular disease (Office for National Statistics, 2004). It is notable that as well as having worse health and shorter life expectancy, people in lower socio-economic groups, are more likely to experience disability. Physical ill health and disability are the most consistent factors linked to depression among older people (Victor, 2005). Most studies find that rates of depression are approximately double for older people suffering from ill health compared to their healthy counterparts. It has been estimated that 70% of new cases of depression in older people are related to poor physical health (Godfrey et al, 2005). Older people with mobility problems are particularly at risk, being three to four times more likely to be depressed than those without (Godfrey et al, 2005). This point highlights the important fact that it is not age per se, which creates vulnerability but the impact of disability and chronic ill health, which are simply more common among older people. Further, that it is specifically their role in increasing immobility, reducing opportunities to go out, and undermining independence that creates mental health problems. That many older people retain good quality of life in spite of these challenges underscores the point made earlier about successfully ageing despite adversity. Higher levels of education appear to be 'protective' (Victor, 2005).

Bereavement is a loss commonly experienced in later life, particularly for women who are especially vulnerable to the loss of intimate relationships, such as the death of a spouse. Around half of older women are widowed compared with a fifth of older men, a gender gap that widens with age (Victor, 2005). It has been estimated that between 10% and 20% of older people suffer 'complicated grief', which is grief that lasts for a long period, is intense, and is associated with severe depressive symptoms. If left untreated this may develop into a mental health problem; risk is heightened in contexts where the bereaved person was supported intensively by the person who died (Godfrey & Denby, 2004). Bereaved men appear to be at greater risk of death than women, particularly during the first year; higher educational status and income levels may play a protective role (Byrne & Raphael, 1994). Bereavement is certainly one of the most widely cited causes of isolation, which when combined with disability and dependency on the deceased person, may place an older person at risk of loneliness and vulnerable to depression (Victor et al, 2009).

Another significant loss – or life course 'transition' – which often has an impact on mental health, is retirement. While for some, retirement heralds an era of new opportunities, it can also lead to the loss of a valued role, identity and status. Living on a reduced income is also a concern for many, particularly women living alone who are less likely to have built up an occupational pension during their working life (Milne & Williams, 2003). Working beyond retirement can be protective of mental health, particularly for those in valued occupations eg. doctors (Phillipson, 1993). As it is income and social engagement that older people most often cite as the 'things they miss' about working rather than the job per se, ensuring an adequate income in later life as well as enhancing social support for the newly retired, may go some way to resolving the so called 'retirement crisis' (Victor, 2005).

Later life offers opportunities for growth and development as well as losses. Noted advantages include increased self-acceptance and confidence, the easing of domestic responsibilities and more time for leisure and social activities (Help the Aged, 2004b). It is also notable that while losses may be relatively common among older people it is the management of those losses that affects mental health. Most older people successfully adjust to the many changes that late life brings, bolstered by personal resources, social networks and social support – three of the most important factors in protecting mental health and the focus of the following sub sections.

Personal capabilities and resources

There is increasing evidence that resources internal to the individual, including self-esteem, self-efficacy and resilience play a significant role in helping an older person adjust to losses and cope with changes effectively (Milne & Peet, 2008). The effect of an illness or loss such as bereavement is mediated by the psycho-social resource of mastery – being able to take charge of one's life; high perceived self-mastery and an optimistic outlook are related to better coping mechanisms and are protective of mental health (Bowling, 2005).

The psychological literature on coping and adjustment makes a helpful distinction between so-called 'daily hassles' such as changing light bulbs and sorting out bills, and major stressors such as bereavement or physical illness (Godfrey & Denby, 2004). Daily hassles emerge, or become visible, when an older person has few social contacts to call upon for help; they also act as a constant reminder of reduced ability (Holahan et al, 1984, cited in Godfrey & Denby, 2004). They are also likely to deepen when the older person's health deteriorates, for example, more severe arthritis makes it even harder to open a jar or operate a cooker. There is additional evidence that daily hassles are more strongly correlated with psychosocial distress than major life events. The implication of this finding is that addressing the 'small things' may be a more useful and achievable stress relieving intervention than tackling the 'big issues'. It also suggests that learning about the strategies employed by those older people who do manage to accommodate the 'big issues' would, potentially at least, be a useful way to help others develop effective coping responses and protect their mental health. The ability of some older people to develop 'compensatory strategies' when facing a new challenge or loss is a widely noted coping strategy (Baltes & Baltes, 1990). Moving to a bungalow when stairs are no longer possible, or paying a cleaner when bending becomes difficult are two examples of ways in which a person can compensate for physical deficits. Recourse to this type of strategy, however, depends on the older person having access to economic resources.

One of the main psychological strategies proposed for maintaining well-being and promoting self-mastery and control in the face of age related challenges is the use of self-enhancing social comparisons (Ryff, 1999). It is believed that if people make comparisons 'upwards' with those whose status they cannot attain they are more likely to be unhappy than those who compare their lot 'downwards' with people who are worse off.

Social relationships and networks

As noted in the first part of this chapter socially embedded individuals tend to have better life quality (Phillipson et al, 2001). Research has consistently demonstrated the importance of social and family relationships in enhancing well-being and mental health; social participation is linked to reduced risk of common mental health problems (Mentality, 2004). Having close friends is important for maintenance of morale, self-esteem and mastery; feeling loved and secure; and for prevention of loneliness: this is especially the case if relationships are reciprocal (Bowling et al, 2002). The existence of an 'intimate, confiding relationship' is a major factor in ameliorating the impact of age-related losses such as ill health; higher levels of social support have specifically been identified as a buffer against 'excess risk of depression' in the presence of disability (Brown & Harris, 1978). Conversely, lack of social integration can decrease an individual's resources for dealing with psychological and social stress; isolation increases vulnerability to loneliness and depression and is implicated in alcohol abuse and suicide (Bowling, 2005). One in 10 people aged 65, living in the community, report feeling often or always lonely, increasing to one in four people aged 80 years or over (Social Exclusion Unit, 2006). People attain old age with the social networks they have built up over a lifetime; women tend to have larger groups than men and people in lower socio-economic groups report weaker friendship ties but stronger links with kin.

Older people themselves additionally identify 'meaningful engagement' as an important facet of social relationships. Specifically, that having a role and helping others promotes a person's identity and purpose and increases levels of personal satisfaction; it also reinforces a 'sense of belonging' to a community or social group (Godfrey et al, 2005). On a related note there is increasing evidence of the benefits and value of befriending and volunteering – older volunteers have been shown to have greater life satisfaction, improved morale and self-esteem as well as larger social networks (Mentality, 2004). How public agencies can actively enhance engagement and participation levels among older citizens remains a key challenge and an issue to which the author returns in **chapter 3**.

Support networks and caring

It is important to make a distinction between a social and a support network, the latter being a more limited entity than the former and one directed at providing 'support' when help is needed (Victor, 2005). Although the two kinds of network interrelate they are not, necessarily, co-terminus. The strength and constituency of a support network is directly related to the older person's ability to retain independence, and cope with frailty, illness or loss. As relatives tend to provide the majority of instrumental help, for example, shopping, driving the person to a hospital appointment, those older people whose networks consist primarily of relatives tend to be supported for longer and more effectively (Maher & Green, 2002).

The provision of informal care – that is support beyond the instrumental – can lead to considerable physical and emotional strain. Caring intensively is a known risk factor for mental ill health; a recent survey of carers found that those caring intensively (ie. for 20 or more hours per week) were twice as likely to experience depression or anxiety as other carers (Office for National Statistics, 2002). Further, a third of people who provide care to a relative with dementia have depression. As older carers disproportionately provide intensive care and dementia care, and over 20% of the UK's six million carers are aged 65 and over, this is a concern. While the proportion declines with age, this still leaves 5% of people aged 85 years and over providing care (Office for National Statistics, 2004; Milne & Hatzidimitriadou, 2002). Most older carers support a spouse or very elderly parent (Carers UK, 2004).

Community and neighbourhood issues

The positive role of 'social capital' in promoting mental health and well-being is widely noted (Le Mesurier, 2003). That the term incorporates both the characteristics of an individual's social support system – discussed above – and their access to 'enabling community resources' suggests that the nature and type of community is a key element. Communities that offer members opportunities to join groups and clubs, take up voluntary work, and access social and leisure opportunities, have high levels of social capital; these tend to promote inclusion, reciprocity and trust. Community facilities, civic and social opportunities and accessible leisure and educational resources all protect against isolation and enhance opportunities for participation (Age Concern England, 2007). Taking an IT course or joining an aqua fit class provides activity, learning and may facilitate new relationships. Having a role in the local neighbourhood such as being a school governor, or running a club, is routinely identified as fulfilling; this dovetails with evidence about the benefits of volunteering (Help the Aged, 2004b). Membership to an accepting faith community can also have positive effects on mental health (Mentality, 2004).

At a more physical level, neighbourhood disadvantage is likely to have a negative impact on mental health. Issues that specifically contribute to elder well-being include the attractiveness of the area, levels of crime and security, and availability and safety of public transport (Walker & Walker, 2005). Around 44% of people aged 65 and over do not have access to a car and 17% do not use public transport due to poor health, inconvenience or cost (Age Concern England, 2005). The accessibility of resources within the immediate environment such as shops and services, not only affects how easy it is for an older person to sustain independence but also informal opportunities for social interaction (Godfrey & Denby, 2004).

Research indicates that 'excluded' older people tend to experience poverty, social isolation, minimal engagement with community activities, exclusion from basic services, and fear of crime and antisocial behaviour in the local neighbourhood (Phillipson & Sharf, 2004; Social Exclusion Unit, 2006). It is therefore important that community safety programmes, crime policies and regeneration strategies take proper account of the needs and interests of older people (Age Concern & Mental Health Foundation, 2006).

Age discrimination

Stereotypes about old age are an important element of the way in which older people experience later life and gain access to, or not, socially valued roles and resources; they function to reinforce age-related norms and perpetuate assumptions about old age and ageing as a process (Bytheway, 1995). Old age stereotypes are almost universally negative and are associated with dependency, isolation, limited social and sexual lives, and incapacity to exercise informed choice, control or self-determination (Victor, 2005). Ageism is a manifestation of systematic age stereotyping and '…*is an ideology, which condones and sanctions the subordination and marginalisation of older people within society and legitimises (or at least ignores) poor quality care, neglect, and social exclusion*' (Victor, 2005: 156). Ageism is, in turn, a defining feature of age discrimination, a process that has been identified as having a pernicious impact on the mental health and well-being of older people in the UK and as a multi-level barrier to opportunity and inclusion (Age Concern & Mental Health Foundation, 2006). Specifically, age discrimination contributes to feelings of worthlessness, despair and being non-deserving, it lowers self-esteem and expectations, limits access to services and underpins lack of respect shown to older people (Age Concern & University of Kent, 2005). Poor mental health itself amplifies the risk of experiencing age discrimination, which not only hampers recovery but contributes to the perpetuation, or deepening, of distress (Social Exclusion Unit, 2004).

Age discrimination has been identified in a recent national survey as the most common type of prejudice experienced in later life (Age Concern & University of Kent, 2005). In particular, it is experienced in relation to access to health and social care, welfare benefits, education, financial and retail services, and through the portrayal of older people in advertising and the media (Help the Aged, 2004a). Age discrimination can also intersect with other dimensions of social inequality such as gender, race or disability. Older women, for example, report that they feel 'overlooked' and 'useless', a manifestation of the 'double discrimination' of sexism and ageism, while black elders experience the combined disadvantages of racism and ageism (Moriarty & Butt, 2004).

A note on dementia

The author recognises that the discussion to date has considerably more explanatory power in relation to functional mental ill health, particularly depression, than for organic disorders. However, it is important to recognise that dementia, especially vascular dementia, does have some of its roots in life course disadvantage, specifically those linked to diet, level of education and lack of exercise (Alzheimer's Society, 2007; Butler *et al*, 2004). Even with Alzheimer's disease, where the dominant risk factor is very old age, there is recent evidence that environmental factors do play a role (*ibid*). Specifically, smoking seems to increase the risk of Alzheimer's disease as well as vascular dementia (Ott *et al*, 1998). Long-term follow-up studies show that high blood pressure (Skoog *et al*, 1996; Kivipelto *et al*, 2001) and high cholesterol levels (Kivipelto *et al*, 2001) in middle age each increase the risk of developing Alzheimer's disease in later life. Further, evidence from cross-sectional and case-control studies suggests associations between Alzheimer's disease and limited education, and recent research suggests that vascular disease predisposes people to Alzheimer's disease as well as to vascular dementia (Hofman *et al*, 1997). Space does not permit detailed analysis of these issues here but suffice to say that the causes of dementia do not lie entirely out with the mental health risks discussed above; nor is it helpful to view dementia as an illness that has no relationship to risk reduction or health promotion. Further, that there is emerging evidence that quality of life of people with dementia is as amenable to enhancement as that of those without dementia makes its inclusion both appropriate and timely (Livingstone *et al*, 2008).

Conclusion

This chapter has identified the dimensions of, and links between, mental health, well-being and quality of life, and has outlined the key determinants of mental health in old age. While the majority of older people do not have mental illness, it is instructive to foreground the role of both lifelong and age-related factors that challenge, or protect, mental health in later life. Mental health – much like health more broadly – can be viewed as a product of a wide range and number of intersecting factors located at the level of the individual and their family, the community and neighbourhood, and wider society. This perspective not only makes visible the issues that create particular vulnerability to mental ill health but also provides a lens through which to consider ways to promote mental health and reduce risk. This is the focus of the next chapter – addressing the challenges to mental health and well-being in later life – which complements, and builds upon, the synthesis of evidence presented here.

References

Age Concern England (2003) *Adding Quality to Quantity: Older people's views on quality of life and its enhancement*. London: Age Concern England.

Age Concern England (2004) *Policy Position Paper: Income*. London: Age Concern England.

Age Concern England (2005) *Policy Position Paper: Transport*. London: Age Concern England.

Age Concern England (2007) *Improving Services and Support for Older People with Mental Health Problems*. London: Age Concern.

Age Concern & Mental Health Foundation (2006) *Promoting Mental Health and Well-being in Later Life*. London: Age Concern.

Age Concern & University of Kent (2005) *Age Discrimination*. London: Age Concern England.

Albrecht GL & Devlieger PJ (1999) The disability paradox: high quality of life against all odds. *Social Science and Medicine* **48** 977–988.

Alzheimer's Society (2007) *Dementia UK*. London: Alzheimer's Society.

Anderson D (2005) Preventing delirium in older people. *British Medical Bulletin* **73** (1) 25–34.

Baltes P & Baltes M (1990) *Successful Ageing: Perspectives from the behavioural sciences*. Cambridge: Cambridge University Press.

Beeston D (2006) *Older People and Suicide*. London: Care Services Improvement Partnership.

Bond J & Corner L (2004) *Quality of Life and Older People*. Maidenhead: Open University Press.

Bowling A, Banister D, Sutton S, Evans O & Windsor J (2002) A multi-dimensional model of the quality of life in older age. *Aging and Mental Health* **6** (4) 355–371.

Bowling A (2005) *Ageing Well: Quality of life in old age*. Berkshire: Open University Press.

Brown G & Harris T (1978) *Social Origins of Depression: A study of psychiatric disorder in women*. London: Tavistock.

Butler R, Orrell M, Okoumunne O & Bebbington P (2004) Life events and survival in dementia: a five-year follow-up study. *Australia and New Zealand Journal of Psychiatry* **38** (9) 702–705.

Byrne GJA & Raphael B (1994) A longitudinal study of bereavement phenomena in recently widowed elderly men. *Psychological Medicine* **24** (2) 411–421.

Bytheway B (1995) *Ageism*. Milton Keynes: Open University Press.

Carers UK (2004) *In Poor Health: The impact of caring on health*. London: Carers UK.

Covinsky KE, Wu AW, Landefeld, CS, Connors Jr AF, Phillips RS, Tsevat J, Dawson JL & Fortinsky RH (1999) Health status versus quality of life in older patients: does the distinction matter? *American Journal of Medicine* **106** 435–440.

Depp CA & Jeste DV (2006) Definitions and predictors of successful aging: a comprehensive review of larger quantitative studies. *American Journal of Geriatric Psychiatry* **14** 6–20.

Godfrey M & Denby T (2004) *Depression and Older People*. Bristol: Policy Press.

Godfrey M, Townsend J, Surr C, Boyle G & Brooker D (2005) *Prevention and Service Provision: Mental health problems in later life*. Leeds: Institute of Health Sciences & Public Health Research, University of Leeds & Division of Dementia Studies, University of Bradford.

Grundy E (2001) *Ageing and Vulnerable Elderly People in Europe*, paper prepared for NIEPS (Network for Integrated European Population Studies) workshop, Rome, 2001.

Health Scotland (2004) *Mental Health and Well-being in later life: Older people's perceptions*. Edinburgh: Scottish Executive, Health Scotland.

Help the Aged (2004a) *Everyday Age Discrimination – What older people say*. London: Help the Aged.

Help the Aged (2004b) *Quality of Life in Older Age, Messages from the Growing Older Programme*. London: Help the Aged.

Henderson A, Korten A, Jacomb P, MacKinnon A, Jorm A, Christensen H & Rodgers B (1997) The course of depression in the elderly: a longitudinal community-based study in Australia. *Psychological Medicine* **27** (1) 119–129.

Hofman A, Ott A, Breteler MMB, Bots ML, Slooter AJC, van Harskamp F, Van Duijn CN, Van Broeckhoven C & Grobbee DE (1997) Atherosclerosis, apolipoprotein E, and prevalence of dementia and Alzheimer's disease in the Rotterdam Study. *Lancet* **349** 151–154.

Holahan CK, Holahan CJ & Belk SS (1984) Adjustment in ageing: the roles of life stress hassles and life efficacy. *Health Psychology* **3** (4) 315–328.

House of Commons Committee of Public Accounts (2008) *Improving Services and Support for People with Dementia*, HC 228. London: The Stationery Office.

Jacoby R, Oppenheimer C, Dening T & Thomas A (2008) (Eds) *The Oxford Textbook of Old Age Psychiatry*. Oxford: Oxford University Press.

Kivipelto M, Helkala EL, Laakso MP, Hanninen T, Hallikainen M, Alhainen K, Soininen H, Tuomilehto J & Nissinen A (2001) Midlife vascular risk factors and Alzheimer's disease in later life: longitudinal, population based study. *British Medical Journal* **322** 1447–1451.

Lawton MP (1991) Background: a multi-dimensional view of quality of life in frail elders In: JE Birren, J Lubben, J Rowe & D. Deutchman (Eds) *The Concept and Measurement of Quality of Life in the Frail Elderly*. San Diego, CA: Academic Press.

Le Mesurier N (2003) *The Hidden Store: Older people's contributions to rural communities*. London: Age Concern.

Livingstone G, Cooper C, Woods J, Milne A & Katona C (2008) Successful ageing in adversity – the LASER longitudinal study. *Journal of Neurology, Neurosurgery and Psychiatry* **79** 641–645.

Maher J & Green H (2002) *Carers 2000*. London: Office of National Statistics.

Mental Health Foundation (2003) *Fact Sheet: What is mental health?* London: Mental Health Foundation.

Mental Health Foundation (2007) *Fundamental Facts*. London: Mental Health Foundation.

Mentality (2001) *Making it Happen: A guide to delivering mental health promotion*. London: Department of Health.

Mentality (2004) *Literature and Policy Review on Mental Health Promotion in Later Life*. London: Age Concern and the Mental Health Foundation.

Milne A & Williams J (2000) Meeting the mental health needs of older women: taking social inequality into account. *Ageing and Society* **20** (6) 699–723.

Milne A & Williams J (2003) *Women at the Crossroads: A literature review of the mental health risks facing women in mid-life*. London: Mental Health Foundation.

Milne A & Hatzidimitriadou E (2002) The caring in later life report: a secondary analysis of the 1995 general household survey. *Quality in Ageing* **3** (3) 3–15.

Milne A & Chryssanthopoulou C (2005) Dementia caregiving in black and Asian populations: reviewing and refining the research agenda. *Journal of Community and Applied Social Psychology* **15** 319–337.

Milne A, Hatzidimitriadou E & Wiseman J (2007) Health and quality of life among older people in rural England: exploring the impact and efficacy of policy. *Journal of Social Policy* **36** (3) 477–495.

Milne A & Peet J (2008) *Challenges and Resolutions to Psychosocial Well-being for People in Receipt of a Diagnosis of Dementia: A literature review*. London: Alzheimer's Society.

Moriarty J & Butt J (2004) Inequalities in quality of life among older people from different ethnic groups. *Ageing and Society* **24** (5) 729–753.

Office of the Deputy Prime Minister (2006) *The Social Exclusion of Older People: Evidence from the first wave of the English longitudinal survey of ageing*. London: OPDM.

Office for National Statistics (2002) *Mental Health of Carers*. London: ONS.

Office for National Statistics (2004) *Focus on Older People*. London: ONS.

Ott A, Slooter AJC, Hofman A, van Harskamp F, Witteman JCM, Van Broeckhoven C, Van Duijn CM & Breteler MMB (1998) Smoking and risk of dementia and Alzheimer's disease in a population-based cohort study: the Rotterdam Study. *Lancet* **351** 1841–1843.

Phillipson C (1993) The sociology of retirement. In: J Bond, P Coleman and S Peace (Eds) *Ageing in Society* (2nd ed). London: Sage.

Phillipson C, Bernard M, Phillips J & Ogg J (2001) *The Family and Community Life of Older People*. London: Routledge.

Phillipson C & Sharf T (2004) *The Impact of Local Government Policy on Social Exclusion of Older People: A review of the literature*. London: Social Exclusion Unit.

Reed J, Glenda C, Childs S & Hall A (2003) *Getting Old is Not for Cowards: Comfortable, healthy ageing*. York: Joseph Rowntree Foundation.

Robinson L, Clare L & Evans K (2005) Making sense of dementia and adjusting to loss: psychological reactions to a diagnosis of dementia in couples. *Aging and Mental Health* **9** (4) 337–334.

Ryff CD (1999) Psychology and ageing. In: W Hazzard, J Blass, W Ettinger, J Halter & J Ouslander (Eds) *Principles of Geriatric Medicine and Gerontology* (4th ed). New York: McGraw-Hill.

Skoog I, Lernfelt B, Landahl S, Palmertz B, Andreasson LA, Nilsson L, Persson G, Oden A & Svanborg A (1996) 15-year longitudinal study of blood pressure and dementia. *Lancet* **347** 1141–1145.

Social Exclusion Unit (2004) Mental Health and Social Exclusion. London: Office of the Deputy Prime Minister.

Social Exclusion Unit (2006) *A Sure Start to Later Life, Ending Inequalities for Older People*. London: Office of the Deputy Prime Minister.

Stastny P & Amering M (1997) Integrating consumer perspectives in quality of life in research and service planning. In: H Katschnig, H Freeman & N Sartorius (Eds). *Quality of Life in Mental Disorders*. Chichester: Wiley.

Thompson L & Kingston P (2004) Measures to assess the quality of life for people with advanced dementia: issues in measurement and conceptualisation. *Quality in Ageing* **5** (4) 29–39.

Veenhoven R (2000) The four qualities of life. *Journal of Happiness Studies* **1** 1–39.

Victor C (2005) *The Social Context of Ageing: A textbook of gerontology*. Abingdon: Routledge.

Victor C, Scambler S & Bond J (2009) *The Social World of Older People: Understanding loneliness and social isolation in later life*. Maidenhead: McGraw Hill.

Walker A & Walker C (2005) The UK: quality of life in old age. In: A Walker (Ed) *Growing Older in Europe*. Maidenhead: Open University Press.

World Health Organization (2001) *Mental Health: New understanding, new hope*. Geneva: WHO.

World Health Organization (2003) *Investing in Mental Health*. Geneva: WHO.

Chapter 3

Addressing the challenges to mental health and well-being in later life

Alisoun Milne

This chapter will focus on how, given what we know about the determinants of mental health outlined in **chapter 2**, mental health can be promoted and mental ill health prevented. A lengthy exposition of all the myriad ways in which threats can be addressed is outside the remit of a single chapter but outlining a framework to take forward mental health promotion will be offered alongside examples of good practice. That some mental health determinants are located at the level of the individual and family, for example, physical health, some at the level of the community or neighbourhood, such as social engagement, and others at the level of society, such as age discrimination, is a pivotal underlining issue (see **figure 1**). These can be conceptualised as concentric circles extending outwards from the individual. They also overlap and intersect; some are additionally a product of the life course. That the dimensions of mental health and well-being also exist in a number of different spheres – income, housing, transport, neighbourhoods, health care – means that action is required within and across agencies and policy arenas (Age Concern England, 2007). It is axiomatic that if threats to mental health exist in each of these dimensions and spheres, interventions to promote mental health and prevent mental illness are directed at addressing these threats at each level and across multiple domains (Mentality, 2001).

Figure 1 incorporates these key dimensions and offers a model, originally developed by Godfrey and Denby (2004), to review the promotion of mental health in later life. The model foregrounds the levels at which activity needs to be targeted – the individual and family or micro level, the community and neighbourhood or meso level, and the societal or macro level. Its capacity to incorporate multidimensionality reinforces the argument that mental health is 'everybody's business' and underscores the links, made earlier, between mental health and quality of life; the enhancement of one will improve the other (Care Services Improvement Partnership, 2005).

Before highlighting examples of particular initiatives it is instructive to provide a definition of mental health promotion. 'Mental health promotion' is any activity or action that strengthens or protects the mental health and well-being of individuals, families and communities and reduces structural barriers to participation or opportunity (see **box 1**) (Age Concern England, 2007). Mental health promotion activities tend to be most effective when targeted at either a specific population or group (eg. older people), individuals at risk (eg. bereaved older people), or those with existing mental health problems (eg. people with dementia). It is notable that this framework dovetails to a considerable degree with **figure 1**.

Figure 1: Addressing threats to mental health and well-being

Domain	Elements of quality of life	Risk factors	Interventions
Individual and family	Physical health Personal/social relationships Social activities	Loss of function/ mobility Loss of role/ connectedness No/few social activities	Early diagnosis of ill health and support Volunteering opportunities Community facilities/ resources Befriending activities
Community	Participation and engagement Quality of physical environment Crime and fear of crime	Lack of engagement Poor physical/social environment High levels of crime	Enhancing social and physical capital Neighbourhood improvement Crime prevention schemes
National/society	Material resources Inclusion Equality	Poverty/poor housing Exclusion/ marginalisation Age discrimination	Raise level of state pension Social inclusion initiatives Age equality/tackle age discrimination

(Source: Godfrey & Denby, 2004)

Box 1

Mental health promotion can:

- strengthen individuals – by increasing emotional resilience through interventions designed to promote self-esteem, life and coping skills
- strengthen communities – by increasing social inclusion and participation, improving neighbourhood environments, developing a range of interventions that support mental health for people of all ages such as self-help networks, safety measures or reducing social isolation
- reduce structural barriers – by tackling inequalities through initiatives to reduce age and other types of discrimination, promote access to services, education and benefits and facilitate inclusion for those who are vulnerable.

(Source: Age Concern England, 2007 citing Mentality, 2001)

Promoting mental health in later life: services and strategies

Micro level: individuals and families

At the individual level essential to older people's life quality is maintaining a positive sense of self, maintaining physical function, engagement in meaningful social activities, and participation as valued members of a family and/or social networks. It is the extent to which the losses that accompany old age stunt and limit those opportunities that represents the greatest risk to mental health and well-being. Conversely, interventions that are geared towards reducing such threats are likely to support, or promote, well-being (Godfrey et al, 2005; Mentality, 2004).

Interventions focused on alleviating the impact of major life stressors such as bereavement or acute illness are likely to be of particular benefit. In their book on late life depression, Manthorpe and Iliffe (2005) outline two examples of initiatives: emotional support following early diagnosis of dementia, and intervention after the death (or admission to care home) of a cared for relative.

The first example views diagnosis as the first stage in a process that includes specific follow-up support. For the early diagnosis of dementia to be managed well and risk of depression minimised, it needs to be supported by at least the following: support groups for those with dementia; carers groups; counselling; individual tailored information; access to specialist advice and help; and assistance with practical, financial and legal matters (Alzheimer's Society, 2008).

The second example relates to long-term carers being at particular risk of mental ill health following the death – or admission into a care home – of their relative. Carers have often become chronically isolated in their support role and when no longer actively 'caring' are likely to feel emotionally and socially adrift. The existence of a family carer may be known about by NHS or social care staff, for example a GP or care manager, but as their focus is most often the cared for person, when that person dies the carer may be 'abandoned' by services (Milne et al, 2004). It is at this juncture that proactive help for the carer is vital: to provide emotional support; pick up social contacts; and facilitate engagement with a life not defined by caring activities. This help can either be provided by the voluntary sector such as via a carers' agency or by professionals.

Although **box 2** describes a service for those currently caring for a relative with dementia it shares a number of the dimensions of the type of intervention just described.

Box 2

Carers befriending support

The aim of the 'carers befriending service' is to deliver an effective befriending scheme across the city of York for carers of people with dementia. Trained befrienders do not only provide social support and friendship but also information and advice to ensure that the person with dementia is cared for appropriately and at home for as long as possible. Workers use a combination of counselling skills, anger management training, and relaxation techniques to help support carers. Outcomes of the project include: appropriate referrals of people with dementia to health and social care services; increased social support networks; and reduced levels of depression, anxiety and isolation among carers.

(Source: Jane-Llopis & Gabilondo, 2008)

A fourth example of an intervention relates to physical health. Enhancing physical health not only increases functional capacity but also contributes to good mental health (Jane-Llopis & Gabilondo, 2008). Regular exercise is correlated positively with a reduction in depressive symptoms and an association with lower rates of dementia has recently been found (Butler et al, 2004). Exercise is also an inexpensive activity; a particular example of a health initiative is outlined in **box 3**.

Box 3

Walking the Way to Health initiative: Hambleton Strollers Walking for Health

Walking the Way to Health initiative has enabled the creation of more than 350 health walk schemes across the UK. One is based in Hambleton, Yorkshire. The aim is to encourage sedentary, disadvantaged and older people to take up walking through led walks of less than an hour. The project has been the subject of extensive evaluations, including a randomised controlled trial, resulting in increased walking by 50% of participants and significant improvements in the vitality, emotional and physical function scores. In addition, the social element of taking part in this programme was highly valued by walkers.

(Source: Jane-Llopis & Gabilondo, 2008)

Self-help is also an important and under-recognised facet of mental health maintenance. The Mental Health Foundation (2003) has identified a number of key things individuals of any age can do to help themselves:

- making time to do the things they enjoy
- taking moderate exercise
- cutting down on coffee, tea, alcohol and smoking
- celebrating the good things about ourselves
- keeping things in perspective
- developing and sustaining friendships
- listening to and respecting other people
- asking for help if we feel distressed or upset
- taking as much care of ourselves as the people we care for.

Psychological interventions specifically targeted at improving an older person's self-efficacy have also been evidenced as effective, particularly at times of 'stress' (Milne & Peet, 2008). Cognitive behavioural therapy for example can strengthen a person's capacity to adapt to change and to manage the challenges associated with old age, although it is notable that these are interventions that tend to be more acceptable, and available, to educated, middle class elders rather than those in 'greatest need' (Ryff, 1999).

Meso level: community and neighbourhood

There is some evidence to suggest that social capital is in decline in the UK and that this has had a disproportionately negative impact on older citizens (Phillipson & Sharf, 2004). Action required to facilitate community enrichment involves designing interventions that encourage interpersonal interaction within 'ordinary' communities and promote social connectedness. At the locality level, the provision of support and resources to facilitate or enhance the social integration of older people can improve life quality significantly. Recent research by Godfrey and Randall (2003) evidenced the pivotal role of small scale locally based organisations to promote the social inclusion of relatively fit older people – via social clubs, educational opportunities and outings – while also meeting the needs of elders with disabilities who are housebound (Cotterill & Taylor, 2001). By combining a range of activities which both develop and draw upon the capacities and expertise of local people, levels of social participation increased, friendships were developed and skills (re)learned. At the same time, specific initiatives such as befriending and small neighbourhood groups for people with disabilities meant that the 'social worlds' of those living with restrictions could be sustained, or even extended, contributing to well-being and inclusion.

Addressing the needs of 'at risk' groups such as those who are isolated or lonely – due for example to being recently widowed or having an existing mental illness – is evidenced as effective at enhancing participation and improving mental health. One such initiative, adopting a community development approach, is showcased below (see **box 4**).

Box 4

Reducing social isolation among older people in Bromley: adopting a community development approach

In 2002 a community development project, led by Age Concern, was rolled out in the London Borough of Bromley specifically targeting isolated older people. By facilitating a range of social and educational opportunities and building on existing networks, the project reduced levels of isolation, enhanced levels of participation, enriched civic and community activities, and improved overall well-being among project users. In particular it increased levels of social engagement and involvement in local decision-making, increased the use of local facilities, trained local volunteers to act as 'community leaders', and through early intervention delayed the need for mainstream services.

(Source: Milne et al, 2002)

The quality of the physical environment is a key contributor to older people's sense of dissatisfaction with, and alienation from, the places in which they live. As older people, particularly those with disabilities, tend to be more dependent than others on their locality, 'neighbourhood initiatives' such as the provision of green areas and meeting places, crime reduction schemes, well-lit streets, and accessible public transport, have the potential to have a significant positive impact on their mental health (Age Concern England, 2007). In terms of tackling crime and fear of crime, one initiative – the Neighbourhood Warden Scheme – has proved particularly effective at reducing fear among older citizens living in deprived areas (see **box 5**).

Box 5

Neighbourhood warden schemes

The schemes (over 50) shared the aims of crime prevention – reducing levels of crime, antisocial behaviour and fear of crime, environmental improvements, including the removal of litter and graffiti, improving the appearance and general state of repair of properties and public areas, and community development. In the main, they achieved all three aims especially bringing down levels of crime and fear of crime; wardens were found to be particularly successful at reducing fear among older people. Schemes that encompassed environmental and community based aims, together with crime prevention elements, appeared to have the potential to reverse the social and physical decline of poor areas.

(Source: Neighbourhood Renewal Unit, 2004)

Macro level: policy and societal

Age Concern England's (2003) policy report on quality of life among older people, emphasised the need for local and central government to undertake an overarching policy review – a coherent 'stock take' – of the impact of policy on those areas of older people's lives that contribute most significantly to mental health and well-being. This includes policies that focus on pensions and benefits, housing and neighbourhood renewal, the development of low level preventive services, as well as improved health and social care provision, community involvement and social engagement, promotion of independence, inclusion and social capital, and those that address stigma, exclusion and discrimination (Bowling, 2005).

Drawing on the very recent reports from the *Age Concern Mental Health and Well-being in Later Life Inquiry* (Age Concern & Mental Health Foundation, 2006; Age Concern England, 2007) it is clear that while much remains to be done, the trajectory of policy development is in the right direction. The current policy emphasis on promoting independence and well-being for all older people, including those with mental frailty, is a positive shift as is the explicit incorporation of older people in the recent focus on social exclusion eg. Social Exclusion Action Plan, 2006 (Social Exclusion Task Force, 2006; Department of Health, 2005). Prevention of ill health, once viewed simply as avoidance of use of tertiary services, is now viewed as a policy aim closely aligned with that of promotion of health and well-being; this explicitly includes mental health (Godfrey *et al*, 2005). *The National Service Frameworks for Older People* (Department of Health, 2001a) and *Mental Health* (Department of Health, 1999) have also set standards relating to promoting mental health in later life although these have been somewhat undermined by the invisibility of older people in the 2004 public health white paper *Choosing Health* (Department of Health, 2004; Mental Health Foundation, 2005). The growing policy emphasis on individualism, so beloved of the baby boom generation(s), is also an issue (Williamson, 2008).

A number of social policy initiatives specifically endorse active ageing. For example, *Opportunity Age* (2005), a strategy produced by the Department for Work and Pensions, aims to ensure that later life is active and fulfilling; it also recognises the contribution older people make to families, communities and UK society. This links with Ageing Well a cross-cutting health promotion initiative, which targets all older people as well as those at risk of mental ill health (see **box 6**). The programme was developed in response to the government's Health of the Nation targets, one of which was mental health (Department of Health, 1998), and was rolled out by Age Concern England and Wales.

Box 6

Ageing Well

Ageing Well is a health promotion initiative developed across England and Wales that enables older people to take control of their own health and promote healthy lifestyles (88 projects in total). The programme recruits and trains volunteers who are aged 50 years or over to become senior health mentors. Volunteers then make contact with isolated older people and community groups, providing vital links to health services and local social or educational opportunities. The programme offers advice on a range of issues: diet/nutrition, physical activity, mental and emotional well-being, and early intervention eg. health screening. Evaluation findings show that both users and volunteers have benefited physically, socially and psychologically from participating. Particularly, levels of isolation have reduced and levels of participation in a whole range of activities have increased facilitating the achievement of 'ageing well'.

(Source: Lambert *et al*, 2007)

The Partnerships for Older People Programme (POPP) is a large scale Department of Health funded initiative tasked with delivering and evaluating 29 local authority led schemes for older people (Personal Social Services Research Unit, 2008). The schemes explicitly aim to promote health, well-being and independence for older people and prevent the need for more intensive care; 14% (64) of projects are specifically focused on older people with mental health problems. Interim evidence suggests that as a result of using a POPP, project users' quality of life is enhanced; also, almost half the staff working in the projects are older volunteers. The National Programme for Improving Mental Health and Well-being in Scotland is a complementary example of a population-wide policy initiative that incorporates a specific dimension relating to older people (see **box 7**).

Box 7

National Programme for Improving Mental Health and Well-being

The National Programme for Improving Mental Health and Well-being was launched in October 2001 to raise the profile of, and support action to promote mental health and well-being, eliminate the stigma of mental illness, recover from mental illness and prevent suicide. One of its six key priority areas is improving mental health and well-being in later life. Relevant initiatives include: the programme's investment in public health campaigns focusing on promoting mental health; training to raise awareness about mental health issues among frontline staff in a range of agencies; and a three-year programme entitled Doing Well by People with Depression, which aims to improve support and access to early interventions. Specific activities include the development of regional 'health in later life interest groups', which share information and experiences and influence policy development, and a 'small projects scheme' to fund local initiatives to support the promotion of mental health among older people.

(Source: Hogg, 2005; Scottish Executive, 2003)

At least two other key policy areas emerge as worthy of note. Ensuring universal access to an adequate state pension is a primary policy goal that has the capacity – more than any other single intervention in the view of some critics – to enhance participation and well-being, provide financial security over the long-term, and promote independence. That an older person, when poor at 60, will be poor for the rest of their lives is a defining feature of old age poverty and one that marks 'the state pension' out as pivotal to the promotion of late life quality. Differential access to economic and social resources over the life course, persist into older age; reducing inequality is therefore an essential component of promoting mental health and well-being in older age (Help the Aged, 2007).

The government now recognises the discrimination faced by older people and the negative impact it has on their lives (Social Exclusion Unit, 2006). A Commission for Equality and Human Rights started work in 2007 and will be fully established by 2009; it will have responsibility for ensuring equal treatment across the six areas of equality: race, gender, physical and mental disability, age, sexual orientation, and religion and belief. The introduction of the equality bill will help in achieving the goal of age equality – securing equality in citizenship, access to opportunities and outcomes for people of every age (Age Concern England, 2007). At a societal level, addressing the embedded ageist attitudes and images that populate the media and popular press would go some way to engaging the wider public in recognising the damage that negative stereotypes can do in reinforcing marginalisation and feelings of worthlessness (Age Concern & University of Kent, 2005). Addressing age discrimination in the workplace and in health and social care services, and tackling stigma related to mental ill health, are also relevant issues.

The Age Concern and Mental Health Foundation Inquiry report (2006) suggests the following as key elements in any strategy to promote mental health and well-being in later life:

- promote age equality, particularly within mental health promotion and health and social care services
- recognise the skills and knowledge that older people have to contribute and provide opportunities for older people to share these with people of all ages, for example, through volunteering
- remove or reduce barriers to participation in later life, such as mandatory retirement ages, fear of crime and appropriate public transport
- help people to manage key transitions such as retirement eg. by offering planned flexible retirement
- encourage the development, and facilitation of, lifelong interests and social networks
- ensure the provision of an adequate state pension and the reduction, or removal, of structural barriers to participation.

Even the 'policy snapshot' offered here makes it clear that the policy picture is uneven and fragmented; while progress is being made in some areas such as social inclusion, other areas are just beginning to acknowledge the relevance of mental health issues eg. policies on discrimination. The picture is complex, impact is challenging to evaluate, and relevant initiatives myriad; this is a field that needs considerably more research attention, particularly on outcomes, than it currently receives (Age Concern England, 2007).

Before reviewing ways to move forward with this multidimensional agenda, a word about prevention is required.

Developing a preventative approach

It is notable that the model outlined here dovetails, to some degree at least, with what has been called a preventative approach, one that is most often understood as operating at three levels – primary, secondary and tertiary (Godfrey, 2001; Godfrey *et al*, 2005). Broadly, primary prevention focuses on causes or risk factors for ill health, secondary prevention on bolstering coping strategies or accessing help for an illness at an early stage, while tertiary prevention relates more to amelioration of symptoms or prevention of 'excess disability' in the face of an existing health problem (Manthorpe & Iliffe, 2005). The majority focus of this chapter has been primary prevention, which overlaps conceptually, and in practice, with the notion of promotion; addressing those factors that create vulnerability to mental ill health and reducing risks is an activity that has the potential to both promote mental health and prevent mental illness. Further, the focus of **chapter 2** – mental health and well-being and the common risks, stressors and transitions faced by older people – inevitably steers the discussion towards primary prevention for 'ordinary' older people rather than those who have a diagnosed mental illness. That is not to suggest prevention has no place in work with older people with enduring mental ill health, including dementia, but rather that to address the needs of the total population of older people with mental health problems is a task beyond the boundaries of this, relatively focused, chapter. Additionally, that risks to mental health have been presented through the lens of inequality has left limited room for discussion on the role these play in deepening disadvantage for those who are already mentally ill (Milne & Williams, 2000).

Although there has been some recent policy emphasis on developing preventive strategies and early intervention, there remains limited investment in low-level services, those whose aim it is to prevent physical and mental ill health (Department of Health, 2006). The kinds of services that promote well-being described above eg. those that target the relief of isolation or enhance social activity, can as easily be conceptualised as preventative; it is the other side of the same coin (Association of Directors of Social Service/Local Government Association, 2003). The tendency to equate older people's mental health issues with dementia inhibits the development of a focus on prevention and promotion. As we have reviewed here, not only is it evidently the case that much can be done to address or ameliorate risks to mental health in later life, but that efforts to prevent mental illness and promote mental health should target all those who experience late life challenges, including people with dementia.

Promoting mental health and well-being – moving forward

This chapter has outlined some examples of how risks to mental health in later life might be addressed at the level of the individual and family, community and neighbourhood, and policy/society (Godfrey & Denby, 2004). How to move the process forward is a significant challenge and one that remains cited at the margins of policy targeting older people. While greater acknowledgement is now made of the importance of promoting 'good mental health and well-being in later life' than hitherto, there is little evidence of a 'joined up' approach to mental health promotion for older people. For example, the mental health promotion framework for England *Making it Possible* stated: '*It is widely acknowledged that the mental health and well-being of older people has been neglected across the spectrum of promotion, prevention and treatment services*' (National Institute for Mental Health in England, 2005). Similarly, the ageing policy agenda marginalises mental health. Active ageing initiatives tend to focus on the promotion of physical health and well-being despite the evidence that depression and dementia can have a greater impact on quality of life than chronic physical illnesses (Age Concern England, 2007).

Thus, there is a government level need to foreground mental health in later life issues and knit together existing policies, located in different policy spheres, under this single topic head. A wide-ranging review of policy efficacy at regular intervals would also ensure that changes were being monitored and gaps identified. Much can be learned from approaches and interventions developed for younger adults and children in the mental health field (Department of Health, 2001b). The Age Concern and Mental Health Foundation Inquiry (2006) had gone some way to identifying 'what needs to be done' to ensure that a coherent and multidimensional approach is adopted to promote mental health and well-being in later life. In particular, it recommends action be taken in the following key areas:

- removing discrimination is central to success; it limits opportunities to participate in activities that would improve physical health, extend social contacts and reduce isolation
- poverty among older people limits opportunities to maintain decent housing, pay for heating and a healthy diet, join in social and other activities and support a standard of living commensurate with facilitation of choice and independence
- good physical health enables people to maintain relationships, get out and about and engage in meaningful activities
- inequalities in health and well-being within the older population are considerable; addressing inequalities across the life course, as well as within the older cohorts, should be a key policy and public health concern.

National level policy needs to be taken forward, and complemented, by local government and council-led local strategies. As is clear from this chapter, this process would need to involve a range of agencies – housing, social services, voluntary sector, public health, community groups, education – working together to agreed targets and timetables. The focus of such activity would be the development of interventions and programmes aimed at reducing the impact of threats to mental health; particular attention would also be directed at those experiencing a multiplicity of risk factors (Godfrey et al, 2005). This multifaceted approach would form the basis of an integrated and comprehensive service response to support well-being in older age, and address those risk factors that create mental health vulnerability in later life (Godfrey et al, 2005; Godfrey & Denby, 2004). Examples of existing mechanisms to take this kind of approach forward include 'Local Area Agreements' (Office of the Deputy Prime Minister, 2005).

There are other issues that need addressing. While research has helped to identify the risks, transitions and challenges commonly associated with later life, as well as opportunities and protective factors, more investment is needed to extend understanding about the features of the ageing process that are amenable to change and the kinds of action that must be taken to enhance positive adaptation (Godfrey & Denby, 2004). Providing robust evidence of the impact and efficacy of low-level services to address risks to mental health is also needed. The current relatively weak evidence base makes statutory commitment to the development of such services difficult, although it could be argued not only that prevention is better, and cheaper, than cure but also enhances well-being over the longer run (Godfrey, 2001). An additional issue relates to the user voice. The benefits of drawing on the experiences of older people in research and service development cannot be overstated; an approach that has considerably strengthened the work and credibility of the *UK Inquiry into Mental Health and Well-being*, and a core feature of many of the initiatives outlined above (Age Concern England, 2007). There is also a key ideological tension embedded in policy that cannot be ignored. The foregrounding of emphasis on informed choice, personalisation, and individual responsibility for health sits uncomfortably alongside policy drives to improve the mental health of populations, reduce health inequalities and promote social inclusion (Williamson, 2008). Whatever its benefits, a focus on individualisation is not a substitute for public health initiatives whose lens accommodates the needs of all older people, including those who are disadvantaged, and which target the socio-economic and life course determinants of mental ill health.

While the challenge remains considerable and the issues complex, three overarching conclusions emerge. The first is that most of the actions that are needed to promote mental health in later life can be integrated into existing policy and service developments and once added, will strengthen the existing 'momentum for change' (Age Concern and Mental Health Foundation, 2006: 63). The second is that while the task looks large and multidimensional – and it is in the round – many of the ingredients are relatively small scale, affordable, inclusive and local. The third challenge relates to the need to ensure that policy developments retain a focus on population-wide public health initiatives alongside those that emphasise individual choice and responsibility for mental health and well-being. Time is of the essence with this important agenda, our ageing society demands that we pay attention – now – to the pressing need to address the threats to mental health facing current, and upcoming, cohorts of older people. Mental illness is not an inevitable part of the ageing process but it is more likely if we neglect the potential of older people to contribute and participate, fail to challenge discrimination, do not invest in risk reducing interventions, and ignore opportunities to promote, and enhance, mental health and well-being in later life.

References

Age Concern England (2003) *Adding Quality to Quantity: Older people's views on quality of life and its enhancement*. London: Age Concern England.

Age Concern England (2007) *Improving Services and Support for Older People with Mental Health Problems*. London: Age Concern.

Age Concern & Mental Health Foundation (2006) *Promoting Mental Health and Well-being in Later Life*. London: Age Concern.

Age Concern & University of Kent (2005) *Age Discrimination*. London: Age Concern England.

Alzheimer's Society (2008) *Out of the Shadows*. London: Alzheimer's Society.

Association of Directors of Social Service/Local Government Association (2003) *All Our Tomorrows: Inverting the triangle of care*. London: Association of Directors of Social Service/Local Government Association.

Bowling A (2005) *Ageing Well: Quality of life in old age*. Maidenhead: Open University Press.

Butler R, Orrell M, Okoumunne O & Bebbington P (2004) Life events and survival in dementia: a five-year follow-up study. *Australia and New Zealand Journal of Psychiatry* **38** (9) 702–705.

Care Services Improvement Partnership (2005) *Everybody's Business –Integrated mental health services for older adults: a service development guide*. London: Department of Health.

Cotterill L & Taylor D (2001) Promoting mental health and well-being among housebound older people. *Quality in Ageing* **2** (3) 32–46.

Department of Health (1998) *The Health of the Nation: A policy assessed*. London: Department of Health.

Department of Health (1999) *National Service Framework for Mental Health*. London: Department of Health.

Department of Health (2001a) *National Service Framework for Older People*. London: Department of Health.

Department of Health (2001b) *Making it Happen: A guide to delivering mental health promotion*. London: Department of Health.

Department of Health (2004) *Choosing Health: Making health choices easier*. London: Department of Health.

Department of Health (2005) *Independence, Well-being and Choice*. London: Department of Health.

Department of Health (2006) *Our Health, Our Care, Our Say: A new direction for community services*. London: Department of Health.

Department for Work and Pensions (2005) *Opportunity Age*. London: Department of Work and Pensions.

Godfrey M (2001) Prevention: developing a framework for conceptualising and evaluating outcomes of preventive services for older people. *Health and Social Care in the Community* **9** (2) 89–99.

Godfrey M & Denby T (2004) *Depression and Older People*. Bristol: Policy Press & Help the Aged.

Godfrey M & Randall T (2003) *Developing a Locality Base Approach to Prevention for Older People*. Leeds: Nuffield Institute for Health.

Godfrey M, Townsend J, Surr C, Boyle G & Brooker D (2005) *Prevention and Service Provision: Mental health problems in later life*. Leeds: University of Leeds & University of Bradford.

Help the Aged (2007) *Social Inclusion and Older People*. London: Help the Aged.

Hogg E (2005) United Kingdom: Scotland. In: E Jané-Llopi & P Anderson (Eds) *Mental Health Promotion and Mental Disorder Prevention across European Member States: A collection of country stories*. Luxembourg: European Communities.

Jane-Llopis E & Gabilondo A (Eds) (2008) *Mental Health in Older People, Consensus paper*. Luxembourg: European Commission.

Lambert S, Granville G, Lewis J, Merrell J & Taylor C (2007) *As Soon as I Get My Trainers on I Feel Like Dancing – Age Concern's Ageing Well programme in England and Wales, Final evaluation report*. London: Age Concern England.

Manthorpe J & Iliffe S (2005) *Depression in Later Life*. London: Jessica Kingsley.

Mental Health Foundation (2003) *Fact Sheet: What is mental health?* London: Mental Health Foundation.

Mental Health Foundation (2005) *Choosing Mental Health: A policy agenda for mental health and public health*. London: Mental Health Foundation.

Mentality (2001) *Making it Happen: A guide to delivering mental health promotion*. London: Department of Health.

Mentality (2004) *Literature and Policy Review on Mental Health Promotion in Later Life*. London: Age Concern and the Mental Health Foundation.

Milne A, Falloon M & Bradshaw S (2002) *Reducing Social Isolation amongst Older People: Adopting a community development approach.* London: Age Concern.

Milne A, Hatzidimitriadou E & Chryssanthopoulou C (2004) Carers of older relatives in long-term care: support needs and services. Generations review. *Journal of the British Society of Gerontology* **14** (3) 4–9.

Milne A & Peet J (2008) *Challenges and Resolutions to Psycho-social Well-being for People in Receipt of a Diagnosis of Dementia: A literature review.* London: Alzheimer's Society.

Milne A & Williams J (2000) Meeting the mental health needs of older women: taking social inequality into account. *Ageing and Society* **20** (6) 699–723.

National Institute for Mental Health in England (2005) *Making it Possible: Improving mental health and well-being in England.* London: National Institute for Mental Health in England.

Neighbourhood Renewal Unit (2004) *Research Summary 8, Neighbourhood Warden Scheme Evaluation: Key findings and lessons.* Wetherby: Office of the Deputy Prime Minsiter.

Office of the Deputy Prime Minister (2005) *Local Strategic Partnerships: Shaping their future, consultation paper.* London: Office of the Deputy Prime Minister.

Personal Social Services Research Unit (2008) *National Evaluation of Partnerships for Older People Projects: Interim report of progress.* Canterbury: University of Kent.

Phillipson C & Sharf T (2004) *The Impact of Local Government Policy on Social Exclusion of Older People: A review of the literature.* London: Social Exclusion Unit.

Ryff CD (1999) Psychology and ageing. In: W Hazzard, J Blass, W Ettinger, J Halter & J Ouslander (Eds) *Principles of Geriatric Medicine and Gerontology* (4th ed). New York: McGraw-Hill.

Scottish Executive (2003) *National Programme for Improving Mental Health and Well-being Action Plan 2003–2006.* Edinburgh: Scottish Executive.

Social Exclusion Task Force (2006) *Reaching Out: An action plan on social exclusion.* London: Cabinet Office.

Social Exclusion Unit (2006) *A Sure Start to Later Life: Ending Inequalities for Older People* London: Office of the Deputy Prime Minister

Williamson T (2008) From the 60s to their sixties: baby boomers – challenges and choices for public mental health. *Journal of Public Mental Health* **7** (1) 4–8.

Chapter 4

What do you expect at your age?

Philip Hurst

'I feel I am treated differently because of my age. It feels like I'm invisible now and I think sometimes I don't get offered services because I'm old.' (Age Concern, 2007)

Introduction

It has become an established convention to plan and organise mental health services separately for younger and older adults, with age cut-off points set at or around age 65. Mental health services are now unique in this approach, which has increasingly been recognised as anachronistic in a health and care system that is meant to be needs-led and based on equality of access. Many studies have found that the separation of services is discriminatory and does not serve older people well, but there are concerns that a simplistic approach to change could lead to the loss of specialist services that some older people need.

Our identities are clearly not determined by age alone, but by many factors including race, gender, gender identity, disability, religion, belief and sexual orientation. Although people may face discrimination as a result of any of these aspects of identity or any combination of them, there is a tendency to 'classify' older people simply according to age. Yet all of these factors can be as relevant to older people as younger people – and, in some cases, even more relevant. For example, the majority of people living with disabilities are older people.

It can also be useful to think about the issue of discrimination in the context of human rights. Here the key legal requirement is that people must not be discriminated against on any ground such as sex, race, colour, religion, or any other status (which can include age) in securing their human rights. Over a period of time, a range of separate legal measures has been taken to protect people against discrimination in relation to race, gender, disability, sexual orientation, gender reassignment, religion and belief. Legal duties have been introduced for public bodies to promote equality of opportunity in relation to race, gender and disability. Age has tended to lag behind in terms of legal protection but the introduction of an Equality and Human Rights Commission in 2007 brought together work to tackle discrimination and promote equality across all strands, including age, and the government has introduced an equality bill to Parliament, which aims to outlaw age discrimination in the provision of goods, facilities and services.

While recognising that all equality strands are potentially important to older people – and that some older people face multiple discrimination – this chapter will focus on the nature of age discrimination and age equality in mental health and will propose some actions for change.

Age discrimination

Ageism is the most commonly experienced form of discrimination in Britain across all age groups. A 2004 Age Concern survey showed that 29% of people reported having been unfairly treated because of their age in the previous year. Although older people are the least likely age group to report any form of discrimination, those who do experience discrimination are more likely to encounter age discrimination than any other type. There has also been a change in the public perception of the seriousness of age discrimination. In 2004 the majority of the public believed that ageism was not a serious issue but, by the time the survey was repeated in 2006, there had been a shift to a slight majority (51%) believing it was very or quite serious (Age Concern, 2008a). Yet, despite the fact that ageism is experienced across the whole of society, people continue to regard it as less serious than discrimination on the grounds of race, religion or disability.

Although there has been relatively little examination of the specific impact of age discrimination on mental health, it is well established that discrimination in any form is a risk factor for poor mental health (Thornicroft, 2006). It can lower self-esteem, sometimes leading to feelings of worthlessness and despair. The result may be lowered expectations of rights and capabilities that prevent people from contributing to society and enjoying life to the full.

Promoting good mental health and well-being among older people has also been a relatively neglected area in both research and policy. A UK inquiry into mental health and well-being in later life sought to fill some of the gaps in the evidence base by seeking the views of older people, organisations and professionals on the key factors that either promote or hinder good mental health (Age Concern/ Mental Health Foundation, 2006). The responses from older people stated strongly that feeling valued, respected and understood was crucial for good mental health. Tackling age discrimination and improving public attitudes towards older people was therefore, unsurprisingly, a key priority for action.

> '*Older people need to be needed and valued. This country doesn't teach children to value older people as they do in other countries. They should start teaching children how important older people can be in their lives.*'

Organisations responding to the call for evidence also recognised the importance of tackling this issue. One in five organisations mentioned that, in order to achieve real change in mental health and well-being in later life, one of the crucial areas of work would be around public attitudes.

> '*Society as a whole has to recognise ... that old age is not the final destination in our journey through life, but a point in our growth and progression!*'

Individual older people and organisational responses showed striking similarities but also some subtle differences. One of the most important areas of difference was in the importance they attached to older people's continued contribution to society. Whilst organisations recognised that older people wish to remain active and engaged in interests, they gave less weight to older people's contributions.

For older people, the themes of both voluntary work and formal employment were strongly emphasised as being important to their sense of self-worth. Individuals, particularly in the younger age group, expressed the wish that they should be able to continue in formal employment beyond the age of 65. Some people who had passed retirement described feeling forced out of responsible jobs, which they were deemed capable of on the eve of their birthday. There was no universal reason why people wished to remain in paid employment for longer, but individuals' responses included financial concerns, inactivity and potential boredom, feeling valued and contributing to society. People were keen to pursue their voluntary work for similar reasons, though clearly not for financial gain. Whatever people's reasons for undertaking voluntary work in the first instance, it seemed to also have a personal benefit.

In terms of responsibility for action to tackle age discrimination, older people saw roles for the media, to improve the portrayal of ageing, and for advertising and marketing, including improving product design. It was often the 'casual', day-to-day age discrimination in older people's encounters with shop assistants, receptionists and health care workers that had a very negative impact on how they felt. There were calls to improve the education and training of all those who were in regular contact with older people to counter ingrained ageist attitudes and beliefs.

Older people with mental health problems can face the combination of age discrimination with the stigma attached to mental illness. The Social Exclusion Unit has identified discrimination against people with mental health problems as 'the greatest barrier to social inclusion, quality of life and recovery'. The National Dementia Strategy for England (Department of Health, 2009b) emphasises the importance of tackling the stigma associated with dementia to ensure that people seek help at an early stage of their illness, as well as improving the understanding of the wider society in which people with dementia will spend most of the rest of their lives.

Mental health policy and practice

In spite of the negative impact of age discrimination on mental health, mental health policy and practice has followed a path of age discrimination, which has been hard to shift. This may tell us much about the stigma attached both to mental health problems and to old age.

Public policy on older people's mental health has often remained confused and disjointed, demonstrated perhaps most obviously by the two National Service Frameworks (NSFs). In 2001 the first priority of the NSF for Older People was to root out age discrimination so that NHS services would be provided, regardless of age, on the basis of clinical need alone; and social care services would not use age, in eligibility criteria or policies, to restrict access to available services. This should perhaps have led to a review of the scope of the earlier (1999) NSF for Mental Health, which gave an explicit focus to 'adults of working age'. The two NSFs were clearly contradictory from the outset but rather than recognising and reconciling these contradictions, public policy for mental health has been pursued along a path that has now been recognised as explicitly age discriminatory. New investment in mental health services has been targeted on additional services available only to adults up to the age of 65. At the same time, services developed under the banner of the NSF for Older People, such as intermediate care, were often designed to exclude people with mental health needs.

The original establishment of separate services for older people with mental health problems often arose from an acknowledgement that there was little in the way of appropriate provision either for people with dementia or for those with complex, multiple physical and mental health problems. Historical underinvestment in mental health services encouraged the maintenance of boundaries to ensure that services would not be overwhelmed by demand. The distinction between services for 'adults' and those for 'older people' has continued in policy and in practice as if normal and natural. However, in health and social care services, mental health services now stand alone in making a distinction based on chronological age – although few attempt to offer a rational justification of it. Even when the problem is recognised it can be challenging to develop practical solutions that avoid unintended, negative consequences.

Calls to remove age discrimination in policy can focus on the problem as one of systems and management without having a clear and explicit understanding of the effects on people's lives. Yet the impact of age discrimination in policy can be devastating for individuals on the receiving end of services.

> *'Going to a group and mixing with others who had similar problems as me was good. And having someone to talk to – I liked my support worker. But I can't get that now because of my age…. I feel alone and isolated. I feel as if there's no reason to get up. I feel terrible…. I feel suicidal. I was going to harm myself recently.'*

Why should age discrimination have been so persistent in mental health? It is perhaps telling that the emphasis in mental health policy has been on defining adults in relation to work – or their potential for it. In spite of the prevalence of mental health problems in the population, mental health policy has continued to be a poor relation in terms of prioritisation of health and care services. Unlike other health services, investment in mental health appears to need justification in terms that demonstrate the benefits that society will reap from getting people back into work, or into work for the first time. Although work can indeed reinforce good mental health, there are wider societal reasons to achieve the best possible level of health and well-being for all citizens, not just those of so-called 'working age'. If economic arguments have to be used, they should be defined more widely than is currently the case. At the moment the economic arguments for investment in mental health services can be seen as another example of disjointed policy-making, ignoring the facts of demographic change.

We live in an ageing society. The fastest growing section of the population is in the older age group and the UK has already passed the point at which the number of people over 60 exceeds the number of those under 16. By 2031 almost a quarter of the population will be over the state pension age. At one level the government has recognised that our society will increasingly rely on the contributions of older people in both paid employment and in a range of other roles. Opportunity Age sets out the cross-government strategy for an ageing population, aiming to end the perception of older people as dependent, ensuring that later life is healthy and fulfilling, and enabling older people to be full participants in society. Already around one million people in the UK work beyond state pension age. People aged 50 and over contribute £230 billion a year (around a quarter of the UK economy) through work, and this is supplemented by contributions valued at £24 billion through contributions as unpaid carers, grandparents and volunteers. It is essential for our society that older people should be well enough to make these contributions whether in paid employment or in other roles.

Yet mental health policy has remained largely immune to the overall policy direction for an ageing society. For example, a white paper on community health and social care (Department of Health, 2006) included a general commitment to age equality and zero tolerance on discrimination but this was made alongside the announcement of two demonstration sites for the expansion of psychological therapies that were to have a focus on 'people of working age'.

The facts and consequences of this age discrimination have not gone unnoticed. In 2005 the National Institute for Mental Health in England reported that, '*It is widely acknowledged that the mental health and well-being of older people has been neglected across the spectrum of promotion, prevention and treatment services*'. And in 2006 a joint inspectorate report (Audit Commission, CSCI & Healthcare Commission, 2006) on progress with the National Service Framework for Older People in England stated that the division of services between 'adults of working age' and 'older people' has resulted in '*the development of an unfair system, as the range of services available differs for each of these groups*'. The report identified in particular that older people who had made a transition between services around the age of 65 had witnessed noticeable differences in the quality of services. In 2009 a final report from the Healthcare Commission found older people's mental health services falling behind those for younger adults in terms of prioritisation and evidence of age discrimination in access to services, age-appropriateness and lack of specialist input.

In response to such reports, the government has declared that ending age discrimination in mental health is a priority. Policy documents (Department of Health, 2005; Care Services Improvement Partnership, 2005) promote the principle of age equality in mental health services and commit to ensuring that, wherever older people with mental health problems appear in the health and social care system, they will not experience discrimination. Key policy developments have, however, continued to focus on younger adults, although there have been some developments, such as the Department of Health's (2009a) commissioning guide for improving access to psychological therapies, which have emphasised the need to ensure equity of access. The end of the 10-year programme associated with the NSF for mental health in 2009 will provide the ideal opportunity to set a future direction that it is truly age equal and age inclusive. To date there is little evidence of the overarching commitment to age equality finding its way into most of the detail of mental health policy or practice.

Age equality has proved to be a difficult concept to grasp within mental health services. A misunderstanding of the nature of age discrimination, coupled with a difficult financial climate, has been a catalyst for some service commissioners or providers to declare that the provision of any separate services for older people is discriminatory and must be removed. However, just as it is wrong to determine access to services on the basis of chronological age, it is equally wrong to deny that some groups of older people need specialist support, particularly where they have complex needs resulting from multiple health and social problems. In some cases there has been a move from direct age discrimination to indirect age discrimination by developing apparently neutral services, which nonetheless continue to disadvantage older people, for example, by mixing adults of all ages on inpatient units or opening up services to older people but making no changes to make the service truly accessible. Alongside this, services for people with dementia, often assumed to be the only services that are relevant to older people, are often inaccessible to younger people who develop dementia.

Consequences for older people

The lack of understanding of age equality is often combined with a general aura of defeatism – the idea that mental health problems are an inevitable part of ageing and that, in any case, there is not much that can be done. Both of these are misconceptions: the majority of older people do not have a mental health problem and evidence has shown that interventions, such as psychological therapies, are as effective for older people as they are for younger people, when they can gain access to them. The risk factors for many of the mental health problems faced by older people are well known and it remains possible to intervene to prevent or reduce risks as well as to alleviate the impact of those that cannot be avoided.

The consequences of these attitudes and beliefs result in a significant mismatch between population health needs and the strategies and services in place to respond to them.

- Some of the highest suicide rates are among people aged 75 and over. Yet suicide prevention strategies pay little attention to the prevention of suicide among older people. Such deaths are often portrayed in the media as heroic rather than tragic (especially in the cases of older couples who enter into 'suicide pacts' as a result of levels of pain or disability).

- Depression is the most common mental health problem among older people, as in younger people. Around one in four older people living in the community has a level of depression that could benefit from some intervention and 10–15% have clinical depression (Department of Health, 2001). This rises to 40% among people living in care homes (Audit Commission, 2000). Yet, although it is a common condition in primary care, depression in older people is significantly under-diagnosed and under-treated by GPs and others (Age Concern, 2008b).

- Approximately one-third of beds in general hospitals are occupied by older people who have mental health problems, or who develop them during their admission (Royal College of Psychiatrists, 2005). Yet few professionals working in general hospitals have been trained to recognise or respond to such needs.

Future opportunities

In the face of problems of this scale it can be challenging to know which policy initiatives could be most effective in bringing about change. However, there is light on the horizon. Aspirations for healthy ageing have been given a boost by the inclusion of the aim to increase healthy life expectancy for older people in the latest set of public service agreements, which set out the government's top priorities, how they will be achieved and how progress will be measured. This will need to address good physical and mental health – and the interplay between the two – if the objective is to be met in a way that is meaningful for older people.

Perhaps even more significantly, the government has introduced an equality bill, which provides for a new duty on public sector organisations to promote age equality and will start the process of outlawing age discrimination in goods, facilities and services (including health and social care services). Research commissioned by the Department of Health has estimated the costs of achieving age equality in mental health services at around £2 billion. At the very least, this establishes that there is a large-scale problem to address.

The opportunity to set a new agenda lies with the development of a vision for the mental health of people of all ages to replace the National Service Framework for Mental Health.

Money, although it is crucial, will not solve the problems alone. The promotion of good mental health and well-being in later life and the prevention of problems will need to move much higher up the agenda at both a national and local level. The needs of older people who experience mental health problems, and the needs of their carers, must be better understood, taken seriously, given their fair share of attention and resources, and met in a way that enables them to lead full and meaningful lives.

To achieve this transformation, the key priorities are as follows.

■ The principle of age equality must be driven through all mental health policy and practice. This will mean developing specialist services that can meet the specific needs of some groups of older people as well as ensuring that access to services is not determined by chronological age.

■ Local authorities must take up their positions as community leaders to promote 'healthy ageing' programmes, designed in collaboration with older people and working in partnership with private sector, statutory and voluntary organisations.

■ Tackling depression, particularly among older people must become a public health priority, along with opening up access to effective treatments to all who can benefit.

■ The education and training of the health and social care workforce must be transformed so that all those who work with older people are able to recognise and respond to mental health needs.

■ The experiences of older people and carers must be routinely sought and their views must become the basis for planning improvements in services.

An ageing society is inevitable – it is in all our interests that it should be a society that ages with good mental health.

Terms

Direct age discrimination is explicit unequal treatment that cannot be justified, for example, mandatory retirement ages (where these are not justified by public interest), recruitment practices that exclude people over a particular age, or offering inferior services to people over the age of 65.

Indirect age discrimination is apparently neutral practice that disadvantages people of a certain age, for example, designing services around the needs of younger adults without taking older people's needs into account.

Age equality means securing the equal participation in society of people of all ages, based on respect for the dignity and value of each individual. It aspires to achieve equality in citizenship, access to opportunities and outcomes, as well as respect for differences related to age.

References

Age Concern (2004) *How Ageist is Britain?* London: Age Concern.

Age Concern (2007) *Improving Services and Support for Older People with Mental Health Problems – The second report from the UK Inquiry into mental health and well-being in later life.* London: Age Concern.

Age Concern (2008a) *Ageism in Britain 2006 – An Age Concern research briefing.* London: Age Concern.

Age Concern (2008b) *Undiagnosed, Untreated, at Risk – The experiences of older people with depression*. London: Age Concern.

Age Concern/Mental Health Foundation (2006) *Promoting Mental Health and Well-being in Later Life – A first report from the UK Inquiry into mental health and well-being in later life*. London: Age Concern.

Audit Commission (2000) *Forget-me-not: Mental health services for older people*. London: Audit Commission.

Audit Commission, Commission for Social Care Inspection & Healthcare Commission (2006) *Living Well in Later Life – A review of progress against the National Service Framework for Older People*. London: Healthcare Commission.

Care Services Improvement Partnership/Department of Health (2005) *Everybody's Business. Integrated mental health services for older adults: a service development guide*. London: Department of Health.

Department of Health (1999) *National Service Framework for Mental Health – Modern standards and service models*. London: Department of Health.

Department of Health (2001) *National Service Framework for Older People – Modern standards and service models*. London: Department of Health.

Department of Health (2005) *Securing Better Mental Health for Older Adults*. London: Department of Health.

Department of Health (2006) *Our Health, Our Care, Our Say: A new direction for community services*. Cm 6737 London: Stationery Office.

Department of Health (2009a) *Commissioning IAPT for the Whole Community: Improving access to psychological therapies*. London: Department of Health.

Department of Health (2009b) *Living Well with Dementia: A national dementia strategy*. London: Department of Health.

Healthcare Commission (2009) *Equality in Later Life – A national study of older people's mental health services*. London: Healthcare Commission.

National Institute for Mental Health in England (2005) *Making It Possible: Improving mental health and well-being in England*. London: Department of Health.

Royal College of Psychiatrists (2005) *Who Cares Wins: Improving the outcome for older people admitted to the general hospital*. London: Royal College of Psychiatrists.

Thornicroft G (2006) *Actions Speak Louder: Tackling discrimination against people with mental illness*. London: Mental Health Foundation.

Part 2:
Care and support of older people with mental health problems

Chapter 5

The older people's mental health legal and policy framework

Jill Manthorpe

Scarcely a day goes by without discussion of law and policy about older people featuring on the television, radio or in the newspapers. What is important for those working with older people who have mental health problems to know? How do the law and policy impact on practice? Surely all this is not important, compared to getting on with the job?

In this chapter, we suggest that setting your work in context can be helpful and we outline some of the key legal and policy frameworks that affect practitioners supporting older people who have mental health problems. Other chapters of this handbook cover aspects of policy so the concentration here is on the law. The two interconnect, of course. Some important aspects are not covered here for reasons of space; others feature in later chapters (see **chapter 10** on carers' rights and **chapter 16** on elder abuse).

We start with a brief overview of the Human Rights Act, which is important in underpinning people's rights. We then discuss two important laws: the Mental Capacity Act (2005) and the Mental Health Act (2007). We end with social care policy and law, including personalisation. The chapter focuses on the law as it applies in England and Wales. The examples of practice draw on real but disguised situations and individuals.

Part 1: setting the scene

The rule of law, in simple terms, means that neither an individual nor the state is above the law. People cannot take action in connection with another person if the law prevents them from doing so. Organisations such as local councils and the NHS, and people such as nurses, social workers or doctors, cannot take action unless the law gives them authority to do so. This applies even where the action is for the person's own good.

Legal authority derives from common law or statute. Common law is established by the courts and developed from precedents. It is judge-made law and is different from statute law (law that has been passed by Parliament).

Court decisions are the source of common law and equity (meaning that they aim to ensure fairness in the way the law is applied). They also have a crucial role to play in the interpretation of statutes. Of course, courts are both bound by and uphold the rule of law. They must either interpret the will of Parliament expressed in statute or decide what principles of common law and/or equity are relevant to the issues in front of them.

As society becomes more complicated, the role of common law diminishes, since more and more laws are passed dealing with more and more areas of behaviour. Acts of Parliament start life as bills. These may be bills sponsored by government ministers, or private members' bills (the Chronically Sick and Disabled Persons Act (1970) was one of these originally).

Delegated legislation

No matter how long Parliament sits, it cannot consider the working of legislation in detail. Therefore, most Acts of Parliament allow for delegated legislation. This gives the power to some person or body to pass legislation that has the same effect as if it had been passed by Parliament. Delegated legislation is also known as secondary legislation, or statutory instruments.

Guidance

In the field of social care and health services, a particularly important government output is guidance issued by the relevant Secretary of State (Minister). While statutory instruments have the full force of a law, the role of guidance is not so clear-cut. It is not, in law, mandatory. Statutory guidance – guidance issued under an express statutory power – must be followed unless there are powerful and justifiable reasons for not doing so. It is perhaps the clearest expression of the government's intentions of what the law should mean. However, it remains the function of the court actually to decide what the legislation means.

Example

No Secrets (England) (Department of Health, 2000) and *In Safe Hands* (National Assembly for Wales, 2000) have guidance status under the Local Authority Social Services Act (1970), section 7. These cover adult safeguarding (see **chapter 16**).

Other guidance may be published in the form of circulars and other documents that are not issued under statutory provision. If such guidance is not followed, then actions can be criticised. However, it may be possible for public officials, such as social workers or health professionals, to justify not following guidance.

Good practice

Good practice is different from delegated legislation or guidance. It can be very helpful, and can provide principles for making decisions. It is not, however, law, and much good practice is not issued in the form of either regulations or statutory guidance. Therefore, good practice must always give way to the requirements of statute, regulations, and guidance, if the requirements conflict. For more information on the basic operations of the law in this area, see Moriarty (2006).

Note

The law and policy are not easily summarised. This is because the law in this area is a patchwork of acts and guidance. Many of the laws that we are working under in health and social care services were passed a long time ago and some have to be thought about in new circumstances and in line with a greater emphasis on people's rights. Many of these new emphases are seen in policy documents (for example, the *National Service Framework for Older People* (Department of Health, 2001) and Opportunity Age (Department for Work and Pensions, 2005). These are seeking to challenge the ageism, age discrimination and social exclusion that are so commonly found in older people's mental health services (Milne *et al*, 2007).

The Human Rights Act (1998) (HRA)

The HRA enables people to enforce – in British courts – 16 of the fundamental rights and freedoms contained in the European Convention on Human Rights (ECHR). These include rights that impact directly upon services in health and social care (British Institute for Human Rights, 2008). The HRA builds upon the mechanisms in the ECHR that recognise that a balance has to be reached between rights and responsibilities. Not all rights are absolute and practitioners are often required to balance competing rights.

Some of the Convention rights are especially relevant to older people's mental health services and to the policy emphasis on dignity in care (Cass *et al*, 2006).

Article 2 establishes a right to life. The Article could be relevant to the providers of care and adult services if those services failed, for example, to protect a vulnerable person who was killed by an abusive relative, or if there is a failure to properly investigate any such death. It could also be relevant if a public authority, like a local authority, prison or health service, fails to assess and treat someone in its care who is at risk of suicide. There are positive obligations on public authorities to protect life, so failure to observe necessary procedures to reduce the risk of infections in hospital and care settings may be a breach of Article 2. Decisions to move frail older people from a care home may result in illness and death and lead to a breach of Article 2. Organisations might be in breach of Article 2 if, for example, a day centre user died following administration of medication by unqualified staff or if a doctor had recommended checking on a care home resident hourly during the night and staff had failed to do this.

What this means in practice is that organisations should:
■ ensure that the health and safety of service users are prioritised
■ undertake regular risk assessments of the premises and of routine practices so that all risks are identified and managed
■ have strategies for identifying, minimising and managing the risks of transfers of service users from one care home or hospital to another location
■ check that health and safety requirements are met by staff
■ provide training on health and safety so that all staff understand the importance of these procedures.

Practice example

Some people with dementia require help to eat their food or to drink. Failing to provide that help could potentially be a breach of Article 2.

Miriam cannot manage to eat her food in hospital without help. This is recorded in her notes but the nurses fail to offer this or to find someone to help Miriam. If there is no system in place to ensure that help is given, then there is a risk of a breach of Article 2. Her family might wish to make a complaint to the hospital if they cannot get this resolved on the ward.

Article 3 is the right not to be subjected to torture, inhuman or degrading treatment. The threshold for breach of the Article is high – so not all examples of poor practice might be classified as inhuman or degrading treatment. The Article could be relevant to failures by public services to protect vulnerable adults from abuse or neglect. In social or health care settings, it could be argued that failure to prevent and treat bedsores could be a breach of Article 3, and, for example, a regime where food is given at the same time as a person is using the toilet is likely to be seen as degrading. Practices such as tying residents of a care home into chairs so they do not 'wander' would almost certainly be inhuman. Local authorities have a responsibility under this Article to ensure that any care home in which they place residents has policies and procedures in place to protect vulnerable adults from abuse and to provide redress should abuse occur. Relevant policies and procedures would include a robust complaints procedure and a 'whistle-blowing' procedure. Dignity in care policy emphasises this important area.

Inhuman and degrading treatment can arise as a result of failure to assess an individual's need for services and a failure to provide necessary services in a timely manner and at a level appropriate to the needs of the service user. Under the National Health Service and Community Care Act (1990) (NHSCCA), local authorities have a duty to provide information and a duty to assess (Section 47) and a duty to promote equality under the Race Relations Amendment Act (2000). It is not good enough to say, for example, that because a person with dementia has savings then they cannot have an assessment under the NHSCCA because they would be likely to have to pay for any services.

The Mental Capacity Act (2005) offers another route to challenge willful neglect and mistreatment by making these criminal offences when looking after a person who lacks mental capacity.

Practice points (see also chapter 16)

- Every local authority and health care organisation should have adult protection or safeguarding systems to help practitioners deal with concerns about inhuman and degrading treatment.
- Staff's rights to whistle-blowing may be important to remember and respect when they feel that they are witnessing inhuman or degrading treatment.
- Local policies about adult protection or safeguarding give details of local contacts or ring a helpline such as Action on Elder Abuse (www.elderabuse.org.uk, tel. 080 8808 8141).

Article 5 provides a right to liberty and security of person. This means that a person can be detained only in certain circumstances, following a proper, lawful procedure that provides the detainee (person being detained) with opportunities to challenge their detention.

The significance of Article 5 has been illustrated by an incident that has become known as the Bournewood case that concerned L, a 49-year-old man with learning difficulties and autism, who lacked capacity to consent to arrangements made for his care.

The man was detained under common law powers in Bournewood Hospital during 1997 as an informal patient, on the grounds that he required treatment for a mental disorder. He did not have capacity (ability) to consent to or to refuse admission and treatment. In 2004 the European Court of Human Rights (ECtHR) held that his detention under common law was incompatible with Article 5 because it was arbitrary and lacked appropriate safeguards. Compliance with the European Convention required the process to be formalised. It needed to be clear, for instance, who could propose deprivation of liberty for people like L and for what purpose. There needed to be procedures for review of the detention and formal mechanisms – such as an appeal – by which detention could be challenged.

In 2007 the government amended the Mental Capacity Act (2005) (discussed below) to introduce safeguards against illegal deprivations of liberty for people who have a mental disorder, if they do not have the capacity to consent to arrangements made for their care that would deprive them of liberty. The deprivation of liberty safeguards are explained in the code of practice (www.publicguardian.gov.uk). This is an essential read for practitioners working with people with 'mental disorders' in care home and hospital settings.

Briefly, the managers of care homes or hospitals that identify that a person who lacks capacity is being, or risks being, deprived of their liberty, must apply to a 'supervisory body' for authorisation of the deprivation of liberty unless it would be more appropriate to detain the person under the Mental Health Act (2007) (usually when it is clear that the person is receiving assessment or treatment and meets the other criteria for detention under the Act).

When a person in this position is in a care home the supervisory body is the relevant local authority. Where the person is in a hospital it is the relevant primary care trust, or, in Wales, the National Assembly for Wales. In an emergency, the care home or hospital management can itself provide an urgent authorisation supported by written reasons for a maximum of seven days.

Practice points

- It may be difficult for care homes or hospitals to recognise that someone is being deprived of their liberty. Organisations must ensure that they have systems in place to consider whether care plans in fact deprive the 'incapacitated' adult of his or her liberty. Staff must keep these cases under review and ask the question about deprivation of liberty explicitly whenever a change is made to the care plan. This should be recorded in the person's health and care records.
- Staff working in care homes and hospitals need to be able to tell the difference between 'restraint' (which the Mental Capacity Act does permit in certain circumstances – see below) and 'deprivation of liberty' and, if they are not clear, know where they can seek advice.
- Indications that liberty has been deprived could include: sedating a patient who is resisting admission, any decision that the person would be prevented from leaving if they made a meaningful attempt to do so and refusals of requests by carers for the person to be discharged to their care.
- The code of practice is invaluable and should be easily accessible to staff in care homes and hospitals and training should be available and taken up.

Practice example

Mrs Japp made arrangements herself to enter a care home. She is increasingly confused. She often tries to leave the home to 'go to school' and staff have to persuade her to come back. In supervision, her key worker raises this with the home's manager and they decide to contact the local adult services as they feel that they may now be depriving Mrs Japp of her liberty and would like to have the legal position clarified.

Article 6 provides the right to trial and of innocence until proved guilty. This concerns the requirement for civil rights to be fairly determined, and for criminal trials to contain full procedural safeguards. The basic right is to a fair and public hearing within a reasonable time by an independent and impartial tribunal established by law.

Practice points

Organisations should:

- ensure that service users and carers have information about their legal rights
- maintain a list of local services with experience of working with or advocating for people who may have communication difficulties or other needs (eg. for translation)
- provide service users with advocates and communication specialists where necessary
- provide staff with practical training on legal developments when this is appropriate to their role and responsibilities
- develop procedures that mean that decision-making that affects a service user's or carer's rights is transparent and fair and there is sufficient opportunity for the service user or carer to put their case to the decision maker.

Article 8 provides that everyone has the right to respect for private and family life, his or her home, and correspondence. Any interference with this right must be lawful, necessary, and proportionate. This Article is the most open to interpretation; a court has to balance society's interests against those of the individual. This means staff of public bodies, such as nurses or care assistants, must respect individual decisions unless interventions are legally sanctioned and required.

Article 8 affects social and health care practices in many ways. It impacts on the ways in which we obtain and keep confidential information – so asking someone for details of their medical or mental health condition where those details can be overheard by other people may be a breach of Article 8.

In certain circumstances, it might be necessary and proportionate to share confidential information. What is required is an assessment of the reasons for disclosing information and a balance between the common law duty of confidentiality and a service user's Article 8 rights to privacy.

However, disclosure of confidential information has to be proportionate, meaning people should only be given the information on a 'need to know' basis. The Data Protection Act (1998) sets out principles that safeguard confidential information.

- For general information see
  http://www.justice.gov.uk/whatwedo/datasharingandprotection.htm
- For health care see http://www.dh.gov.uk/en/Policyandguidance/Informationpolicy/Patientconfidentialityandcaldicottguardians/index.htm
- And for social care see
  http://www.dh.gov.uk/en/Publicationsandstatistics/Legislation/Actsandbills/DH_4015584

Service users' rights to live in the home of their choice are obviously critical to Article 8 rights. Local authorities should take into account both the service user's wishes and those of their family/friends when making decisions about care homes. Under the National Assistance Act (1948) (Choice of Accommodation) Directions (1992) when a person is eligible for residential accommodation, they can choose the care home as long as certain conditions apply – it has to be suitable, would not cost more than the council would usually pay (but someone else can make up the difference), a place is available and the home will accept the person, and it has to be in England and Wales.

Practice points

- Personal information should be stored properly and should only be accessed by people with authority to have it (based on clear 'need to know' organisational policies and inter-agency protocols).
- Clear information for service users should be available about their rights to access their own records – how is this communicated in your setting?
- Practitioners should stress the importance of confidentiality and model good practice in their own behaviour.
- Effective complaints procedures need to be in place and understood by all.
- Assessments should be timely and appropriate services should be provided.
- Available options and choices need explaining and exploring.

Mental capacity and Article 8

Particular difficulties may arise when a service user lacks capacity to consent to a particular intervention. The Mental Capacity Act (2005) (discussed below) helps resolve these difficulties and is built upon human rights principles. It protects and empowers people who may lack capacity to make decisions or to consent to care and treatment in a variety of ways. It requires that staff act in the best interests of the person who is not able to make specific decisions. The code of practice (http://www.justice.gov.uk/guidance/mca-code-of-practice.htm) is a key document for practitioners who must have regard to it and other people, for example, lay people, such as relatives who have been granted Lasting Power of Attorney (to make decisions on someone's behalf) or have been appointed to do so.

The Mental Capacity Act (MCA) says that any decision or action taken on behalf of a person who lacks capacity to make this decision, or consent, must be in his or her best interests. What are someone's best interests depends upon the circumstances.

Restraint

A person who lacks capacity to make a decision or to consent to care and treatment can only be restrained where there is a reasonable belief that it is necessary to prevent harm to him or her. Any restraint must also be proportionate to the risk, and of the minimum level necessary to protect the person.

In the rare circumstances that restraint needs to be used, staff restraining a person who lacks capacity will be protected from liability (for example, criminal charges) if certain conditions are met. There are specific rules on the use of restraint, both verbal and physical, and the restriction of liberty and these are outlined in the MCA code of practice (Sections 5.36 – 5.49), which notes that restraint should only be used as a last resort, or in exceptional circumstances.

Restraint can include physical restraint, locking a door and verbal warnings to stop someone going somewhere or doing something but cannot extend to depriving someone of their liberty. Staff must record when and why they have restrained a person. Restraint may also be used under common law (as distinct from the MCA) in the rare circumstances where there is a risk that the person lacking capacity may harm someone else. Again, staff must record when and why they used restraint.

Staff working in care homes and hospitals need to be aware that should there be a need to use restraint to treat someone for a mental disorder, or to detain them in a care home or hospital, then the Mental Health Act or Deprivation of Liberty Safeguards may have to be used. These may not take away people's rights but can defend them.

Practice examples

1. Terry and Gloria, who live in a group home for people with long-term mental health problems, start a sexual relationship. Gloria's social worker talks to her independently about this decision. Terry's community nurse has a similar conversation with him. The practitioners ensure as far as possible that both have consented to the relationship and see their role as supportive. This helps to uphold their dignity – the practitioners are working with both tenants to try to ensure that their best interests are considered and that their autonomy is respected. Practitioners should record their discussions.

2. Wilfred Hall, who lives in a care home, might be putting his health at risk by eating an excessive amount of crisps and sweets. The staff worry about whether their duty of care means that they should restrict his spending money so that he cannot overeat. Mr Hall has capacity to make decisions, it is just that the staff think that he is at risk of not eating properly and they are worried about their responsibilities. His key worker talks to him about why they are concerned, and puts those concerns in writing in the notes; however, his Article 8 rights mean that he has a right to his money and to make decisions about how it should be spent. Perhaps the staff team should also ask for advice for themselves about the best way to provide more information to Mr Hall, for example, from the local health promotion service or a dietician? But this may be fruitless; people have a right to choose what they do with their lives.

3. Miss O'Brien, a volunteer befriender of a care home resident, reports her distress to the Care Quality Commission that she has heard care home workers often talk about personal details of residents in public settings. She feels that this does not show respect for the residents' privacy. The inspector takes this up with the home manager.

Part 2: key laws that affect practice with older people with mental health problems

The Mental Capacity Act (2005) (MCA) (England and Wales)

The MCA provides a statutory framework to protect and empower adults who may lack capacity to make all or some decisions about their lives. It also governs the way decisions can be made for an individual who lacks capacity. Section 1 of the MCA sets out five principles to support decision-making either by or on behalf of a person who may lack capacity.

- There is a presumption of capacity – every adult has the right to make his or her own decisions and must be assumed to have capacity to do so unless it is proved otherwise.
- Individuals should be supported to make their own decisions.
- People have the right to make unwise decisions and making an unwise decision does not mean they lack capacity to make that decision.
- If someone lacks capacity then an act done or a decision made for them under the Act must be done in their best interests (see above).
- Anything done for or on behalf of a person who lacks capacity should be the less restrictive option (providing it is still in their best interests).

These principles promote the human rights of people who may lack capacity because they enshrine respect for individual autonomy. They make it clear that we should always presume that a person has capacity to make decisions unless it is established otherwise. Some people may have used the MCA to draw up statements about treatment they would not wish to receive if they lacked capacity to consent at the time it was about to be provided (advance decisions to refuse treatment), or who they would like to make decisions on their behalf about their care and treatment if they lacked capacity (Lasting Powers of Attorney). They may also have made written statements about what they would wish to happen to them if they become unable to make their own decisions and lose capacity to do this (advance statements).

Practice points
- Staff should ask a person or their carers if the person has made any plans or expressed any views for their future or has appointed someone to make decisions on their behalf by giving them Lasting Power of Attorney.
- These should be part of the person's records.
- All staff should know about a person's wishes and what these mean for the delivery of care.
- If major decisions about care and treatment are being considered and the person does not have capacity to make decisions about them, and there is no family, friends or supporter to consult, then an Independent Mental Capacity Advocate (IMCA) must be consulted – responsibility for making this link needs to be clear.
- Care plans need to be regularly consulted, monitored and amended as necessary.

The code of practice provides guidance and information on how the Act works on a day-to-day basis for anyone who works with or cares for people who lack capacity to make decisions, including family, friends and unpaid carers. Certain people are legally required to 'have regard to' the code including people acting in a professional capacity for, or in relation to, a person who lacks capacity and people being paid for acts for or in relation to a person who lacks capacity. This includes a variety of health care staff and social care staff (social workers, care managers, care assistants and home care workers).

Practice questions for organisations and managers

- Where is the code of practice in your work setting and is it consulted?
- Is information about the MCA available to staff and service users and carers?
- Who is the local source of expertise on the MCA?
- Which staff need knowledge about the MCA and how many of them are confident in their practice?
- Is the role of the IMCA service known and understood?
- How would your service stand up to an inspection in this area?

The MCA defines a lack of capacity as an inability to make a particular decision, due to *'an impairment of, or a disturbance in the functioning of, the mind or brain'* (section 2). The impairment or disturbance can be either temporary or permanent. Capacity is therefore both time specific and decision specific (so 'blanket' assessments of capacity based on diagnosis, for example, are not acceptable). It can change over time, for example, a person's mental health problems may be short-term or fluctuating. Since capacity is decision specific, professionals also need to be prepared to assess capacity in relation to particular decisions and to recognise that a lack of capacity in one area of life does not mean that an individual cannot make decisions in another field. This requires some careful consideration, based on knowledge of the individual concerned. For instance, someone with severe dementia may have strong views and be able to exercise choice about what food they want. In the context of mental health services, a person in great distress because of hallucinations or psychosis, may perceive threats in their environment where none exists, but they may still be able to make decisions concerning arrangements for their pets to be cared for while they are in hospital.

Section 3 of the MCA identifies the key components of an assessment of capacity, which does not have to be done by a specially trained professional. In addition to having a mental impairment or disturbance (such as severe dementia), people assessing capacity need to establish whether the person being assessed is able to:

1. understand the information relating to a particular decision
2. retain the information related to the decision to be made
3. use or weigh that information as part of the process of making the decision
4. communicate that decision – by any means, including blinking an eye or squeezing a hand.

If any one of these applies, then the person lacks capacity to make the decision in question.

Best interests decisions

The MCA does not define 'best interests' but Section 5 of the Act offers protection from liability to people (including family carers, professionals and other staff) carrying out acts of care and treatment in a person's best interests as long as they have not acted negligently and that they:

1. have taken reasonable steps to assess the person's capacity to consent to the act in question
2. reasonably believe that the person lacks the capacity to consent
3. reasonably believe that the act they are carrying out is in the person's best interests.

Much of this is about shifting practice culture (Stanley & Manthorpe, 2009). Prior to the MCA, many of the small best interests decisions made on behalf of people lacking capacity would not previously have been recognised as such and would not generally have been written down. It is not feasible or practicable for staff to write down every time someone is assisted with dressing, bathing, feeding or toileting and the decision-making processes that all these actions entail, but the decision to undertake these tasks for a person in the absence of the person giving consent could be recorded the first time they are done in a new setting.

The Mental Health Act (2007)

The Mental Health Act (2007) (which significantly changes the MHA (1983)) enhances the human rights of people who have a mental disorder (see the main amendments in **box 1**). Some people see the MHA as controlling – but it does have the capacity to protect people's rights as well as to limit them in some circumstances. Its code of practice (Department of Health, 2008) (issued as an amendment to the MHA (1983)) includes a statement of the principles informing decisions made under the Act that highlights:

- respect for patients' past and present wishes and feelings
- respect for diversity generally including, in particular, diversity of religion, culture and sexual orientation
- minimisation of restrictions on liberty
- involvement of service users in planning, developing and delivering care and treatment appropriate to them
- avoidance of unlawful discrimination
- consideration of the effectiveness of treatment
- taking into account the views of carers and other interested parties
- respect for patients' well-being and safety
- taking into account public safety.

If you work with older people with mental health problems, such as depression or dementia, you might not be familiar with the MHA. This means that if it is being considered that an older person needs to be compulsorily admitted to hospital for assessment or treatment, or if they should be detained there, or if the older person wishes to be discharged or to make an appeal, then there may not be much experience to draw on in some services or teams. Space does not permit a lengthy discussion of the sections of the MHA (see Golightly, 2004 and Johns, 2007 for accessible guides) so practitioners should make sure they are well-trained and receive regular updating if it is commonly a part of their work and should know local sources of expertise if not. The implementation of the Mental Health Act (2007) is a good opportunity to refresh knowledge and practice and many local events will be available.

Box 1: Main amendments introduced under the 2007 Mental Health Act

- Introduction of a single definition of mental disorder
- Introduction of an appropriate medical treatment test
- Broadening of social work and medical roles
- Increased patient rights to apply to the County Court of the removal of their nearest relative (these include civil partners)
- Widening of grounds to displace a nearest relative
- Earlier reference to the Mental Health Review Tribunal
- Introduction of a single tribunal for England alongside its Welsh counterpart
- Introduction of Independent Mental Health Advocacy (IMHA) service
- Introduction of new safeguards for patients where electro-convulsive therapy is contemplated (older people are one of the major groups affected).

Practice points

Organisations should:

- provide support for staff if they are asked to provide their views about the older person they are working with who is being assessed under the MHA
- ensure staff know who to contact when they have high levels of concern eg. about risk of suicide or possible harm to other people
- seek advice if they are not sure about the legal status of the person they are working with
- know the scope of local advocacy (especially the IMHA) and interpreting services and how to contact them or be able to identify sources of this knowledge and expertise
- be aware of any advance plans or statements about what a person might want to happen to them if a crisis arises and they are not able to make decisions
- ensure that the circumstances and needs of older people feature in training and practice learning opportunities.

Practice example

Cora is a home care worker who helps Mrs Fisher with personal care and some housework. Mrs Fisher has been in hospital following a suicide attempt. The community mental health nurse asks Cora to let her know if she discovers that Mrs Fisher is keeping stocks of pills, or seems to be making preparations as if she is going away. Cora is not sure what to do as telling the community nurse seems like being disloyal to Mrs Fisher, who has told her that the suicide attempt was not really one at all, but an accident.

Cora discusses this with her manager and they ask the community nurse to talk this over with them as neither is certain what to do. The nurse explains the situation as she sees it and helps Cora to think about what would be best for Mrs Fisher. She tells them about the very high risks of suicide if an older person has made an attempt previously (Manthorpe & Iliffe, 2005) and suggests ways in which Cora can be a very important part of the care team supporting Mrs Fisher.

Part 3: social care

The third part of this chapter looks briefly at social care although much of the discussion about the Human Rights Act has touched upon this area.

Much social care law relates to social services authorities, often now called adult services. Local authorities or councils have particular powers and responsibilities, given to them by Parliament. They can arrange, pay for or provide services for adults – among whom are disabled people and older people, people with mental health problems and carers. Not all councils are able to do this; they have to be councils with social services responsibilities. This means that if you live in a rural area, there may be a district council that has responsibilities for housing while the county council is responsible for social care services. Just to complicate matters, in some areas, provision for older people with mental health problems is very much a joint activity between local government and the NHS. The new Dementia Strategy (Department of Health, 2009) stresses the importance of providing support across agencies.

Nowadays, we talk more about social care but the term used in legislation has generally been community care. Much of what happens in social care today in England and Wales is governed by the National Assistance Act (1948) and the NHS and Community Care Act (1990). These set in place many of the roles that we are familiar with today, such as social services provisions and community care assessments and care managers. The National Assistance Act enables local authorities to provide a range of welfare services to disabled people – and has provided a safety net of care for many older people across the decades. It is the only part of Beveridge's post-war foundations of the welfare state still in force. Over time, ideas about 'need' and disabilities have changed with growing emphasis on rights, as we have seen in part 1 of this chapter.

Other laws since have added to local authorities' powers and duties, such as the Mental Health Act (1983) extending the duties on social services and the NHS to provide aftercare for people who have been detained in hospital (for which they are not charged). The NHS and Community Care Act (1990) (NHSCCA) was also one of the most important of these changes, setting out rights to an assessment of social need in a policy context that changed local authorities from being providers of social care (home helps and old people's homes, for example) to purchasers or commissioners of services from the private and voluntary sector (see Clements & Thompson, 2007 for an extensive guide).

These laws affect adults of all ages and with a range of disabilities or long-term conditions. Initially, older people were excluded from the Community Care (Direct Payments) Act (1996) that allowed local authorities to make payments to people who are eligible for social care services ('cash for care'). Older people are now eligible and local authorities have a duty to provide direct payments in certain circumstances (Health and Social Care Act (2001)). Under the Health and Social Care Act (2008) people who lack the capacity to consent to direct payments, for example, a person with severe dementia, a payment can be made to a suitable person (such as a close relative) to manage the direct payment on their behalf.

The current policy of personalisation builds on the take up of direct payments. This is a way of enabling people to live more independently, to have greater choice in social care support and to have control over the support they purchase (see *Putting People First*, Department of Health, 2007; Carr, 2008). Older people are being affected by this policy in many ways and practitioners will need to keep abreast of all the many developments. Assessments are ways of identifying and evaluating an individual's needs but they have to be considered in light of Fair Access to Care Services (FACS) and the Unified and Fair System for Assessing and Managing Care in Wales, which offer statutory guidance and set out local priorities about eligibility criteria or thresholds. Other elements of personalisation include greater investment in prevention services and commitments to providing information and advice to everyone, including people who pay for their own care.

Practice example

Mr Vincent, a former professional footballer, has severe Parkinson's disease and depression. His wife is finding it hard to cope but the couple want him to stay at home as long as possible. Following a community care assessment, which finds that his needs are 'substantial' according to his local authority's FACS criteria, the family decide that direct payments might be suitable and work out what the budget allocated will afford. The couple use a local bookkeeping service to do all the paperwork and employ two personal assistants to provide support on a weekly rota. One is keen on football and spends many hours with Mr Vincent talking about this while helping him with personal care. The other takes Mr Vincent to and from the day centre twice a week and comes in most Wednesdays so that Mrs Vincent can go out.

Personal budgets are an important part of personalisation and extend direct payments by offering people more choice about the mix of possible arrangements. Under a personal budget, a person is told how much money is available and they can use this as a direct payment or choose to 'spend' all or some of it on local authority services. Means testing still applies. In some areas, personal budgets can be made up of social care finance and money from housing related support (eg. Supporting People money) from the local council (for discussion of the pilot individual budgets scheme see Glendinning et al, 2008). Proposals around using NHS money in a similar way for people's health care are currently being developed by government).

Practice points

Organisations should ensure that their staff:

- are aware of the implications of personalisation for their practice, including their duty to provide information about direct payments and personal budgets to people using services and carers
- receive information, training and support around the changes arising from personalisation
- are consulted about the process and substance of change
- have opportunities to discuss the impact of change on their roles and are accurate and confident in explaining changes to people using services and carers.

Conclusion

This chapter has illustrated how the law and policy impact on practice. No one is suggesting that we should all become lawyers but if we are working with older people with mental health problems then they may need support to maintain their rights, and practitioners need to know the limits of their considerable power. The law is under review in this area and so it is important to keep up-to-date with the legal underpinnings of practice.

Acknowledgments

This chapter draws on material used in the SCIE Dignity in Care law guide (2007) (www. scie.org.uk) written by Jill Manthorpe and Helen Carr. The material in this chapter is a brief summary and readers should consult legal practitioners for accurate advice.

References

British Institute for Human Rights (2008) *The Human Rights Act – Changing lives.* London: King's College London.

Carr S (2008) *Personalisation: A rough guide.* London: SCIE.

Cass E, Robbins D & Richardson A (2006) *Dignity in Care.* London: Social Care Institute for Excellence.

Clements L & Thompson P (2007) *Community Care and the Law.* London: Legal Action Group.

Department of Health (2000) *No Secrets: guidance on developing and implementing multi-agency policies and procedures to protect vulnerable adults from abuse.* London: Department of Health.

Department of Health (2001) *National Service Framework for Older People.* London: Department of Health.

Department of Health (2007) *Putting People First.* London: Department of Health.

Department of Health (2008) *Mental Health Act 1983: Revised code of practice.* London: Department of Health.

Department of Health (2009) *Living Well with Dementia: National dementia strategy.* London: Department of Health.

Department for Work and Pensions (2005) *Opportunity Age.* London: Department for Work and Pensions.

Glendinning C, Challis D, Fernandez JL, Jacobs S, Jones K, Knapp M, Manthorpe J, Moran N, Netten A, Stevens M & Wilberforce M (2008) *The Evaluation of the Individual Budget Pilots.* York: Social Policy Research Unit, University of York.

Golightly M (2004) *Social Work and Mental Health.* Exeter: Learning Matters.

Johns R (2007) *Using the Law in Social Work.* Exeter: Learning Matters.

Manthorpe J & Iliffe S (2005) *Depression in Later Life.* London: Jessica Kingsley.

Milne AJ, Gearing B & Warner J (2007) *Ageism, Age Discrimination and Social Exclusion, Learning Materials.* London: SCIE.

Moriarty J (2006) *SCIE Guide 3: Assessing the mental health needs of older people.* London: SCIE.

National Assembly for Wales (2000) *In Safe Hands.* Cardiff: National Assembly for Wales.

SCIE (2007) *Dignity in Care within Mental Health – SCIE Guide 15: Dignity in care.* London: SCIE.

Stanley N & Manthorpe J (2009) Small acts of care: exploring the potential impact of the Mental Capacity Act (2005) on day-to-day support. *Social Policy and Society* **8** (1) 37–48.

Chapter 6

Working with older people who have dementia

Ruth Bartlett

Introduction

Whatever your role in health and social care – general nurse, community or hospital physiotherapist, occupational therapist, paramedic, rehabilitation worker, learning disability nurse, social worker, residential care worker, care home liaison worker, support worker, radiographer, optometrist, podiatrist, dentist, even midwife – you will come into contact with an older person who has dementia. This is because dementia is a condition that affects most families to some degree at some point in their lives, and also because men and women with dementia have problems other than dementia. For example, a person with dementia is also likely to have a physical health condition such as diabetes, stroke, osteoporosis, heart disease, breast, prostrate, or lung cancer, Parkinson's disease, sight problems (such as cataracts, age related macular degeneration) or be hearing impaired. In addition, older people occupy some 60% of acute hospital beds, of these up to 40% will have dementia and so staff in acute hospital services will also certainly come into contact with people who have dementia (National Audit Office, 2007). Similarly, two-thirds of care home residents have some form of dementia (244,000) but only 60% of these will be in a dementia registered bed (Alzheimer's Society, 2007a) and so everybody working in and visiting a care home for older people will meet a person with dementia. A person with dementia may also have a learning disability, such as Down's syndrome, or a pre-existing mental health condition like depression. A person with dementia may also have socio-economic problems related to long-term poverty, unemployment, poor housing, homelessness or unclaimed benefits, and so people working in the wider public sector, including housing officers and benefit advisers, will come into contact with families affected by this condition as well. For these reasons, the needs and concerns of people with dementia should be considered 'everybody's business', not just specialist mental health staff, and it is in this context that this chapter is written (Department of Health, 2005).

In this chapter it is recognised that mainstream staff have not only an important role to play in supporting people with dementia but also a particularly challenging one for several reasons. First, so much has been written and said about dementia and people with dementia in the past 20 years that it might be difficult for those working in mainstream services to know where to begin or what to regard as good practice. Compounding this, it is generally assumed in the dementia care literature that care staff are working with people with dementia on a full-time ongoing basis, with few exceptions, very little has been written specifically for mainstream staff for whom dementia and people with dementia may not be a professional interest or priority. One of the aims of this chapter is to orientate readers to the dementia care literature, highlighting current best practice in the field and outlining basic ways of helping and supporting people with dementia. A second challenge for mainstream staff is that contact with an older person with dementia is likely to be infrequent and limited, as opposed to regular and long-term, and so it might not be possible, or appropriate, to develop a long-term relationship and really get to know a person with dementia and their family. The chapter will therefore focus upon interactions and practices that are important and achievable regardless of how much is known about a person. Wherever possible, discussion will be illustrated by real life examples to show how good practice is achieved in a practical sense.

The focus of this chapter is on people with dementia, as opposed to the causes or aetiology and progression of dementia as a disease process (see McKeith & Fairburn, 2001 for a full discussion of these issues). In particular, the chapter suggests ways of understanding and responding to older people with dementia, which are essentially kind and helpful – kind and helpful in the sense that the response a person receives, maintains or restores their overall sense of well-being, rather than hindering it or making it worse. Drawing on current research and the growing body of anecdotal evidence created by people with dementia themselves, such as conference presentations and pamphlets, the chapter briefly explains what it is like to have a dementia, outlining the effects it has on a person in both a neurological and social sense, before describing some of the key features of working with people with dementia. The importance of involving family members is a given, plus it is dealt with elsewhere in this book, and so it will not be discussed in this chapter.

What is dementia and what is it like to have this condition?

Dementia is an umbrella term used to describe various different brain disorders that have in common a loss of cognitive function that is usually progressive and severe. Alzheimer's disease is the most common type of dementia, accounting for 62% of cases, but to date over 200 subtypes of dementia have been identified, including vascular dementia, dementia with Lewy bodies, Pick's disease, and Korsakoff's syndrome – an alcohol related dementia (Blossom & Brayne, 2008: 11). The most common subtypes are vascular dementia and mixed dementia (such as Alzheimer's and vascular dementia), accounting for almost one-third of all cases (Alzheimer's Society, 2007b). It is beyond the remit of this chapter to go into detail about the different types of dementia. Besides, the Alzheimer's Society produce a very good fact sheet about rarer types of dementia, which can be downloaded from their website (www.alzheimers.org.uk), and McKeith and Fairburn (2001) provide a useful summary of the main subtypes. Moreover, there is always a danger, when talking about types of dementia, of paying too much attention to the disease process rather than the person's experience of life generally.

Whatever type of dementia a person has, they are likely to experience a significant decline in memory, reasoning and communication skills, as well as a gradual loss of skills needed to carry out day-to-day activities such as shopping, counting money, independent travel and socialising (Scottish Dementia Working Group, 2007). Unlike conditions such as depression and delirium, which can have a relatively sudden onset, the onset of dementia is insidious over months, even years. Some people may speak of 'not feeling themselves' and notice physical or psychological changes rather than poor cognitive function. Take for example, the early experiences of Christine Bryden (2001) who was diagnosed with dementia:

> 'Our journey begins with a struggle with daily life, of tiredness, irritability, stress, a feeling that not all is well. There may be gaps in memory but that is not always the first sign we feel. It is more like a kaleidoscope of small problems, of not quite being ourselves. We don't do everything we used to do, It all seems so much trouble. It's what you on the outside might call apathy. But it's not a lack of interest, but a lack of energy.'

Similarly, a 42-year-old woman with Down's syndrome, who was eventually diagnosed with a dementia, initially had problems with dressing and remaining calm in social situations. The early signs of dementia are often wrongly attributed to stress, bereavement or normal ageing (National Audit Office, 2007), or in the case of the woman with Down's syndrome, to the onset of the menopause and need for more personal space (Kerr, 2007). It is clearly important that practitioners are open to the possibility that someone may have dementia, even though loss of memory may not be the first sign either they or the person themselves, notices or complains about. Likewise, loss of memory is not necessarily proof of having dementia, as there are many other causes of memory problems in older people, including alcohol misuse and depression. The need to improve public and professional awareness of dementia and to ensure that those affected are diagnosed early and appropriately are aims of the National Dementia Strategy for England (Nazarko, 2009).

Other changes that a person might experience are changes in personality and behaviour, which are out of character for that person. These changes can be particularly dramatic and frightening to witness, as they can make people behave in a way that might seem odd or strange and without apparent cause or reason. Here, a former GP who now has Pick's disease describes how the condition affected him:

> '(Pick's disease) affects the personality and social behaviour. Memory is affected but it's not the salient feature that it is in Alzheimer's. So, considering the personality changes the person affected may become more outgoing, or conversely, withdrawn. He or she may lose the ability to empathise with others, becoming a cold fish, and being selfish and unfeeling. Aggressive behaviour may develop. He becomes less flexible, and will be irritated by being contradicted. He may develop obsessive routines, or get over absorbed in one particular idea. He may lose his inhibitions and become sexually inappropriate. In other ways he may become inappropriate, making tactless comments, joking at the wrong moment or being rude, and generally being an anxiety and embarrassment to his wife.' (Fay, 2008).

The experience of dementia is unique, as different people will have different experiences of the dementia they have. It is therefore important that you do whatever you can to find out what the particular person you are working with is experiencing (Kitwood, 1997a). For more individual examples of the subjective experience of dementia see Harris (2002) and Phinney (2008) who provide a useful summary of work on the subjective experience of dementia. For insights into how people feel about and cope with being diagnosed with dementia see Alzheimer's Society (2008).

Several factors affect a person's experience of dementia and their rate of decline in cognitive function, including the type of dementia the person has, their physical health and emotional strength and quality of support available from family, friends and formal care services (National Audit Office, 2007). In addition, cultural factors such as ethnicity (Mackenzie, 2007), and geographical factors like rural living, which can affect the receipt of services (Wenger, Scott & Seddon, 2002), will also impact on a person's experience of dementia. It is not possible in this short chapter to discuss or explain any of these factors in any detail. Suffice to say, a great deal has been written about the different factors affecting a person's experience of dementia. In particular, Kitwood (1997b) and Brooker (2007) shed much light on how the quality of formal care services impacts on a person's experience.

One aspect of the experience that people with dementia do have in common is that the changes a person is experiencing will have a concrete cause in damage to the brain. Thus, there is actually a good reason why the person has changed and finds it hard to behave in a way that we consider 'normal'. As the dementia progresses, and the brain becomes more and more damaged by a build up of tangles and plaques, a person will need extra support with everyday activities such as eating, washing and dressing; they are also likely to become increasingly forgetful and more at risk to themselves (for example, by leaving taps running and the gas on, leaving their house in night clothes and/or getting lost). These changes are commonly referred to as the middle stage symptoms of dementia (National Audit Office, 2007). As the dementia becomes more advanced, the person is likely to have trouble recognising familiar objects and surroundings, or people; the person may start to shuffle or walk unsteadily and become physically frail generally, eventually becoming confined to a bed or wheelchair. The person is also likely to have difficulty with eating and swallowing, and may lose weight, as well as the ability to communicate verbally. At this point, palliative care approaches should be adopted to ensure that the person remains as comfortable and supported as possible (Small, Froggatt & Downs, 2007). It is important to remember that however cognitively impaired a person is or seems to be, they will always being trying to make basic sense of what is going on around them. It is therefore important to try and find ways of facilitating this.

How many people are affected?

Latest data on the prevalence of dementia estimates there to be a total of 683,597 people in the UK with a dementia; 574, 717 in England; 56,106 in Scotland; 36,924 in Wales and 15, 850 in Northern Ireland. This represents one person in every 88 (1.1%) of the entire population (Alzheimer's Society 2007b). Age is the single biggest risk factor for dementia and **table 1** shows how the chances of getting dementia increases with age.

Table 1: Prevalence rates among the general population for dementia in the UK	
Age (years)	Prevalence
30–59	0.1%
60–64	1.0%
65–69	1.4%
70–74	4.1%
75–79	5.7%
80–84	13%

(Hoffman, 1991, quoted in Kerr, 2007)

Assuming a cure is not found, and this seems unlikely in the foreseeable future, the number of people with dementia is expected to double in the next 30 years. Hence the need to make dementia a national priority (Alzheimer's Society, 2007b).

While dementia is strongly associated with growing older, the condition is not restricted to older people, neither is it an inevitable part of the ageing process. For example, there is estimated to be 18,500 people under the age of 65 with dementia in the UK (Alzheimer's Society, 2003), and certain forms of dementia, like variant Creutzfeldt-Jakob disease (CJD) are more likely to affect younger people. Families, and individuals like Clive Beaumont who was 45 when he was diagnosed with early onset dementia in 1993 (http://www.thecliveproject.org.uk) are likely to have very different concerns, expectations and needs than a much older person with dementia. Hence the need for more services for younger people with dementia (see Cox & Keady, 1999). Many younger people with dementia will also have Down's syndrome, as this group of people are known to be more susceptible to early onset Alzheimer's (Kerr, 2007). **Table 2** shows the prevalence rates among people with Down's syndrome; note how over half of people with Down's syndrome aged 60 years and over are likely to develop Alzheimer's.

Table 2: Prevalence rates among people with Down's syndrome for dementia in the UK	
Age (years)	Prevalence
20–39	2%
40–49	9.4%
50–59	36.1%
60–69	54.5%

Whichever group of people you are working with it is important to remember that there is a huge under-diagnosis of dementia. Nazarko (2009) reports on work that suggests that more than half the people who have dementia in the UK do not have this formal diagnosis.

Helping and supporting people with dementia

Given the rising numbers of people with dementia, it is important that those affected are given appropriate help and support. In the past decade there has been a great deal of research into the most effective pharmacological, cognitive and psychosocial interventions in treating and supporting people with dementia. Much of this work is reported in the National Institute for Health and Clinical Excellence (NICE) and the Social Care Institute for Excellence (SCIE) comprehensive guide *Dementia: Supporting people with dementia and their carers in health and social care* (2006). It is worth spending time familiarising yourself with this work, as not only does it provide guidance for professional staff, it also provides a booklet on treatments and support written specifically for people with dementia and their family members. The main message in this guidance is that while there is no cure for dementia, there are many things that can be done to maintain and improve the quality of life for those affected. It is important to remember that people will need different types of help and support at different times, and the kind of help and support you offer will depend on the person's individual circumstances.

Person-centred support

The work of Professor Tom Kitwood (1945–1998) in the 1980s and 1990s began a cultural shift in the way we see and treat people with dementia that continues to this day. His book, *Dementia Reconsidered* (1997) paved the way for thinking about people with dementia as people and remains a formative text in this field. His untimely death interrupted the development of thinking about dementia, but his work on personhood and person-centred care has been carried on by others and incorporated into UK health and social care policy (Baldwin & Capstick, 2007). There is now a (growing) body of knowledge about how best to work with people with dementia in a person-centred way, which is usefully summarised and articulated by Brooker (2007) and others including Epp (2003) and Davies and

Nolan (2008). Underpinning this work is the value and importance of focusing on the individual person (rather than the disease) in the context of their family and wider social networks.

Creative communication

Learning to communicate effectively and in a creative way is arguably the single most important way a practitioner can help and support a person with dementia. Evidence is growing on how best to do this. One useful resource is the SCIE research briefing on aiding communication with people who have dementia (SCIE, 2004), which can be downloaded from the SCIE website. In addition, Killick and Allan (2001) have written extensively on the importance of communicating with people with dementia. Here are some practical tips on communicating with people with dementia, which have been drawn from these sources.

■ Avoid chronological questions like how old are you or when did you last see your doctor or get your eyes tested? Ask a family member for this information.
■ Use short sentences and avoid jargon like 'single assessment'.
■ Deal with strong emotion, listen and accept what someone is telling you, don't try to placate – 'everything will all be alright' or 'I will get you a cup of tea'.
■ Learn to sit in silence.
■ Remember, it is not what you say but how you say it. A person with dementia can be very perceptive, and will sense impatience and negativity.
■ Talk about yourself (but not too much); it can bring equality into a relationship.
■ Go with the flow of a conversation, even if it does not make any sense and accept the messiness of conversations.
■ Give instructions in a way that is helpful; so rather than saying it is time to get dressed, try laying out clothes in sequence and handing them to the person.
■ Try communicating with people using other than spoken dialogue – for example through song, humming, dance, painting or other arts based approaches (for examples see Innes & Hatfield, 2002).

Dealing with challenging circumstances

Earlier in this chapter it was suggested that mainstream staff face particular challenges when working with people with dementia. One of the main challenges that this sector of the workforce face is having to support people who display unusual or strange behaviours, when they may lack the confidence, knowledge or expertise to do so. For example, staff may know very little about the person or they may have had very little, if any, dementia care training. Whenever a person with dementia is behaving or communicating in a way that either you or your colleagues find strange, challenging or unusual (such as shouting, screaming, taking clothes off in public, trying to eat inedible objects, talking to someone who is not there), it is important to try and find out why they are doing it, rather than to simply put it down to 'their dementia', or worse, deride or scold them for doing it. Work by Graham Stokes (2003) and others encourages service providers to see behaviours and comments that challenge (eg. shouting, screaming, hitting, 'I want to go home') as a form of communication – a sign of an unmet need, rather than as a manifestation of the disease. **Table 3** identifies a number of other common circumstances that you might encounter when working with people with dementia, and offers practical solutions, based upon best available evidence, about how to help. Whenever you are working with people with dementia in challenging circumstances, it is helpful to bear in mind the following.

■ Find out as much as you can about the person, either from the person directly or ask a family member.
■ Be especially kind, patient and good-natured; be prepared to go that extra mile.

■ Treat people with dignity and respect at all times.

■ Offer support, understanding, reassurance, comfort and touch if appropriate.

■ Whenever you are in doubt, or if the person's behaviour is putting themselves or others in serious danger, seek specialist help and support.

Table 3: Suggested ways of responding to particular circumstances		
Circumstances	Best approach	Evidence base
1. Person is distressed when you try to help them with daily activities (such as bathing, going to the toilet, dressing and eating).	Rather than explaining what you are trying to do, try humming, singing and/or playing the person's favourite song or melody while you are helping them. If you do not know what the person likes, try one of these popular Western songs: 'Oh what a beautiful morning, oh what a beautiful day' 'Take me home country road' (John Denver) 'You are my sunshine (my only sunshine)'	The singing of songs that are familiar and liked by the person, at times when intimate tasks are being performed has been shown to help people feel more at ease (Clair, 1996, Gottel 2003).
2. Person is distressed by changes in their ability to remember.	Help the person to function to their maximum capacity, for example, with the use of visual cues such as photographs, memory boards and wallets, or personalised signs. Use audio cues if person is visually impaired.	Research suggests that cognitive rehabilitation is possible for people with dementia (Clare, 2008). For more ways of supporting intellectual functioning see Oyebode and Clare (2008).
3. Person repeatedly asks to go home or to see their mother.	Validate and focus on the emotions and sentiment behind what someone is saying, rather than what they are actually saying. So for example, in the case of someone who is asking to go home, acknowledge that they may be feeling insecure and lost.	Validation approaches can help a person with dementia (Miesen & Jones , 2007). The more you know about a person the easier it will be to use validation techniques (Morton, 1999).
4. Person has advanced dementia and becomes easily agitated and irritated.	Use different forms of stimulation to arouse and maximise each of the six senses (eg. sight, smell, hearing, touch, taste, movement).	Short-term improvements in mood and behaviour can be brought about by multi-sensory stimulation; effects are lost once intervention is stopped (Baker et al, 2001).

Maintaining physical health and well-being

The importance of attending to and maintaining the physical health and well-being of someone with dementia cannot be over-emphasised. Often, this will simply be about making sure a person has enough to eat and drink. While this may sound too simplistic, a recent report by Age Concern (2006) found that malnourishment is still a major problem in UK hospitals. Take the following case, cited in the report (2006: 18):

> *'92-year-old "V", who suffered from dementia, was admitted to hospital in January 2005. Her daughter told Age Concern that V was not given the help she needed to eat. Many times, V's food was left untouched on her bedside table and taken away by the catering staff at the end of mealtimes. It was established at the start of V's stay on the ward that her food had to be pureed, as this was the only way she could ingest her food. However, she was often offered meals that were not pureed and, if she was present at the mealtime, V's daughter would have to ask for an appropriate meal. On one occasion, V was given mashed potato and lumpy bits of meat despite the fact that some people with dementia cannot swallow lumpy bits of food. On another occasion, an auxiliary tried to feed her macaroni cheese. V's family resorted to bringing in food she could eat, like yoghurt and soup. The catering staff were often impatient with serving food to the patients and their behaviour was not challenged by the nursing staff.'*

Unfortunately, this kind of incidence is not restricted to hospitals, as there was a case relatively recently of a woman with dementia dying from dehydration and malnourishment because the deputy manager could not spell Alzheimer's and so care staff did not realise she needed help with eating and drinking (*Laurance*, 2002). Fortunately, this kind of incidence is rare and there are many cases of good practice in care homes. Take for example, staff at a care home in Suffolk who started a 'water club' for their residents, which involved encouraging residents to drink eight to 10 glasses of water a day; water coolers were installed and a jug of water was provided in each room (Hughes, 2008). Making sure a person with dementia is hydrated and nourished are the most important ways of maintaining health and well-being. For more ideas on how to do this see the Alzheimer's Society fact sheets on eating, and other publications from their Food for Thought project.

Sometimes a person with dementia will need specialist medical care. As stated in the introduction, people with dementia have health problems other than dementia, and as many of these are treatable, it is important that a person's physical health is routinely assessed and monitored. This includes routine health promotion checks (such as breast screening and eye tests), as well as investigations as and when a person complains of feeling unwell, or in pain, or just seems off colour. It is all too easy, once someone has been diagnosed with dementia, to overlook physical health and well-being, and instead, put everything down to the dementia. For a good overview of best practice in relation to physical health issues see Young (2008). Finally, and this applies whenever a person has to make a decision concerning their care and treatment, the Mental Capacity Act (2005) requires you to begin by assuming that a person can make their own decision about whether to consent to receiving specialist medical care – regardless of their age or dementia (Mental Health Foundation, 2005).

Summary

Helping and supporting a person who has dementia can be highly rewarding and extremely challenging. For some people, the rewards will outweigh the challenges, while for others the opposite may well be true. However you feel about working with people with dementia, you have a responsibility to reflect on your values and attitudes, and to treat those affected fairly and with dignity and utmost respect. You also have a duty to do whatever you can to alleviate any pain or distress that a person is experiencing. This chapter has provided a very brief introduction to how best to help and support people with dementia, and made some suggestions for further reading and sources of information. In this chapter, several key points have been made about helping and supporting people with dementia. These are summarised as follows:

- You have a responsibility to respond to and deal sensitively with people who have memory and other cognitive problems.
- People with dementia are likely to have other problems, as well as those related to dementia. It is important that you recognise and help the person to manage and cope with these as well.
- There are lots of ways to help and support someone with dementia – you have a responsibility to find out what is the best way to help the particular person you are working with – doing nothing is not an option.
- The most important thing you can do to help and support a person with dementia is to get to know as much as you can about that person – even if it is only their favourite song or place in the world.
- There is always hope – even when a person is reaching the end of their life, they and their family will have wishes, desires and expectations about how they would like things to be (and end).

Acknowledgements

The author would like to acknowledge the work of colleagues and former colleagues in the Bradford Dementia Group, particularly Dr Elizabeth Anderson, whose work on the brain and behaviour was drawn upon to write some of this chapter.

References

Age Concern (2006) *Hungry to be Heard: The scandal of malnourished older people in hospitals*. London: Age Concern.

Alzheimer's Society (2003) *Numbers of Younger People with Dementia*. London: Alzheimer's Society.

Alzheimer's Society (2007a) *Home from Home: A report highlighting opportunities for improving standards of dementia care in care homes*. London: Alzheimer's Society.

Alzheimer's Society (2007b) *Dementia UK*. London: Alzheimer's Society.

Alzheimer's Society (2008) *Dementia: Out of the shadows*. London: Alzheimer's Society.

Baldwin C & Capstick A (Eds) (2007) *Tom Kitwood on Dementia: A reader and critical commentary*. Buckingham: Open University Press.

Baker R, Bell S, Baker E, Gibson S, Holloway J & Pearce R (2001) A randomised controlled trial of the effects of multi-sensory stimulation (MSS) for people with dementia. *British Journal of Clinical Psychology* **40** 81–96.

Blossom S & Brayne C (2008) *Prevalence and projections of dementia*. In: M Downs & B Bowers (Eds) Excellence in Dementia Care: Research into practice. Buckingham: Open University Press, pp 9–34.

Brooker D (2007) *Person-centred Dementia Care: Making services better*. London: Jessica Kingsley Publishers.

Bryan K & Maxim J (2006) *Communication Disability in the Dementias*. Oxford: Wiley Blackwell.

Bryden C (2001) *Presentation given at the Alzheimer's Disease International conference*, New Zealand. Available at: http://www.dasninternational.org/conferences/2001NZ/ADI_2001_NZ_christine1.php (accessed February 2009).

Clair A (1996) *The Therapeutic Uses of Music with Older Adults*. Baltimore, MD: Health Professions Press.

Clare L (2008) *Neuropsychological Rehabilitation and People with Dementia*. Hove: Psychology Press.

Cox S & Keady J (Eds) (1999) *Younger People with Dementia: Planning, and practice and development*. London: Jessica Kingsley Publishers.

Davies & Nolan M (2008) Attending to relationships in dementia care. In: M Downs & B Bowers (Eds) *Excellence in Dementia Care*. Maidenhead: McGraw Hill/Open University, pp483–455.

Department of Health (2005) *Everybody's Business: Integrated mental health services for older adults – a service guide*. London: Stationery Office.

Epp T (2003) Person-centred dementia care: a vision to be redefined. *The Canadian Alzheimer's Disease Review* **5** (3) 14–18.

Fay B (2008) *Pick's From the Inside Out. Pick's Disease Support Group: carer's stories*. [online]. Available at: http://www.pdsg.org.uk/caregiver_stories/picks_from_the_inside_out/ (accessed February 2009).

Gottell E (2003) *Singing, Background Music and Music Events in the Communication between Persons with Dementia and their Caregivers*. Thesis, Blekinge Institute of Technology, Karlskrona, Sweden.

Harris PB (2002) The perspective of younger people with dementia: still an overlooked population. *Social Work in Mental Health* **2** (4) 17–36.

Hughes J (2008) How care home keeps elderly healthy. *BBC News* [online]. 23 June. Available at: http://news.bbc.co.uk/l/hl/health/7466457.stm (accessed September 2009).

Innes A & Hatfield K (2002) *Healing Arts, Therapies and Person-centred Dementia Care*. London: Jessica Kingsley Publishers.

Killick J & Allan K (2001) *Communication and the Care of People with Dementia*. Buckingham: Open University Press.

Kitwood T (1997a) The experience of dementia. *Ageing and Mental Health* **1** (1) 13–22.

Kitwood T (1997b) *Dementia Reconsidered: The person comes first*. Buckingham: Open University Press.

Kerr D (1997) *Down's Syndrome and Dementia: Practitioner's guide*. Birmingham: Venture Press.

Kerr D (2007) *Understanding Learning Disability and Dementia: Developing effective interventions*. London: Jessica Kingsley Publishers.

Laurance J (2002) Woman, 71, dies of thirst because carer couldn't spell Alzheimer's. *The Independent*, 19 Oct.

Mackenzie J (2007) Ethnic minority communities and the experience of dementia: a review and implications for practice. In: J Keady, C Clarke & S Page. *Partnerships in Community Mental Health Nursing and Dementia Care*. Buckingham: Open University Press, pp 76–89.

McKeith I & Fairburn A (2001) Chapter 1. Biomedical and clinical perspectives. In: C Cantley (Ed). *A handbook of Dementia Care*. Buckingham: Open University Press, pp 7–25.

Mental Health Foundation (2005) *Mental Capacity Act Briefing* [online]. Available at: http://www.mentalhealth.org.uk/publications/?EntryId5=40155 (accessed February 2009).

Miesen B & Jones G (Eds) (2006) Care Giving in Dementia: *Research and applications* (Vol 4). London: Routledge.

Morton I (1999) *Person-centred Approaches to Dementia Care*. Milton Keynes: Speechmark Publishing.

National Audit Office (2007) *Improving Services and Support for People with Dementia*. London: Stationery Office.

Nazarko L (2009) Policy: an update on the dementia strategy. *Nursing and Residential Care* **11** (1) pp 45–48.

NICE and SCIE (2006) *Dementia: Supporting people with dementia and their carers in health and social care*. London: NICE & SCIE.

Oyebode J & Clare L (2008) Supporting cognitive abilities. In: M Downs & B Bowers (Eds) *Excellence in Dementia Care: Research into practice*. Buckingham: Open University Press.

Phinney A (2008) Towards understanding subjective experience of dementia. In: M Downs & B Bowers (Eds) *Excellence in Dementia Care: Research into practice*. Buckingham: Open University Press, pp 35–51.

Social Care Institute for Excellence (2004) *Research Briefing 03: Aiding communication with people with dementia*. Available at: www.scie.org.uk/publications/briefings/index.asp (accessed April 2009).

Scottish Dementia Working Group (2007) *What Disempowers Us and What Can be Done*. Available at: www.sdwg.org.uk/downloads/index.php?file=what-disempowers-us.pdf (accessed February 2009).

Small N, Froggatt K & Downs M (2007) *Living and Dying with Dementia: Dialogues about palliative care*. Oxford: Oxford University Press.

Stokes G (2003) *Challenging Behaviour in Dementia Care: A person-centred approach*. Milton Keynes: Speechmark Publishing.

Wenger G, Scott A & Seddon S (2002) The experience of caring for older people with dementia in rural areas: using services. *Ageing and Mental Health* **6** (1) 30–38.

Young J (2008) Supporting health and physical well-being. In: M Downs & B Bowers (Eds) *Excellence in Dementia Care*. Maidenhead: McGraw Hill/Open University Press, pp 230–249.

Chapter 7

Depression and anxiety in later life: making visible the invisible

Mary Godfrey

This chapter examines the nature and prevalence of depression and anxiety in later life, the contributory risk factors in their onset, the resources which assist with securing a 'good life' in older age that reduce vulnerability, and the challenges in responding appropriately to facilitate 'recovery'.

Nature and prevalence of late life depression and anxiety

Depression in later life

Depression is the most common mental health problem in later life, a significant factor causing severe health problems and a major public health concern. Depression affects how people feel about themselves and the world around them, engendering a sense of the self as worthless, the surrounding world as meaningless and the future as hopeless. It can influence every aspect of a person's life including appetite, sleep, energy levels, interest in relationships, social activities and social participation. Later life depression prevents a person from enjoying things in which they previously found pleasure and can impact on memory and concentration. It has a negative affect on quality of life and functional abilities, and is a major contributory factor in morbidity and mortality (Alexopoulos et al, 1996; Murray & Lopez, 1997). Depression not only causes pain and suffering for those who are depressed, but for the people who care about them (Sewitch et al, 2004).

Much of the research and service focus is on major depression – distinguished by the number and severity of symptoms and their prolonged duration (World Health Organization, 1992; 1993). There is increasing interest in minor depression and mood disorders that do not reach case level for major or minor depression (Geiselmann et al, 2001; Pincus et al, 1999). This has, in part, been fuelled by evidence to suggest that non-major depression may also result in poor physical and mental health outcomes, and can benefit from intervention.

Minor depression is a diverse group of syndromes that may indicate either an early or residual form of major depression, a chronic, though mild form of depression that does not present with a full array of symptoms, or a response to an identifiable stressor. While not as severe as major depression, minor depression and mood disorders resulting from physical ill health or disability can still make it difficult for the person to function (Lyness et al, 1999), contribute to physical decline (Penninx et al, 1998) and lead to major depression, if untreated. People with such conditions do respond to treatment and experience significant improvements in their psycho-social functioning as a result (Rapaport & Judd, 1998).

Across the life span, the course of depression is marked by recurrent episodes followed by periods of remission. In later life, recurrences extend over a longer time period and intervals of remission are shorter. Denihan et al (2000), following a community-based sample of older people with depression over three years found that only 10% recovered completely; just under one-third died (30.2%); a further third (34.9%) had persistent or relapsed case level depression; a fifth had sub-case level mental illness; and the remainder had developed other mental health problems. These findings echo others (Prince et al, 1998) that depression in later life is a chronic condition.

Prevalence of depression

The prevalence of depression (the numbers of older people who have the condition at any given time point) varies between major and non-major depression, between settings (community and institutional) and is also affected by socio-economic and demographic factors. The prevalence of major depression from community-based studies is low, averaging 1.8%, that of minor depression is higher (11.2%), with an average prevalence of 13.3% for all case level depression (Beekman et al, 1999). By including sub-threshold depression – and as indicated above, there are strong clinical arguments to do so – prevalence doubles. Thus, between a fifth and a quarter of older people suffer depression that is likely to cause distress of such severity as to affect their concentration, motivation, functioning and sense of enjoyment with life.

Age

While major depression declines with age, depressive symptoms increase (Henderson et al, 1993). This is attributable to age-related changes in risk factors as opposed to ageing per se (Henderson et al, 1997; Beekman et al, 1999).

Gender

Women generally report more depressive symptoms than men at younger ages and continue to do so in later life (Zarit et al, 1999; Prince et al, 1999), although it is not clear why. One explanation is that it reflects women's higher risk of poverty, which in turn increases susceptibility to stress. Another is that it is a consequence of women's higher prevalence of disability because of problems such as arthritis, which also tend to be accompanied by chronic pain. A fuller explanation of patterns of variation in prevalence of depression between older men and women is likely to reflect the gender-related balance of risk and resources.

Ethnicity

Currently, in Britain, there is little research evidence available on either the prevalence or experience of depression among older people from minority ethnic groups. Yet, it is likely that ethnicity may be a risk factor for emotional and psychological problems in later life – the combined effect of the same daily stressors that affect other older people, and the experience of discrimination and loss on account of the migration experience. Poorer physical health and higher levels of poverty have been reported among some ethnic minority groups within the general population and both are risk factors for depression in older age. However, minority ethnic groups facing greatest disadvantage – those of Bangladeshi and Pakistani origin – have one of the youngest age profiles within the population (Nazroo, 1997). While it is in future years that the impact of their disadvantaged situation over the life course will be felt on mental health problems in older age, there is a clear need for systematic exploration of the specific vulnerability and resource factors that operate on different minority ethnic groups.

Long-term residential and nursing care

Prevalence of depression for older people in long-term nursing and residential care is considerably higher than for those in the community and is associated with high functional disability (McDougall *et al*, 2007). It is estimated that around 40 to 45% of older people entering these settings suffer from clinical depression (Ames, 1993; Godlove Mozley *et al*, 2000).

Anxiety

Anxiety disorders include phobias and obsessive-compulsive disorder and generalised anxiety disorder. Anxiety has been defined as '*the apprehensive anticipation of future danger or misfortune accompanied by a feeling of dysphoria or somatic symptoms of tension*' (American Psychiatric Association 1994:764). People suffering anxiety, particularly older people, often express it primarily as physiological (panic attacks, restlessness, hyperactivity or sleep disturbance) or overt behavioural responses (compulsive behaviours or exaggerated startle responses). Among older people, a key problem is distinguishing between normal anxiety relating to the threat of loss of health, independence and valued life opportunities and pathological anxiety. Estimating prevalence of anxiety disorders, as with depression, poses considerable difficulties in part because these often co-occur with depression to a greater extent in older, compared with younger people.

Prevalence of anxiety

Prevalence of anxiety disorders that meet diagnostic criteria is low – around 2–4% of those over 65 years. Prevalence of symptoms of anxiety likely to indicate need for clinical intervention, is considerably higher, around 10% (Beekman *et al*, 1998), with negative impact on disability, well-being and service use (de Beurs *et al*, 1999). As with depression, women are more likely to experience anxiety disorders than men.

Anxiety tends to co-occur with depression especially in later life. Around half of older people with clinical level depression suffer from co-morbid anxiety disorders (Mehta *et al*, 2003) and a quarter of those with anxiety suffer from major depression (Beekman *et al*, 2000). Co-morbid depression and anxiety are also associated with more severe psychopathology (Lenze *et al*, 2001) and a longer time to remission (Alexopoulos *et al*, 2005), even with optimal treatment that goes beyond routine clinical care (Andreescu *et al*, 2007). Thus, not only is anxiety and depression less separable in older, compared with younger people, but their combined and interactive effect exacerbate the experience of distress, chronicity and poor outcomes.

Depression and anxiety: vulnerability and resources

Risk and vulnerability to depression and anxiety

The most significant risk factors for later life depression are losses as a result of ill health, disability and bereavement, transitions (for example, becoming a caregiver), stressful life events and daily hassles. Current evidence relates primarily to depression and there is limited understanding of risk in respect of anxiety disorders.

Chronic ill health and disability

For older people – to a greater extent than for younger adults – physical ill health, pain and disability are the most consistent risk factors in depression, and prevalence rates of depression are approximately double for those suffering ill health and disability compared with people who are healthy.

The general consensus from research is that it is not illness per se that is key in vulnerability to depression but the loss of functional ability, pain, restrictions in valued life activities, including social participation and meaningful relationships (Zeiss et al, 1996; Braam et al, 2005; Prince et al, 1998; Verhaak et al, 2005). Depression also impacts on daily functioning, ability to sustain social networks and quality of life and mortality from other causes (Penninx et al, 2000). There is an interactive and cumulative relationship between ill health, functional abilities, social isolation and depression that in turn lead to increased disability and poor outcomes for recovery of physical and mental health problems (McCusker et al, 2006).

The limited evidence on the impact of illness on anxiety disorders suggests that sudden onset events perceived as a source of threat of further similar events, of ill health and of loss of independence in the future, are significant risk factors for anxiety and particularly late onset agoraphobia. This includes, for example, such conditions as heart attacks and stroke (Burvill et al, 1995). The impact of agoraphobia in the way it restricts people's lives outside the home is likely to increase the risk of depression.

Bereavement

Older people, particularly older women, are especially vulnerable to the loss of intimate relationships through the death of a spouse or partner. While bereavement is a universal experience and a traumatic and stressful life event, the majority of older people who experience the death of a close relative will be able to manage the distress and adjust to a different life. However, a significant minority, estimated at between 10–20%, suffer complicated grief reactions during the first year of bereavement. Complicated grief is defined mainly in terms of duration, intensity and severity of depressive symptoms. Without support and treatment, people experiencing complicated grief may become chronically ill, leading to further disability and impairments in general health (Zisook & Shuchter, 1993). Risk factors that help to explain why some older people experience complicated grief and others adjust to life without the dead person include: the nature and quality of the relationship with the person who died (for example, the more dependent the bereaved person was on the person that died, the greater the likelihood of complicated grief); and where bereavement involves multiple and concurrent losses, as for instance where it is followed by relocation and loss of, or reduction in social contact with family and/or friends.

Transitions: caregiving

An important transition in later life is becoming a caregiver. While older people are frequently viewed as 'care-receivers', some 40% of informal caregivers are older – primarily as spouses but also as siblings, neighbours and friends – often in the context of reciprocal and mutually supportive relationships.

There is considerable research evidence to indicate that caregiving is a risk factor in the onset of mental health problems in later life, especially depression (Aneshensel et al, 1995; Schulz et al, 1995). The factors that increase vulnerability include stages in the caregiving 'career'; the nature of the caregiving task; the relationship between caregiver and care recipient; and the impact of caregiving on social activities and social networks.

Research with caregivers of people with dementia has found that while 35–40% are at risk of developing a depressive disorder, this does vary. The factors distinguishing those who experience a depressive disorder and those who do not are: the higher level of behaviour problems of those being cared for, being physically or emotionally depleted by caregiving activities and feeling trapped by one's responsibilities (Alspaugh et al, 1999; Grant et al, 2002; Bond et al, 2003). A similar pattern of risk emerges from studies that have included those caring for a more diverse group of care recipients: people with stroke, heart disease, or arthritis (Seltzer & Li, 2000; Marks et al, 2002; Burton et al, 2003). Here too, the interaction between length of time caring and transition into heavier caring results in a significant increase in symptoms of depression; and duration of caregiving is associated with declines in leisure activity and more depressive symptoms. It is the link between the demands of caregiving and the restrictions these impose on activities that appear to be central.

Stressful life events

Health related difficulties such as serious illness and hospitalisation of someone close is associated with onset of the first episode of depression among older people (Brilman & Ormel, 2001) and the risk of depression at onset of a serious illness is concentrated in the first six months after the event (Prince et al, 1997). Being a victim of crime is associated with symptoms of both anxiety and depression (de Beurs et al, 2001) and this can persist over a long period of time.

Daily hassles

Several studies have established a link between daily hassles – the 'irritating, frustrating, distressing demands and troubled relationships that plague us day in and day out' (Lazarus & de Longis, 1983:247) and psychological distress (Grzywacz et al, 2004). Daily hassles cause disruption and change to the daily grind of stress. They add new demands and frustrations, many of which are recurrent and chronic in the context of major life events. These include bereavement and loss related to chronic illness and disability, for example, loneliness, managing money, and house maintenance. The frustration generated by these daily hassles is two-fold – in the absence of family, friends or neighbours, there is no obvious source of help, and they foreshadow an escalation of dependence (Godfrey et al, 2004).

Social resources or protective factors

Not all older people who experience risk or stressors implicated in depression and anxiety go on to develop such problems and older people demonstrate enormous resilience in the face of losses that often accompany old age. Resources that have a direct positive effect on mental health or provide a protective function in the presence of stressors have been examined at three levels: internal to the individual; social networks and relationships; and neighbourhood/community.

Internal to the individual

There is considerable evidence on the importance of self-esteem, self-efficacy and mastery (self-confidence and self-sufficiency) in managing stress in older people. These personal coping resources are directly associated with less depressive symptoms in both those with and without chronic illnesses (Zarit et al, 1999; Penninx et al, 1998). Positive self-esteem, mastery, energy, stamina and strength are also important personal resources in the face of bereavement (Prigerson et al, 1993). The main sources of positive well-being are social relationships and social participation (Smith et al, 2002).

Social relationships and networks

A focus of sustained research interest from the pioneering work of Berkman and Syme (1979), is the nature and quality of interpersonal relationships that tie people to each other and meet needs for physical and emotional intimacy, personal support, sociability, stimulation and meaning, and affect health, well-being and life quality in older age.

The existence of an intimate, confiding relationship appears crucial in dealing with such major stressors as chronic illness, buffering its impact on depression (Penninx et al, 1998). Older people without confidantes report more psychological distress and higher rates of depression (Prince et al, 1997). The availability of a confiding relationship is associated with higher morale and lower levels of loneliness and social isolation (Wenger et al, 1996), and loneliness is a risk factor for emotional and physical health problems (Berkman, 2000). Thus, there is a complex, iterative and mutually reinforcing relationship between loneliness, ill health, disability and depression.

The quality of social relationships (perceived closeness, shared confidence, reciprocity and mutual help) are major resources in managing bereavement in later life (Lund et al, 1993) and in mitigating the impact of chronic illness and disability on mental health and life satisfaction (Bisschop et al, 2004).

There is also growing literature on the benefits and value of volunteering or 'befriending' by older people and older volunteers have been shown to benefit through improved health, fewer symptoms of depression, greater life satisfaction, improved morale, self-esteem and larger social networks (for example, Chappell, 1999).

Neighbourhood and community

There is a developing literature on the effects of the physical and social environment on ageing, for example, the opportunities and constraints that physical environments present, the social and physical characteristics of deprived neighbourhoods (such as crime, poor infrastructure and service provision) that impact on health and well-being in later life, and the significance of place in facilitating social networks and relationships.

Knipscheer et al (2000) found that living in a more urbanised environment, associated with complex housing facilities (for example, flats), a higher risk of robbery, more complex traffic situations and having fewer social contacts within the neighbourhood increased depressive mood among older people. They also found that feeling able and being able to influence one's environment increased proactive behaviour and decreased depressive symptoms in older people with poor functional ability. Studies suggest that deprivation may have an effect on residents' social networks (Deeg & Thomese, 2005; Scharf et al, 2005) with older people becoming distrustful and socially isolated.

Even so, it is evident that social and physical characteristics of environments and access to social capital are intertwined in complex ways (Cattell, 2004), and neighbourhoods which to the outside observer may exhibit typical features of urban decay, may nevertheless be a source of significant social resources – in the 'embededness' of older people in social networks, in their engagement and participation in the social life of the community, and in their degree of attachment to, and identity with, people, physical landmarks and places (Godfrey et al, 2004).

Accessing and receiving help

Policy and service development context

The National Service Framework for Older People (Department of Health, 2001) has placed emphasis on the development of an integrated approach to service delivery for older people with mental health problems, spanning acute, primary, community care and specialist mental health services. It has also noted the importance of diagnosis in the treatment of depression and anxiety. Both the National Institute for Health and Clinical Excellence (NICE) guidelines on depression (NICE, 2007a) and anxiety (NICE, 2007b) and the review of mental health service developments for older people (Philp & Appelby, 2005), have argued that older people should be offered the same range of treatments and services available to younger adults with mental health problems. Similarly, good practice guidance on service delivery places emphasis on mental health in later life being 'everybody's business' (Department of Health/CSIP, 2005).

The evidence available on service delivery in later life mental health and summarised from the reviews and evidence to the UK Inquiry into Mental Health and Well-Being in Later Life (Lee, 2007), throws down a major challenge for commissioners, sectors, services and professionals. This is because there has long existed professional, organisational, and institutional barriers that limit access to, and appropriate treatment of, depression and anxiety in later life. Indeed, within and between all service systems – primary health, social care, acute general hospital care and intermediate care/transitional support services – few older people access appropriate support and treatment for their mental health problems – a feature of research studies carried out not just in the UK but in other countries suggesting that the problems are deep rooted and pervasive.

Community health and social care

Primary care

While older people with depression and anxiety are high users of primary care and most are dealt with exclusively at this level, there is poor identification and recognition of the illness. Not only are GPs the main route into specialist services for people with mental health problems and their carers, they also act as significant gatekeepers to a range of health and social care services at primary and community level. Yet, problems of accessing appropriate help from the GP arise at every stage in the pathway from illness to treatment: among older people in recognising the need to seek help; in the interaction between the older person and the GP; in making a diagnosis; in offering treatment to those identified as depressed and anxious.

Most older people with a depressive illness never discuss it with their GP, and even where depression is recognised and diagnosed, only a minority are offered treatment and therapy, primarily antidepressant medication, and few are offered psychosocial interventions, including psychotherapy and other cognitive and behavioural therapies. There is ample evidence too, to indicate that even if antidepressant medication is prescribed, many older people do not receive an adequate course of treatment – either the dosage is set below recommended levels or the length of time for which it is prescribed is too short (Unutzer et al, 2003). Only around one in 17 is referred to specialist mental health services (Banerjee, 1998), and while those with major depression are more likely to be picked up, this leaves considerable undetected illness with profound impact on morbidity and mortality.

Social care

Identifying and responding to late life depression and anxiety in social care presents difficulties at organisational and practitioner levels. First, service use activity data does not routinely include information on mental health problems of older service users unless they are in receipt of specialist mental health services. Second, where research has examined prevalence of depression and anxiety among those older people receiving social care support, as for example, home care, a high level of undiagnosed depressive disorders have been identified (Banerjee & McDonald, 1996).

Acute general hospital and intermediate care

Acute general care

While older people are the main users of acute hospital care, hospitalised older people are known to have a high rate of psychiatric co-morbidity with rates of 27% for depression (Royal College of Psychiatrists, 2005) – much of it undetected. For example, in a recent study, nearly two-thirds of older people referred to a hospital mental health older people's team had no prior involvement with mental health services (Godfrey, 2009). In part, this reflects the fact that illness events giving rise to acute admission contribute to mental ill health as in the case of a life-threatening illness or major trauma (Koenig et al, 1997). For example, specific conditions common in older age such a hip fracture are known to increase risk of depression and co-morbidity carries a significant risk of poorer outcomes including death (Holmes & House, 2000; Lenze et al, 2004). As well as being disabling, depression and anxiety hinder recovery from physical illness and contribute to higher inpatient bed days (Blazer, 2000).

Despite the high prevalence of mental health problems among older people in acute general hospitals, the cumulative and interactive impact of mental health on medical and functional recovery, and the fact that an acute hospital is a major interface location for accessing support with such problems, recognition of mental ill health among such patients is poor (Holmes et al, 2003).

Intermediate/transitional care

A major focus of investment and service development in recent years – particularly in England and Wales – has been in intermediate care services, designed to enhance independence and promote recovery from illness. Although depressive symptoms and low mood frequently accompany major disruption to self-identity and lifestyle as a result of sudden onset of a chronic disability (eg. stroke) or life-threatening illness (cardiac problems or cancer) among older people who were independent prior, studies of intermediate care (Godfrey et al, 2005) found little in the way of specialist psychological support to deal with their loss. Yet, there is evidence to indicate that depression, including minor depressive symptoms, affects recovery of function and the likelihood of return home following rehabilitation (Allen et al, 2004). In part, negative outcomes are mediated by participation in rehabilitation (Lenze et al, 2004) ie. people with depression and anxiety are less likely to engage with such programmes – therefore requiring specific help to do so.

Nursing and residential care

Despite the very high prevalence of depression among long-term nursing and residential care residents, including among those people newly admitted, research paints a picture of under-identification and under-treatment of depression in these settings (Schneider et al, 1997; Bagley et al, 2000). Schneider et al (1997) found that less than a third of older people in long-term care identified with depression were receiving antidepressant medication; and that there was considerable variation between homes in the detection and treatment of such problems. Bagley *et al* (2000) found that qualified nursing staff members were no more likely to recognise depression among residents than other care staff.

Barriers to access

A range of barriers to accessing help and identifying and treating depression (and anxiety) across health and social care services can be discerned: patient, provider and institutional.

Patient barriers

There are many reasons why older people suffering from depressive symptoms tend not to discuss these with their GP or to seek out appropriate help. They may lack the knowledge or information needed to obtain good care, they may be reluctant to express a need for help because of sensitivity to the stigma associated with depression, or they may perceive symptoms of depression as features of physical illness, grief or 'normal' ageing. There may also be cultural differences in the way depression is conceived and understood that present a barrier to seeking help (Marwaha & Livingston, 2002).

Older people may see no meaning in their existence and therefore may be less likely to ask for or use treatment for depression, reflective of ageist attitudes that they themselves may have internalised. These may in turn be reinforced in their encounters with medical professionals. Ageist attitudes undermine people's self-esteem and confidence, making them reluctant to ask for help, and further exacerbating their sense of worthlessness in an accelerating downward spiral.

Provider barriers
Multiple health problems making diagnosis and treatment difficult
Older people often present with multiple, chronic medical conditions in addition to their symptoms of mental ill health and this may impact on diagnosis in different and overlapping ways.

There appear to be real differences in the presentation of symptoms between older and younger people that can make it difficult to distinguish between depression and other health problems in older age. Gallo *et al* (1999), for example, suggest that sadness may be a less significant feature of depressive illness in later life than other symptoms such as sleep and appetite disturbance, slowing of thought, activity and poor concentration. Yet weight loss, sleep disturbance and low energy are common problems associated with diabetes and heart disease; poor concentration and memory loss are characteristic of both Parkinson's disease and Alzheimer's; and fatigue, high or low mood and difficulty with concentration can all occur as side effects of medication.

As one of the hallmarks of depression in older people is co-morbidity with ill health and physical disability, the symptoms of physical or somatic conditions may mimic or mesh with mental health problems, making diagnosis difficult. Regarding anxiety disorders specifically, it may be difficult to separate out phobias from what are rational, adaptive responses to threat (for example, fear of crime) or avoidance reactions due to decreased physical abilities (being afraid to go out at night when visual problems are exacerbated). As Blazer (2000) argues, the boundaries between psychiatry and medicine become inextricably blurred in older age, posing major challenges in the construction of comprehensive and integrated service responses.

The presence of concurrent health problems and medication may make GPs reluctant to prescribe drug therapy because of the possible risk of side effects. These problems pose real challenges for primary care practitioners and should not be under-estimated.

Knowledge, skills and expertise

Although much of the focus on identifying mental health problems in the community focuses on GPs, the challenge is considerably broader. Professionals within general services – whether primary, acute or social care services – are likely not only to lack the knowledge and skills required to identify older people with mental health problems but may also lack the confidence to do so.

Training and support in recognising depression has been emphasised within the *National Service Framework for Older People*, and in the importance attached to the use of screening tools and protocols for depression in primary care. However, while important, the problems of recognition of depression in general services are considerably more complex and pervasive than can be dealt with through the use of screening tools and protocols.

Reviews (Callahan, 2001) have suggested that efforts to educate primary care providers in screening for depression need to be combined with additional approaches that focus on improving rates of evidence-based treatment. These might include an increased emphasis on patient education and self-management of the illness, and greater access to and joint working with, mental health professionals. Goldberg (1992) also argues that more important than the use of screening tools in diagnosing depression is training in the use of more effective communication strategies. He found that GPs adept at detecting depression had a better style of communicating with patients. They listened and looked out for verbal and non-verbal cues, made eye contact, asked direct questions about psychological health and social circumstances and made supportive comments. Those better able to detect depression were also better able to manage it. They offered more information and advice about the condition and the possible ways it could be treated. Goldberg also considered that there should be an emphasis on preventative strategies for high-risk groups.

Models of collaborative care – as for example, involving specialist mental health workers in primary care and liaison psychiatry in general acute care – have been put forward to both enhance knowledge of generic staff and provide specialist expertise in identifying and responding to mental health need.

Institutional and societal barriers

Overlaying both user and provider barriers are institutional or societal barriers reflecting ageist attitudes. Such attitudes can operate in several ways. First, they can close professionals' minds to the existence of the underlying depression and anxiety. After all, is it not natural that older people will feel apathetic and low; or that older people are reluctant to leave their homes? Second, it may lead to 'therapeutic nihilism' – the idea that nothing can be done anyway for what is a 'normal' part of the ageing process.

Multi-level interventions in later life depression and anxiety

There is a robust evidence base to indicate that for older people – to a greater extent than for working age adults – physical ill health, pain and disability are the most consistent risk or provoking factors in depression – primarily on account of the restrictions that these impose on people's engagement in social activities and social relationships. Further, the relationship between functional limitations, reduced participation in social activities and networks and depression is interactive and cumulative. As a consequence, Blazer (2000) argues that interventions to reduce depression must proceed across multiple levels simultaneously. This would tend to include strategies to maintain/improve functioning, sustain and support social networks and improve health-related quality of life as well as therapeutic and pharmacological interventions. There is some supportive evidence for such an approach.

Although older people do not tend to access common treatments for depression and anxiety, particularly psychotherapeutic interventions, systematic reviews of the evidence suggest that behavioural and problem-solving strategies for major depression (focus of most of the research) are effective for older people (Arean & Cook, 2002). For depression linked with chronic illness, however, pharmacological treatments appear to be less effective in reducing depression (Oslin *et al*, 2002) because of the mediating effect of pain and functional impairment. Similar findings emerge from studies using psychotherapeutic approaches (Arean & Miranda, 1996). The authors argue the need for combined strategies such as physical therapy or enhanced pain management, alongside treatment for depression. Indeed, there is evidence to suggest the positive benefits of exercise in securing an improvement in depressive symptoms (Mather *et al*, 2002; Timonen *et al* 2002; Babyak *et al*, 2000). This appears to operate at two levels simultaneously – providing opportunities for people to get together and meet others as well as the positive effect of exercise on morale and abilities (see also NICE Guidelines 2007a,b; Mental Health Foundation, 2005).

Conclusions, policy and practice implications

There are broad sets of implications that emerge from the evidence and discussion on later life depression and anxiety:

- for prevention, independence and well-being in later life – currently at the centre of policy discourse on ageing well
- for collaborative models of service provision; if mental health problems in later life are everybody's business, what does this mean for service development and practice with regard to older people with depression and anxiety?

Prevention and well-being in later life

Depression and anxiety – despite their high prevalence – are not inevitable features of ageing. It is age related changes in risk factors that account for the increased prevalence and it is the dynamic between risk and resources that explains both vulnerability and resilience in the face of risk. For older people – to a greater extent than for younger adults – physical ill health, pain and disability are the most consistent risks or provoking factors in depression. Moreover, it is the restrictions these impose on people's engagement in social activities and social relationships that provide the link between ill health, disability and depression.

Loss of an intimate or partner as a result of bereavement is also a risk factor in depression. This appears to be more significant for major than for minor depression, especially when linked with long-standing vulnerability factors such as family and personal history.

Other risk factors include adverse life events such as chronic difficulties; the daily hassles that are an ever present reminder of loss or increasing disability; sudden, unexpected events like an acute, life-threatening illness and hospitalisation, or being a victim of crime. Although anxiety and depression often co-occur, a specific risk factor relating to anxiety alone is threat and fear of loss, whether of health or ability to manage.

Even so, people exhibit enormous resilience over the ageing process when confronted with stress as a result of loss or threat. Not all those who experience loss go on to develop a depressive illness or anxiety disorder. It depends on the meaning of the loss for the older person. It also relates to the person's degree of vulnerability when exposed to risk or, conversely, their access to resources or protective factors that either buffer stress or mediate its impact on the development of a mental illness. Important protective factors internal to the individual are self-esteem, a positive sense of self and mastery. Significant also, is whether people are enmeshed within reciprocal and interdependent relationships that meet wide ranging needs for physical and emotional intimacy, engagement in social activities and sustaining a sense of belonging and participation in social life. The same factors that buffer risk or reduce its impact in the presence of risk are also those that contribute to well-being in later life. There is an intimate relationship then between services and support to facilitate a 'good life' in older age and primary preventive initiatives to reduce late life depression – whether directed at older people generally, or at those in high-risk groups such as those who are restricted to the home on account of disability.

At the individual level to both reduce risk and shore up protective factors, there is a need for:

■ specific programmes such as rehabilitation, pain management and exercise groups for those experiencing deteriorating mobility and illness
■ services and support that open up opportunities for self-expression, maintaining social relationships and building new ones, and developing new interests
■ practical, social and emotional support in coming to terms with, and managing life changes
■ assistance in dealing with the 'daily hassles' that constrain people's lives.

At the neighbourhood or community level, primary preventive strategies mesh with support and action to create environments that are safe, secure, and easily negotiated. Strategies also need to integrate older people into decision-making structures and systems to effect positive change with older people as active agents in those changes. This needs to link with:

■ opportunities for people to meet and share interests at a very local level
■ enabling those who are restricted to the immediate neighbourhood to participate
■ offering a range of leisure, interest and educational pursuits that are attractive to older men and women within mainstream services.

Mental health in later life: everybody's business

Responding appropriately to the problems and barriers identified in recognising and treating late life depression and anxiety requires considerably more than enhancing the skills of GPs in identifying and diagnosing depression, although that is part of it. Older people with mental health problems can potentially come through many different routes: acute medical care, intermediate care, social care services, such as home care and day care as well as long-term care. Improving recognition and understanding of mental health problems in later life has to engage staff within health, social care, and housing more generally – both through training and use of integrated assessment processes.

However, much more is also required – specifically understanding of the interplay between physical, psychological and social factors in the onset and development of depression among older people, and the development of multidimensional and multi-faceted interventions that take this complexity into account. This is not just about professionals within generic services being able to access specialist mental health workers to provide an assessment of mental ill health but the development of collaborative models of care embracing mental health and older age services in acute, primary, transitional and community care. For later life mental health services, it also means that in order to offer an appropriate breadth of service to meet needs, these must be located in, and create links between, primary and secondary care, health care and social care and between statutory and voluntary/community networks. Translating these linked and combined partnership approaches into service development and practice is the central challenge in constructing an integrated service system for older people with mental health problems – thereby making later life mental health everybody's business. This complements and contributes to the Age Concern campaign to raise the veil of invisibility on late life depression, identifying five priority areas for attention (Age Concern, 2008):

1. meaningful engagement of older people with depression and their involvement with influence
2. a high profile publicity and media campaign on mental health and well-being in later life
3. greater recognition for and access to independent advocacy and support
4. greater focus on self-directed support for older people with mental health needs
5. access to and opportunities for different kinds of support and services; an environment where research, knowledge, best practice and developments are shared, disseminated and implemented.

Questions for consideration

In light of the evidence and issues posed, what would a service system for older people with mental health problems look like? What are the necessary components?

What would a strategy for preventive action on late life depression and anxiety look like at the individual, social networks and community levels?

References

Age Concern (2008) *Down But Not Out*. London: Age Concern England.

Alexopoulos G, Vrontou C, Kakuma T, Meyers B, Young R, Klausner E & Clarkin J (1996) Disability in geriatric depression. *American Journal of Psychiatry* **153** 877–885.

Alexopoulos G, Katz I, Bruce ML, Heo M, Ten Have T, Raue P, Bogner HR, Schulberg HC, Mulsant BH & Reynolds CF (2005) Remission in depressed geriatric primary care patients: a report from the PROSPECT study. *American Journal of Psychiatry* **162** 718–724.

Allen BP, Agha Z, Duthie EH & Layde PM (2004) Minor depression and rehabilitation outcome for older adults in sub-acute care. *Journal of Behavioral Health Services and Research* **31** (2) 189–198.

Alspaugh ME, Zarit SH & Greene R (1999) Longitudinal patterns of risk for depression in dementia caregivers: objective and subjective primary stress as predictors. *Psychology and Ageing* **14** (1) 34–43.

American Psychiatric Association (1994) *Diagnostic and Statistical Manual of Mental Disorders* (4th ed). Washington DC: American Psychiatric Association.

Ames D (1993) Depressive disorders among elderly people in long-term institutional care. *Australia and New Zealand Journal of Psychiatry* **27** (3) 379–391.

Andreescu C, Lenze E, Dew M, Begley A, Mulsant B, Dombrovski, B, Pollock B, Stack J, Miller M & Reynolds C (2007) Effect of co-morbid anxiety on treatment response and relapse risk in late-life depression: a controlled study. *British Journal of Psychiatry* **190** 344–349.

Aneshensel CS, Pearlin LI, Mullan JT, Zarit SH & Whitlatch CJ (1995) *Profiles in Caregiving: The unexpected career.* New York: Academic Press.

Arean P & Cook L (2002) Psychotherapy and combined psychotherapy/pharmacotherapy for late life depression. *Biological Psychiatry* **52** 293–303.

Arean P & Miranda J (1996) The treatment of depression in elderly primary care patients: a naturalistic study. *Journal of Clinical Geropsychology* **2** 153–160.

Babyak MA, Blumenthal JA, Herman S, Khatri P, Doraiswamy PM, Moore KA, Craighead WE, Baldewicz TT & Krishnan KR (2000) Exercise treatment for major depression: maintenance of therapeutic benefit at 10 months. *Psychosomatic Medicine* **62** 633–638.

Bagley H, Cordingley I, Burns A, Mozley C, Sutcliffe C, Challis D & Huxley P (2000) Recognition of depression by staff in nursing and residential homes. *Journal of Clinical Nursing* **9** (3) 445–450.

Banerjee S (1998) Needs of special groups: the elderly. *International Review of Psychiatry* **10** (2) 130–133.

Banerjee S & Macdonald A (1996) Mental disorder in an elderly home care population: associations with health and social services use. *British Journal of Psychiatry* **168** (8) 750–756.

Beekman A, Copeland J & Prince M (1999) Review of community prevalence of depression in later life. *The British Journal of Psychiatry* **174** (4) 307–311.

Beekman AT, Bremmer MA, Deeg DJ, van Balkom AJ, Smit JH, de Beurs E, van Dyck R & van Tilburg W (1998) Anxiety disorders in later life: a report from the longitudinal aging study, Amsterdam. *International Journal of Geriatric Psychiatry* **13** (10) 717–726.

Beekman AT, de Beurs E, van Balkom AJ, Deeg DJ, van Dyck R & van Tilburg W (2000) Anxiety and depression in later life: co-occurrence and commonality of risk factors. *The American Journal of Psychiatry* **157** (1) 89–95.

Berkman L & Syme L (1979) Social networks, host resistance and mortality: a nine-year follow-up of Alameda County residents. *American Journal of Epidemiology* **109** (2) 186–204.

Berkman L (2000) Social support, social networks, social cohesion and health. *Social Work in Health Care* **31** (2) 3–14.

Bisschop MI, Kriegsman DM, Beekman ATF & Deeg D (2004) Chronic diseases and depression: the modifying role of psychosocial resources. *Social Science and Medicine* **59** 721–733.

Blazer D (2000) Psychiatry and the oldest old. *American Journal of Psychiatry* **157** (12) 1915–1924.

Bond MJ, Clark MS & Davies S (2003) The quality of life of spouse dementia caregivers: changes associated with yielding to formal care and widowhood. *Social Science and Medicine* **57** 295.

Braam AW, Prince M, Beekman AT, Delespaul P, Dewey ME, Geerlings SW, Kivela SL, Lawlor BA, Magnusson H, Meller I Peres K, Reischies FM, Roelands M, Schoevers RA, Saz P, Skoog I, Turrina C, Versporten A & Copelan JR (2005) Physical health and depressive symptoms in older Europeans: Results from EURODEP. *British Journal of Psychiatry* **187** (1) 35–42.

Brilman E & Ormel J (2001) Life events, difficulties and onset of depressive episodes in later life. *Psychological Medicine* **31** (5) 859–869.

Burton L, Zdaniuk B, Schulz R, Jackson S & Hirsch C (2003) Transitions in spousal caregiving. *The Gerontologist* **43** (2) 230–241.

Burvill PW, Johnson GA, Jamorozik KD, Anderson CS, Stewart-Wynne EG & Chakara TM (1995) Anxiety disorders after stroke: the Perth Community Stroke Study. *British Journal of Psychiatry* **166** (3) 328–332.

Callahan CM (2001) Quality improvement research on late life depression in primary care. *Medical Care* **39** (8) 772–784.

Cattell V (2004) Social networks as mediators between the harsh circumstances of people's lives and their lived experience of health and well-being. In: C Phillipson, G Allan, DHJ Morgan (Eds). *Social Networks and Social Exclusion: Sociological and policy perspectives.* Aldershott: Ashgate Publishing.

Chappell N (1999) *Volunteering and Healthy Aging: What we know.* Canada: Volunteering Canada.

de Beurs E, Beekman A, van Balkom J, Deeg D, van Dyck R & van Tilburg W (1999) Consequences of anxiety in older persons: its effect on disability, well-being and use of health services. *Psychological Medicine* **29** (3) 583–593.

de Beurs E, Beekman A, Geerlings S, Deeg D, van Dyck R and van Tilburg W (2001) On becoming depressed or anxious in late life: similar vulnerability factors but different effects of stressful life events. *The British Journal of Psychiatry* **179** (5) 426–431.

Deeg D & Thomese G (2005) Discrepancies between personal income and neighbourhood status: effects on physical and mental health. *European Journal of Ageing* **2** (2) 98–107.

Denihan A, Kirby M, Bruce I, Cunningham C, Coakley D & Lawlor BA (2000) Three-year prognosis of depression in the community dwelling elderly. *British Journal of Psychiatry* **176** 453–457.

Department of Health (2001) *National Service Framework for Older People*. London: Department of Health.

Department of Health/CSIP (2005) *Everybody's Business, integrated services for older adults: A service development guide*. London: Department of Health.

Geiselmann B, Linden M & Helmchen H (2001) Psychiatrists diagnoses of sub-threshold depression in old age: frequency and correlates. *Psychological Medicine* **31** (1) 51–63.

Gallo JJ, Rabins PV & Anthony JC (1999) Sadness in older persons: 13-year follow-up of a community sample in Baltimore, Maryland. *Psychological Medicine* **29** (2) 341–350.

Godfrey M, Townsend J & Denby T (2004) *Building a Good Life for Older People in Local Communities*. York: Joseph Rowntree Foundation.

Godfrey M, Keen J, Townsend J, Moore J, Ware P, Hardy B, West R, Weatherly H & Henderson K (2005) *An Evaluation of Intermediate Care for Older People*. Report to the Department of Health. Leeds: University of Leeds.

Godfrey M (2009) *An Evaluation of the Leeds Partnership for Older People's Pilot (POPP): Toward system level change in later life mental health*. Leeds: University of Leeds.

Godlove Mozley C, Challis D, Sutcliffe C, Bagley H, Burns A, Huxley P & Cordingley L (2000) Psychiatric symptomology in elderly people admitted to nursing and residential homes. *Ageing and Mental Health* **4** (2) 136–141.

Goldberg D (1992) Early diagnosis and secondary prevention. In: R Jenkins, J Newton & R Young (Eds). *The Prevention of Depression and Anxiety*. London: HMSO.

Grant I, Adler K, Patterson TL, Dimsdale JE, Zeigler MG & Irwin MR (2002) Health consequences of Alzheimer's caregiving transitions: effects of placement and bereavement. *Psychosomatic Medicine* **64** 477–486.

Grzywacz J, Almeida D, Neupert S & Ettner S (2004) Socio-economic status and health: a micro-level analysis of exposure and vulnerability to daily stressors. *Journal of Health and Social Behaviour* **45** (1) 1–16.

Henderson A, Jorm A, Mackinnon A, Christensen H, Scott LR, Korten AE & Doyle-Phillips C (1993) The prevalence of depressive disorders and the distribution of depressive symptoms in later life: a survey using Draft ICD-10 and DSM-III-R. *Psychological Medicine* **23** (3) 719–729.

Henderson A, Jacomb P, McKinnon A, Jorm A, Christen H & Rodgers B (1997) The course of depression in the elderly: a longitudinal community-based study in Australia. *Psychological Medicine* **27** (1) 119–129.

Holmes J & House A (2000) Psychiatric illness predicts poor outcome after hip fracture: a prospective cohort study. *Psychological Medicine* **30** 921–929.

Holmes J, Bentley K & Cameron I (2003) A UK survey of psychiatric services for older people in general hospitals. *International Journal of Geriatric Psychiatry* **18** 716–721.

Koenig HG, George LK, Petersen BL & Pieper CF (1997) Depression in medically ill hospitalised older adults: prevalence, characteristics and course of symptoms according to six diagnostic schemes. *American Journal of Psychiatry* **154** 1376–1383.

Knipscheer C, Van Groenou M, Leene GJF, Beekman A & Deeg D (2000) The effect of environmental context and personal resources on depressive symptomatology in older age: a test of the Lawton model. *Ageing and Society* **20** (2) 183–202.

Lazarus R & De Longis A (1983) Psychological stress and coping in aging. *Journal of American Psychology* **38** (3) 245–254.

Lee M (2007) *Improving Services and Support for Older People with Mental Health Problems*. London: Age Concern England.

Lenze E, Mulsant B, Shear M, Alexopoulos G, Frank E & Reynolds C (2001) Co-morbidity of depression and anxiety disorders in later life. *Depression and Anxiety* **14** (2) 86–91.

Lenze EJ, Munin MC & Dew MA (2004) Adverse effects of depression and cognitive impairment on rehabilitation participation and recovery from hip fracture. *International Journal of Geriatric Psychiatry* **19** 472–478.

Lyness JM, King DA, Cox C, Yoediono Z & Caine ED (1999) The importance of subsyndromal depression in older primary care patients: prevalence and associated functional disability. *Journal of the American Geriatrics Society* **47** (6) 647–652.

Lund D, Caserta M & Dimond M (1993) The course of spousal bereavement in later life. In: MS Stroebe, W Stroebe & RO Hansson. *Handbook of Bereavement: Theory, research and intervention*, pp240–254. New York: Cambridge University Press.

Marks N, Lambert JD & Choi H (2002) Transition to caregiving – gender and psychological well-being: a prospective US national study. *Journal of Marriage and Family* **64** 657–667.

Marwaha S & Livingston G (2002) Stigma, racism or choice: why do depressed ethnic elders avoid psychiatrists? *Journal of Affective Disorders* **72** (3) 257–265.

Mather AS, Rodriguez C, Guthrie MF, McHarg AM, Reid I & McMurdo M (2002) Effects of exercise on depressive symptoms in older adults with poorly responsive depressive disorder. *British Journal of Psychiatry* **180** 411–415.

McCusker J, Cole M, Ciampi A, Latimer E, Windholz S, Elie M & Belzile E (2006) Twelve-month course of depressive symptoms in older medical inpatients. *International Journal of Geriatric Psychiatry* **22** 411–417.

McDougall FA, Matthews FE, Kvaal K, Dewey ME & Brayne C (2007) Prevalence and symptomatology of depression in older people living in institutions in England and Wales. *Age and Ageing* **36**:562–568.

Mehta K, Simonsick E, Penninx B, Schulz R, Rubin S, Satterfield S & Yaffe K (2003) Prevalence and correlates of anxiety symptoms in well-functioning older adults: findings from the health aging and body composition study. *Journal of the American Geriatric Society* **51** (4) 499–504.

Mental Health Foundation (2005) *Up and Running: Exercise therapy and the treatment of mild and moderate depression in primary care*. London: Mental Health Foundation.

Murray CJ & Lopez AD (1997) Alternative projections of mortality and disability by cause 1990–2020: global burden of disease study. *Lancet* **349** 1498–1504.

Nazroo JY (1997) *The Health of Britain's Ethnic Minorities: Findings from a national survey*. London: Policy Studies Institute.

NICE (2007a) *National Clinical Practice Guidelines: CG 23 depression* (Amended 2007). London: NICE.

NICE (2007b) *National Clinical Practice Guidelines: CG 22 anxiety* (Amended 2007). London: NICE.

Oslin DW, Datto CJ, Kallan MJ, Katz IR, Edell WS & Tenhave T (2002) Association between medical co-morbidity and treatment outcomes in late life depression. *Journal of American Geriatrics Society* **50** 823–828.

Penninx B, van Tilburg T, Boeke AJP, Deeg D, Kriegsman DM & van Eijk J (1998) Effects of social support and personal coping resources on depressive symptoms: different for various chronic diseases. *Health Psychology* **17** (6) 551–558.

Penninx B, Deeg D, van Eijk J, Beekman A & Guralnik J (2000) Changes in depression and physical decline in older adults: a longitudinal perspective. *Journal of Affective Disorders* **61** (1) 1–12.

Philp I & Appelby L (2005) *Better Mental Health for Older Adults*. London: Department of Health.

Pincus H, Davies W & McQueen L (1999) 'Sub-threshold' mental disorders: a review and synthesis of studies on minor depression and other 'brand names'. *The British Journal of Psychiatry* **174** (4) 288–296.

Prigerson H, Frank E, Reynolds C, George C & Kupfer D (1993) Protective psychosocial factors in depression among spousally bereaved elders. *The American Journal of Geriatric Psychiatry* **1** (4) 296–309.

Prince MJ, Harwood R, Thomas A & Mann A (1998) A prospective population-based cohort study of the effects of disablement and social milieu on the onset and maintenance of late life depression: the Gospel Oak project VII. *Psychological Medicine* **28** (2) 337–350.

Prince MJ, Beekman A, Deeg D, Fuhrer R, Kivela S, Lawlor BA, Lobo A, Magnusson H, Meller I, van Oyen H, Reischies F, Roelands M, Skoog I, Turrina C & Copeland JR (1999) Depression symptoms in late life assessed using the EURO-D scale: effect of age, gender and marital status in 14 European centres. *The British Journal of Psychiatry* **174** 4 339–345.

Prince MJ, Harwood R, Blizard R, Thomas A & Mann A (1997) Social support deficits, loneliness and life events as risk factors for depression in old age. *Psychological Medicine* **27** (2) 323–332.

Rapaport MH & Judd LL (1998) Minor depressive disorder and sub-syndromal depressive symptoms: functional impairment and response to treatment. *Journal of Affective Disorders* **48** (2/3) 227–232.

Royal College of Psychiatrists (2005) *Who Cares Wins: Improving the outcome for older people admitted to the general hospital*. Report of a working group for the faculty of old age psychiatry. London: RCP.

Scharf T, Phillipson C & Smith AE (2005) *Multiple Exclusion and Quality of Life amongst Excluded Older People in Disadvantaged Neighbourhoods*. London: Office of the Deputy Prime Minister.

Schneider J (Ed) (1997) *Quality of Care: Testing some measures in homes for elderly people*. Discussion paper 1245, Personal Social Services Research Unit. Canterbury: University of Kent.

Schulz R, O'Brian AT, Bookwala J & Fleissner K (1995) Psychiatric and physical mobility effects of dementia caregiving: prevalence, correlates and causes. *The Gerontologist* **35** (6) 771–791.

Seltzer M & Li LW (2000) The dynamics of caregiving: transitions during a three year perspective study. *The Gerontologist* **40** (2) 165–178.

Sewitch MJ, McCusker J, Dendukuri N & Yaffe MJ (2004) Depression in frail elders: impact on family caregivers. *International Journal of Geriatric Psychiatry* **19** 655–665.

Smith J, Borchelt M, Maier H & Jopp D (2002) Health and well-being in the young old and the oldest old. *Journal of Social Issues* **58** (4) 715–732.

Timonen L, Rantanen T, Timonen T & Sulkava R (2002) Effects of a group-based exercise program on the mood state of frail older women after discharge from hospital. *International Journal of Geriatric Psychiatry* **171**106–1111.

Unutzer J, Katon W, Callahan CM, Williams JW Jnr, Hunkeler E, Harpole L, Hoffing M, Della Penna RD, Noel PH, Lin EH, Tang L & Oishi S (2003) Depression treatment in a sample of 1,801 depressed older adults in primary care. *Journal American Geriatrics Society* **51** 505–514.

Verhaak PFW, Heijmans JWM, Peters L & Rijken M (2005) Chronic disease and mental disorder. *Social Services and Medicine* **60** 789–797.

Wenger GC, Davies R & Shahtahmasebi S (1996) Social isolation and loneliness in old age: review and model refinement. *Ageing and Society* **16** (3) 333–358.

World Health Organization (1992) *The ICD-10 Classification of Mental and Behavioural Disorders: Clinical descriptions and diagnostic guidelines*. Geneva: WHO.

World Health Organization (1993) *The ICD-10 Classification of Mental and Behavioural Disorders: Diagnostic criteria for research*. Geneva: WHO.

Zarit S, Femia E, Gatz, M & Johansson B (1999) Prevalence, incidence and correlates of depression in the oldest old: the OCTOC study. *Aging and Mental Health* **3** (2) 119–128.

Zeiss AM, Lewisohn PM, Rohde P & Seeley JR (1996) Relationship of physical disease and functional impairment to depression in older people. *Psychology and Aging* **11** (4) 572–581.

Zisook S & Shuchter S (1993) Major depression associated with widowhood. *American Journal of Geriatric Psychiatry* **1** (4) 316–326.

Chapter 8

Older people with lifelong mental health problems

Jo Warner and Alisoun Milne

Introduction

People who have experienced episodic or enduring mental health problems throughout their adult lives face a particular set of challenges when they reach retirement age (Jacoby et al, 2008). The term 'graduates' has been used to describe this group in recognition of their journey along the continuum of care, from adult mental health services to old age psychiatry. Many 'graduates' have accumulated a range of long-term, multiple and interlocking health and social care needs. Despite this complex range of needs there is evidence that they are supported incoherently by services and tend to be situated on the margins of mental health care. In fact, a significant number are thought to have fallen out of contact with services altogether as a direct consequence of a systemic failure to ensure continuity of support. Given this emerging profile, and the fact that the number of older people with lifelong mental health problems is increasing, it is surprising how little research has been conducted in relation to this group. It is also notable that they appear to be almost totally neglected in both policy and practice arenas.

This chapter summarises what is currently known about older people with lifelong mental health problems before moving on to explore the ways in which their needs are addressed and managed. Our focus is on the social dimensions of need, rather than on medical issues such as symptomology or treatment. We do, however, explore the impact of physical health conditions given the disproportionate impact these have on users' quality of life. Most of the evidence is drawn from work on those with chronic schizophrenia as this group constitutes the majority. The aim of this chapter is to raise awareness of the nature and complexity of the specific problems faced by older people with lifelong mental health problems and to challenge the pessimism that underpins attitudes towards, and approaches to, their care (Age Concern, 2007). The needs of people with dementia, a condition most often associated with old age, is the subject of other chapters in this book.

What is known about this group of people?

Estimates of the actual prevalence of older people with lifelong mental health problems vary widely, from 11 to 60 per 100,000 population, although the national average is thought to be in the region of 31 per 100,000 (Jolley et al, 2004). A significant proportion of this population are former inpatients of large psychiatric institutions, a cohort that is sometimes referred to as the 'original graduates'. Following the resettlement, which accompanied implementation of community care policies during the 1990s, some limited research was undertaken into the needs and profile of people in this group. Their increased visibility is largely a consequence of the commensurate shift of care from institutions to the community (Department of Health, 1999; 2001). There is also a 'new' population of older people with lifelong mental health problems comprising those who have been transferred from modern community psychiatric services for adults of working age to mental health services for older people in the last 20 years. The number of people in this latter group is increasing due to enhanced longevity and better access to health care, a trend that is mirrored in the UK population more widely (Age Concern, 2006; Karim et al, 2005).

Given the difficulties in establishing the number of older people with lifelong mental health problems, it is hardly surprising that so little is known about the nature and dimensions of their needs. From the limited information that can be reported with confidence, it is thought that between half and three-quarters have a diagnosis of schizophrenia and 10–20% have a diagnosis of a 'mood disorder' such as depression or bipolar affective disorder (Campbell & Ananth, 2002; Royal College of Psychiatrists, 2002). As noted above, most studies have focused on those with a diagnosis of chronic schizophrenia, a group that has been described as being 'small in size but high in need' (Karim et al, 2005: 315). The majority of older people with schizophrenia are women, 60% also experience at least one episode of major depression during the course of their illness (Godfrey et al, 2005). A significant percentage – predominantly men – have alcohol and drug problems. Thirty per cent of older people with bipolar disorder have other mental health problems, 9% have substance misuse problems, 5% have post-traumatic stress disorder, 10% have anxiety and 5% have dementia (Sajatovic et al, 2006). This picture of complexity is even more marked in terms of the interplay between physical and mental ill health, an issue to which we now turn.

Physical and mental health

Old age tends to be associated with additive physical and mental health vulnerabilities (Victor, 2005). In the population with which this chapter is concerned these intersect with, and often amplify, pre-existing mental health conditions. Physical health problems, which may be long-standing, as well as age related, are routinely overlooked by service providers because mental health issues dominate the clinical horizon (Age Concern, 2006). Recognition of co-existing physical illness in older people with schizophrenia has been highlighted as being especially important in the following respects: the symptoms of schizophrenia can affect pain thresholds such that patients tend to underreport medical symptoms; drug treatments for schizophrenia can reduce sensitivity to pain; and there is a well-reported tendency for this group to have inconsistent contact with medical services – even if treatment plans are commenced they may not be completed (Cohen et al, 2000). Further, cognitive deficits are common in this group due to the chronic nature of their illness and associated treatments; these deficits can impair the insight that service users might otherwise have into the significance of their physical condition (ibid). Finally, physical health problems may adversely affect the course and treatment of schizophrenia itself.

Studies have found higher mortality and morbidity rates, greater severity of illness and more untreated disorders among people with chronic schizophrenia compared with the wider population (Royal College of Psychiatrists, 2002; Vahia et al, 2007). Specifically, there are higher rates of cardiovascular disorders, diabetes, and hypothyroidism. Respiratory disorders, and bowel and stomach cancers are also more common and surveys have revealed deficiencies in oral and foot health (Jolley et al, 2004; McCleery, 2008; Royal College of Psychiatrists, 2002). Compared with the mainstream population, deaths resulting from unnatural causes such as suicide, homicide and accidents are also higher among this group (although these risks are high among younger people with mental health problems as well) (Age Concern, 2007). Just as the palliative care needs of people with dementia are distinctive and multiple (Sampson *et al*, 2008), so people in the population under review are likely to have similarly complex needs.

Longitudinal studies have identified two patterns in relation to non-pathological cognitive decline among people with chronic schizophrenia. First, that those patients who spent many years in long-stay institutional care – the 'original graduates' – are at greater risk of experiencing cognitive decline than that expected for their age group (Karim *et al*, 2005). People with a learning disability who would have been described as having a 'dual diagnosis' are likely to be included in this group. Second, in contrast, the community based 'new graduates' appear to be at reduced risk compared with their age matched peers (Vahia *et al*, 2007). These findings powerfully underscore the role played by environment and 'treatment regimes' in promoting, or reducing, cognitive function. In relation to organic Alzheimer-type conditions, evidence is mixed as to whether there is an elevated risk for this population. Some symptoms of dementia mimic the side effects of psychotropic drugs, making its early identification unlikely, and opportunities for preventive treatment are overlooked (Milne *et al*, 2008). Overall, health outcomes for this population are poor, as McCleery states, '*Those patients with severe and enduring mental illness who survive to old age reach it with a high burden of ill health*' (2008: 633).

While unpleasant side effects from psychiatric drugs are experienced by many service users, those who have been on older treatments and/or have been treated long-term often have specific and severe iatrogenic illness ie. illness caused directly by treatment(s). Neurological side effects such as involuntary movements (tardive dyskinesia) are most prevalent among older people with chronic schizophrenia, with studies focusing on hospital populations (in McCleery, 2008: 23). Such side effects can ultimately cause more severe problems with functioning than the original condition for which the medication was prescribed. One recent study demonstrates the increased risk of hip fractures associated with long-term use of neuroleptic medication (Howard *et al*, 2007). Health risks in this population are also compounded by limited opportunities for exercise, poor diet, smoking and limited access to primary care. The prevalence of smoking among people with a diagnosis of schizophrenia is as high as 70%; many people smoke heavily (McCreadie, 2003).

Social needs and community support

Older people with lifelong mental health problems, particularly schizophrenia, tend to have high levels of social need; many are isolated, have poor social skills and have infrequent, or no links with relatives (Graham *et al*, 2002; McNulty *et al*, 2003; Rodriguez-Ferrera *et al*, 2004). Among 'original graduates' this is, in good part, a consequence of the separation from community and family life that is consistent with long-term incarceration. There is additional evidence that this group have limited self-care skills proportionate to their length of stay in institutional care (Abdul-Hamid *et al*, 1998). Their social profile has been compared with that of mentally ill homeless people in that they are '*destitute of personal contacts and supports*' and profoundly lacking in skills for the management of daily life (Jolley *et al*, 2004: 30). Not only are a number of these 'social features' linked directly to poor levels of social functioning but they have also been identified as associated with poor overall outcomes for people with chronic schizophrenia (Jolley *et al*, 2004). In other words, these social factors are a pivotal dimension of need.

Among 'new' graduates, the picture is more complicated. Fewer spend long periods in psychiatric hospital, and modern treatment regimes accommodate, to a varying degree, the social needs of patients. While many users of long-stay inpatient care have limited contact with relatives or friends, the 'new graduates' population have more extensive networks; many have family carers (Department of Health, 1999). Additionally, there is some evidence that nursing staff on short-stay psychiatric wards welcome the input of relatives and encourage their involvement, although it is interesting that relatives themselves consider their role to be negligible (Abdul-Hamid et al, 1998).

Wider evidence about the role of family carers suggests that, unlike carers of disabled children or older people, carers of adults with functional mental health problems do not recognise themselves as 'carers', do not have their needs assessed by professionals and receive little support from services (Milne et al, 2001; Commission for Social Care Inspection, 2008). The limited evidence that does exist about the health and well-being of carers of this population indicates that the majority experience significant levels of burden (Commission for Social Care Inspection, 2008). Concern about who will support their relative when they die or become disabled is a key issue (Rethink, 2004).

In terms of accommodation needs, one study has suggested that the characteristics of supported housing are an important factor in the quality of life of graduates from different diagnostic groups (Depla et al, 2006). Specifically, people with psychotic conditions appear to have social needs associated with more intensive forms of professional support; people with 'mood disorders' appear to value high levels of personal and social autonomy (Depla et al, 2006). One study specifically identified needs associated with inappropriate accommodation in mainstream nursing homes, where most of the residents have severe dementia and consequently very different care requirements from people with lifelong mental health conditions (McNulty et al, 2003).

Social dislocation, stigma and invisibility

An overriding issue for old and new graduates alike is that of social dislocation, a process that is a function both of their condition and social responses to it. Stigma and labelling play a particularly pernicious role, as observed by Keating:

> *'Regardless of the perspective or approach that is taken to understand mental illness, it has to be acknowledged that when a person is assigned a label of mental illness, they take on an identity that is stigmatised and valued negatively'* (2006: 32).

While stigma is a prominent issue for mental health service users in general, it is a particularly powerful facet of the experience of the population under review because of the lifelong nature of their problems. Stigma has been identified both as a contributory risk factor in mental illness, especially relapse, and an obstacle to recovery (Thornicroft, 2006). However, while 'combating stigma' among people with mental health problems has become a priority area for UK policy and practice (Department of Health, 2006), the focus has been working age adults and limited attention has been paid to the needs of older people with mental ill health. That the stigma faced by this group is likely to be particularly entrenched – in that they face the double stigma associated with negative attitudes towards age and mental illness over many years – makes this a significant deficit (Godfrey et al, 2005).

In terms of discrimination, there is evidence that ageism informs the nature and types of therapeutic service allocations. While it may be true that years of chronic illness undermine the preparedness of some individuals to seek therapeutic help, research suggests that psychosocial interventions such as CBT, are rarely, if ever offered to older people with enduring mental health problems when they are routinely offered to younger adults (Karim *et al*, 2005). The fact that there is no evidence to suggest these treatments are any less effective for older patients, supports the argument that ageist assumptions underpin decisions about eligibility rather than 'need' (Boyd, 2007). It is commonly believed, quite erroneously, that older people are less amenable to therapy, that their personalities are more 'fixed' than those of younger adults and that they have a reduced capacity for recovery and/or change (Victor, 2005; Jacoby *et al*, 2008). Notions of 'inevitable decline' in old age and 'dependency' are linked assumptions that permeate attitudes in this area of work. These feed into and deepen the 'enduring pessimism' that has been evidenced as characterising work with older people with long-term mental health problems (McCleery, 2008: 28).

A paradoxical dimension of the dual stigma associated with ageism and mental illness can be seen in constructions of 'risk' and how these differ in relation to older service users compared to younger ones. Rodriguez-Ferrera and Vassilas (1998) suggest that the perceived risk of violence associated with younger service users with schizophrenia accounts for the lack of focus on older people with the same condition. As the construction of 'risk' associated with older people tends to be related to vulnerability to physical harm through accident or neglect, they attract less public attention (Kemshall, 2002). As the Age Concern inquiry report into mental health in later life notes, '*They do not pose a threat. They are often hidden away from public view and therefore easier to ignore*' (2007: 43). For older people with lifelong mental health problems, the absence of behaviour that draws attention to them means they are effectively rendered invisible; that they lack an advocate to champion their cause is an additional deficit (Jolley *et al*, 2004).

The policy framework

Whilst older people with lifelong mental ill health are identified in a range of policies situated in a number of, largely separate, policy spheres, they are not the core focus of any specific policy initiative and occupy a no man's land falling between policies whose main focus is other user groups. In terms of mental health policy, the clinical guidelines on schizophrenia by the National Institute for Health and Clinical Excellence (2002) concentrates on services for adults of working age, thereby omitting any focus on those who will have received services for many years but then been transferred to services for older people on reaching 65 years. The overarching *National Service Framework* (NSF) *for Mental Health* signposts responsibility for managing the needs of older people with mental health problems within the *National Service Framework for Older People* (Department of Health, 1999; 2001). The older people's NSF states that they, '... *will require the packages of care set out in the NSF for Mental Health, and the same standards should apply as for working age adults. For these people care should be provided within the framework of the Care Programme Approach*' rather than the Single Assessment Process, which applies to older people who become mentally ill in later life (Department of Health, 2001: 91). Despite this commitment, and a later attempt to clarify the situation by the Department of Health, there remains considerable confusion about the arrangements for assessing the needs, and managing the care, of older people with lifelong mental health problems (Royal College of Psychiatrists, 2006).

In policies relating to older people with mental health problems, very limited attention is paid to the population under review (National Audit Office, 2007; Care Services Improvement Partnership,

2005). This fast developing policy landscape is dominated by concerns about mental illnesses that develop in old age – primarily dementia – rather than those that have a lifelong trajectory. The recently launched *National Dementia Strategy* is a key example: the key focus of Standard 7 of the *National Service Framework for Older People* entitled *Mental Health in Older People* was dementia and depression (Department of Health, 2008a; 2001). While the 2005 guidance, *Everybody's Business: Integrating mental health services for older adults*, incorporated all older people with mental health needs, it makes only limited reference to those with lifelong mental health problems (Care Services Improvement Partnership, 2005). Implementation of the 2008 equality bill may provide an opportunity for policy and services to review the way in which mental health care for the population under review is designed and delivered (Department of Health, 2008b).

Far from being exceptional, the invisibility of older people with longstanding mental health needs across the board in policy development appears to be an established pattern. In their 2005 audit of research relating to older people with mental ill health, Godfrey *et al* (2005) noted that no studies focused on older people with lifelong mental illness. This selective inattention reflects the marginal position of this population in the existing research portfolio and serves to perpetuate '*the invisibility of later life mental health problems in policy*' (*ibid*, 445).

Service responses

As noted earlier, comorbidity and complexity of need are defining characteristics of the population under review (Karim *et al*, 2005). As their risks of becoming isolated, homeless and neglected are significant, this group of users – perhaps more than any other – require careful assessment and care planning and meticulous support and management (Rodriguez-Ferrera *et al*, 2004). In fact, primarily as a consequence of the poor management of transition from adult services to older people's mental health care, these risks appear to be reinforced and deepened (Jolley *et al*, 2004). The paucity of services available for older people with lifelong mental health problems further compounds the challenge, a situation that, in part, reflects the positive impact of the *National Service Framework for Mental Health* on services for adults of working age. Thus, for a significant number of people in this group, the transfer may mean moving from, '*a generously sponsored programme of support and rehabilitation ... [to] ... a threadbare system shared with large numbers of much older, physically frail patients*' (Jolley *et al*, 2004: 31). While it can prove difficult to provide a national picture of service provision, inequalities have been identified; these are particularly visible around transitions (Beecham *et al*, 2008).

Although it has been common practice in the past to transfer patients with long-term mental health problems from 'adult care' to old age psychiatry when they reach retirement age, there has been increasing pressure to change such institutionalised procedures. Policy has emphasised a needs-based approach: '*When individuals subject to the Care Programme Approach reach old age, switches to the Single Assessment Process are not inevitable, and should only be made in the best interests of individuals and the continuity of their care*' (Department of Health, 2002: 1). Recent guidance on service standards from the Royal College of Psychiatrists advises that a patient's 65th birthday should be used as a '*...trigger for reassessing need, and not a trigger for automatic transfer*' (2006: 32). Its earlier 'interface' document regards the (re)assessment as underpinning decision-making about which service best meets the needs of individuals (Royal College of Psychiatrists, 2004).

Drivers for continuing the transfer of patients when they reach 'old age' include heavy workloads – as one consultant psychiatrist for adults of working age notes, '*When burdened, the natural desire is to shed some of the load. There can be a sense of relief when a patient crosses the threshold criterion for transfer to another service*' (quoted in Jolley *et al*, 2004: 30). That clinical teams vary about whether, and/or when, they transfer patients from adults services to old age psychiatry is an additional issue. It has been criticised for contributing to the uneven and fragmented response to the needs of the population under review (Jolley *et al*, 2004).

While flexibility at the local level is important and should reflect the strength, or not, of old age psychiatry services, the need of the individual service user should be at the centre of decision-making. Within reason, any transfer of care provision needs to be iterative rather than a 'one off' event (Jolley *et al*, 2004). That a significant number of graduates fall out of contact with services altogether supports the contention that there has been a systemic failure to ensure continuity of care for this group of users. It also reflects the marginal status of this population, their invisibility and the lack of a nationally agreed 'care pathway' or 'model of care' (Royal College of Psychiatrists, 2002; 2006).

The fact that there are separate services for 'adults' and 'older people' with mental health problems has been challenged by some critics as discriminatory. The Age Concern inquiry report argues that this artificial age related distinction should be removed; there should be one mental health service for all adults on the basis that, '...*older people are adults too*' (Age Concern, 2007: 37). The report also notes that as 'health' is not related in any precise way to chronological age and as 'retirement' is a shifting concept, the positive role and value of age related mental health services is questionable. Certainly for older people with lifelong mental health problems, the bifurcation of service provision has contributed, albeit indirectly, to inconsistency of provision, differences in practice around transfer and lack of continuity of care. In fact, this bifurcation lays the ground for some of the most serious risks this group faces, including those arising from a lack of specialist provision in social care and housing services. Further, it can be regarded as a reflection of discriminatory assumptions about the needs of older people (Age Concern & Mental Health Foundation, 2006).

Facing the challenge

The aim of this chapter has been to raise awareness of the profile and needs of older people with lifelong mental health problems in the UK (Rethink, 2004). It has highlighted the fact that within the larger population of 'graduates' there are two discrete groups with different needs – the 'older' graduates and a more recent group that is growing rapidly. Although these two sub-populations have different profiles, they share the defining experiences of multiple and complex need, long-term marginalisation and stigma, socio-economic disadvantage and poor physical health. Mismanagement of the transition from adult mental health services to older people's mental health care is also a widely evidenced experience and one that is reinforced by the absence of explicit reference to this population in policies relating to both older people and people with mental health problems (Royal College of Psychiatrists, 2006). That this division is mirrored in the provision of separate services for 'adults' and 'older people' has been criticised by some commentators as inherently discriminatory and as disadvantaging older people with mental health problems (Age Concern, 2007).

The challenges facing services for older people with lifelong mental ill health are, we would argue, both a cause and a consequence of the construction and implementation of policies that marginalise this population and a service system that is designed to meet the needs of the majority. The population under review require priority research and policy attention in order that appropriate forward planning can be undertaken to respond to predicted growth in prevalence, and need, in a way that is proactive rather than reactive and that is integrated rather than fragmented.

References

Abdul-Hamid W, Holloway F & Silverman M (1998) Psychiatric care needs of elderly graduates – unanswered questions. *Aging and Mental Health* **2** (3) 167–170.

Age Concern (2006) *Key Facts and Statistics 2006*. London: Age Concern.

Age Concern (2007) *Improving Services and Support for Older People with Mental Health Problems: The second report from the UK inquiry into mental health and well-being in later life*. London: Age Concern.

Age Concern & Mental Health Foundation (2006) *Promoting Mental Health and Well-Being in Later Life*. London: Age Concern.

Beecham J, Knapp M, Fernandez J-L, Huxley P, Mangalore R, McCrone P, Snell T, Winter B & Wittenberg R (2008) *Age Discrimination in Mental Health Services: PSSRU discussion paper 2536*. Kent: Personal Social Services Research Unit.

Boyd M (Ed) (2007) *Psychiatric Nursing: Contemporary practice*. Philadelphia: Lippincot, Williams & Wilkins.

Campbell P & Ananth H (2002) Graduates. In: R Jacoby & C Oppenheimer (Eds) *Psychiatry in the Elderly* (pp 782–784). Oxford: Oxford University Press.

Care Services Improvement Partnership (2005) *Everybody's Business – Integrating mental health services for older adults: a service development guide*. London: Department of Health.

Cohen CI, Cohen GD, Blank K, Gaitz IR, Leuchter A, Maletta G, Meyers B, Sakauye K & Shamoian C (2000) Schizophrenia and older adults: an overview – directions for research and policy. *American Journal of Geriatric Psychiatry* **8** 19–28.

Commission for Social Care Inspection (2008) *The State of Social Care in England 2006/07*. London: Commission for Social Care Inspection.

Department of Health (1999) *National Service Framework for Mental Health: Modern standards and service models*. London: Department of Health.

Department of Health (2001) *National Service Framework for Older People*. London: Department of Health.

Department of Health (2002) *Fair Access to Care Services: Guidance on eligibility criteria for adult social care*. London: Department of Health.

Department of Health (2006) *Action on Stigma: Promoting mental health, ending discrimination at work*. London: Department of Health.

Department of Health (2008a) *National Dementia Strategy*. London: Department of Health.

Department of Health (2008b) *Equality bill*. London: Department of Health.

Depla MFIA, De Graaf R & Heeren TJ (2006) The relationship between characteristics of supported housing and the quality of life of older adults with severe mental illness. *Aging & Mental Health* **10** (6) 592–598.

Godfrey M, Townsend J, Surr C, Boyle G & Brooker D (2005) *Prevention and Service Provision: Mental health problems in later life – Final report*. Bradford: Institute of Sciences and Public Health Research/University of Bradford Division of Dementia Studies.

Graham C, Arthur A & Howard R (2002) The social functioning of older adults with schizophrenia. *Aging & Mental Health* **6** 149–152.

Howard L, Kirkwood G & Leese M (2007) Risk of hip fracture in patients with a history of schizophrenia. *The British Journal of Psychiatry* **190** 129–134.

Jacoby R, Oppenheimer C, Dening T & Thomas A (Eds) (2008) Mental health in care homes for older people. In: *The Oxford Textbook of Old Age Psychiatry*. Oxford: Oxford University Press.

Jolley D, Kosky N & Holloway F (2004) Older people with longstanding mental illness: the graduates. *Advances in Psychiatric Treatment* **10** 27–36.

Karim S, Overshott R & Burns A (2005) Older people with chronic schizophrenia. *Aging & Mental Health* **9** (4) 315–324.

Keating F (2006) Breaking the spiral of oppression: racism and race equality in the mental health system. In: C Jackson & K Hill (Eds) *Mental Health Today: A handbook* (pp 29–36). Brighton: Pavilion Publishers.

Kemshall H (2002) *Risk, Social Policy and Welfare*. Milton Keynes: Open University Press.

McCleery J (2008) Severe and enduring mental illness in old age. In: R Jacoby, C Oppenheimer, T. Dening & A Thomas (Eds) *The Oxford Textbook of Old Age Psychiatry* (pp627–639). Oxford: Oxford University Press.

McCreadie RG (2003) Diet, smoking and cardiovascular risk in people with schizophrenia. Descriptive study. *British Journal of Psychiatry* **183** 534–539.

McNulty SV, Laing D, Semple M, Jackson G & Pelosi AJ (2003) Care needs of elderly people with schizophrenia. *British Journal of Psychiatry* **182** 241–247.

Milne A, Hatzidimitriadou E, Chryssanthopoulou C & Owen T (2001) *Caring in Later Life: Reviewing the role of older carers*. London: Help the Aged.

Milne A, Culverwell A, Guss R, Tuppen J & Whelton R (2008) Screening for dementia in primary care: a review of the efficacy and quality of tools and measures. *International Psychogeriatrics* **20** (5) 911–926.

National Audit Office (2007) *Improving Services and Support for People with Dementia*. London: Stationery Office.

National Institute for Health and Clinical Excellence (2002) *Schizophrenia: Core interventions in the treatment and management of schizophrenia in primary and secondary care* [online]. Available at: http://www.nice.org.uk/Guidance/CG1 (accessed December 2008).

Rethink (2004) *Lost and Found: Voices from a forgotten generation*. London: Rethink.

Rodriguez-Ferrera S & Vassilas CA (1998) Older people with schizophrenia: providing services for a neglected group. *British Medical Journal* **317** 293–294.

Rodriguez-Ferrera S, Vassilas C & Hague S (2004) Older People with Schizophrenia: A community study in rural catchment area. *International Journal of Geriatric Psychiatry* **19** (12) 1181–1187.

Royal College of Psychiatrists (2002) *Caring for People Who Enter Old Age with Enduring or Relapsing Mental Illness (Graduates): Council report CR110*. London: Royal College of Psychiatrists.

Royal College of Psychiatrists (2004) *The Interface Between General and Community and Old Age Psychiatry: Report of a working group*. London: Royal College of Psychiatrists.

Royal College of Psychiatrists (2006) *Raising the Standard: Specialist services for older people with mental illness. Report of the Faculty of Old Age Psychiatrists*. London: Royal College of Psychiatrists.

Sajatovic M, Blow FC & Ignacio RV (2006) Psychiatric comorbidity in older adults with bipolar disorder. *International Journal of Geriatric Psychiatry* **21** (6) 582–587.

Sampson EL, Thuné-Boyle I, Kukkastenvehmas R, Jones L, Tookman A, King M & Blanchard MR (2008) Palliative care in advanced dementia: a mixed methods approach for the development of a complex intervention, *BMC Palliative Care* **7** (8).

Thornicroft G (2006) *Ignorance + Prejudice + Discrimination = Stigma*. London: Mental Health Foundation.

Vahia I, Bankole AO, Reyes P, Diwan S, Palekar N, Sapra M, Ramirz P & Cohen CI (2007) *Aging Health* **3** (3) 383–396.

Victor C (2005) *The Social Context of Ageing, A textbook of gerontology*. Abingdon: Routledge.

Chapter 9
Older people, suicide and self-harm

Catherine Jackson

'The thing is, if you've got a broken arm you've got people wanting to help... But if you've got a broken heart and a broken head, they just don't want to know.' (Age Concern, 2007)

From the launch of the government's suicide prevention strategy for England in 2002 (Department of Health, 2002), the overriding message has been the need to bring down the high rates in suicide among younger age groups. At the time of the launch, suicide was the most common cause of death among young men aged under 35. Efforts to address suicide have rightly been largely directed at this group, and at the other very high risk groups, people with mental health problems and people in prison (NMHDU, 2008).

But to assume that suicide is not a pressing issue in other age groups would be very wrong. As the most recent age-standardised suicide rates for England and Wales show (see **table 1**), rates of self-inflicted death among older people – and older men in particular – are considerable, and they rise sharply in the very old. The age-standardised suicide rate among young men aged 15–34 (the group considered at highest risk) totals some 261 per million; for men aged 65+ the rate is 414 per million, with the highest rate (175 per million) in men aged 85+.

Table 1: Suicide rates per million population England and Wales 2006–07								
	15–24	25–34	35–44	45–54	55–64	65–74	75–84	85+
Men	87	174	208	171	147	99	140	175
Women	21	42	48	63	50	41	44	46

Moreover, older people are much more successful when they do decide to take their own life. The ratio of suicide attempts to completed suicides in the general population is some 15:1; in older people it is approximately 4:1 (Beeston, 2006).

This risk is only minimally acknowledged in the national suicide strategy, where older people are defined as a 'vulnerable', not high risk, group (NMHDU, 2008).

This chapter will explore the factors that research suggests leads older people to take (or attempt to take) their own lives, what the literature and emerging best practice shows can be done (and is being done) to address these factors, and how national government policy in England is addressing these issues.

Risk factors

The factors that lead to older people seeking to end their lives have been comprehensively reviewed by Beeston (2006). A difficulty highlighted in the Beeston review is that of identifying older people at risk. The research suggests that older people are far less likely than younger adults to have (or to admit to having) suicidal thoughts. Beeston also points to the distinction between passively 'wanting to die' and feeling that 'life is not worth living', and having active suicidal thoughts and plans. A more recent study, using data from a national survey of psychiatric illness in the UK (Dennis, Baillon, Brugha *et al*, 2007), found that younger adults were three times more likely than older adults to have actively considered suicide.

Beeston's review also found that older people who attempt suicide are less likely to have a history of previous attempts (a common risk factor for younger adults) – on average four or fewer attempts, compared with eight (and up to 36) in the general population. Moreover, older people appear less likely than younger adults to have a current diagnosed mental illness and to be in the care of the mental health services (Tadros & Salib, 2007) – again, a common risk factor among younger age groups.

That said, there is some evidence of links between severe mental illness and suicide in older people. One piece of research, conducted in Finland (Karvonen *et al*, 2008), found a higher risk of suicide among people aged 65–75 and 75+ than among a younger group aged 50–64 following discharge from psychiatric hospital. Of the older groups, 42% took their own life within three months of discharge, and 83% used a violent method (ie. they were very determined to kill themselves), indicating a very clear need for intensive follow-up and support in the community.

However, older people at risk of suicide are often in contact with primary care services. Tadros and Salib (2007) reviewed adult suicides in the West Midlands over a four-year period 1995–1999 and found that 41.5% of the older adults had seen their GP within the previous six months, compared with 19% of younger adults. However, the older people were, in most cases, consulting their GP about physical health issues, not their mental or emotional health; they were mainly seeking help with depression, pain and physical ill health, whereas the younger adults were more likely to be seeing their GP about a mental illness or depression.

The very old are no less vulnerable to suicidal wishes and intent, as one Italian study amply demonstrates. Scocco and colleagues (2009) interviewed a random sample of female residents aged 80+ in nursing homes in the north east Veneto region, and found that nearly a third (some 31%) had suicidal thoughts or plans during the previous four weeks, and that suicidal thoughts were most frequent among those aged 85+.

However, dementia (including Alzheimer's disease) does not appear to be a major risk factor for suicide, although the evidence base is limited. For example, Haw and colleagues (2009) found that diagnosis increases the risk of suicide among older people with dementia but, as in the general population, key factors are chiefly depression and a sense of hopelessness. Dementia-specific factors include cognitive impairment, having insight into their mental state, younger age, and failure to respond to anti-dementia drugs.

Suicide risk factors

The Royal College of General Practitioners has produced a checklist of factors that indicate high risk of suicide in older people.

Verbal clues include:
- direct expression of the wish to die ('end-centred' talk)
- indirect statements about 'not being here' for future events.

Behavioural clues include:
- hoarding medication
- making or changing a will
- putting one's affairs in order
- a sudden interest in giving possessions and money away
- suddenly re-establishing contact with church or clergy
- self-neglect and lack of interest in household tasks or social activities
- 'failure to thrive'
- visiting a GP with non-specific medical symptoms.

Situational factors include:
- life changes that might trigger depression, such as retirement, moving home, bereavement and other loss
- diagnosis of a serious illness
- depression or sudden recovery from depression
- changes in sleeping and eating habits
- tension, agitation or guilt
- shunning company and isolating oneself.

Means of suicide

The means chosen by older people to end their lives differs from those taken by younger adults (Tadros & Saleb, 2000; Hawton & Harriss, 2006). The most common means of suicide and suicide attempt among older people across both sexes is overdose by prescribed and over-the-counter medication – a total of 88.6% in the Hawton and Harriss (2006) study, of whom 49.3% used paracetamol, 24% minor tranquillisers and 15.9% antidepressants. The most common means of suicide among older men is hanging; among older women it is self-poisoning. Drowning is more common among older men than among younger men; older women are more likely than younger women to end their lives by self-asphyxiation (tying a plastic bag over their head). Older people much less frequently kill themselves by jumping from a high place, or by carbon monoxide poisoning (from car exhausts, for example). Tadros and Saleb (2000) suggest that the means chosen by older people reflects comparative ease of access – older people are likely to be less physically mobile, may not have a car, and will have very ready access to medication that is often being prescribed for other health problems.

International comparisons support this hypothesis. For example, suicide by firearms is rare in the UK, but very common in the US where many more people have a gun. In Japan, where high-rise buildings are much more common, suicide by jumping from a high place is much more frequent among older people (Chan *et al*, 2007).

However, as Beeston (2006) points out, older people living in rural areas (not only, but particularly those in farming communities) are likely to have access to firearms, and suicide by firearm is thus a risk with this group.

Reasons for suicide

Physical ill health, depression, social isolation, relationship problems and bereavement appear to be the primary factors associated with suicide in older people.

For example, Dennis and colleagues (Dennis, Molloy, Andrews *et al*, 2007) reviewed data on 76 older people referred to a specialist self-harm team and found that most were living alone, were socially isolated and had poor physical health, and 69% were depressed. However, those who were depressed were more actively suicidal than the others, and their main reason for wishing to die was 'to gain relief from an unbearable state of mind', not to put an end to their physical suffering.

Hawton and Harriss (2006), in their 20-year follow-up of over 700 older people who were admitted to hospital following attempted suicide, identified the most common problems preceding the attempts as physical illness (46.1%), social isolation (33.5%), relationships problems with family (29.4%) or partner (25.9%), and bereavement or loss (16.7%).

Harwood and colleagues (2006) identified physical illness, interpersonal problems and bereavement as the three most frequent life problems associated with suicide. Of the 100 suicides reviewed, 82% had physical health problems that were felt to be contributory to their death in 62% of cases; 55% had interpersonal problems that were felt to be contributory to their suicide in 31% of cases, and 47% had been bereaved, which was felt to have contributed to their decision to end their life in 25% of cases.

Deliberate self-harm

Deliberate self-harm is the term commonly used in psychiatric research to describe attempted suicide – although it is also commonly used to describe self-harm that is not inflicted with suicidal intent and is, indeed, a strategy used to stay alive (Mangnall & Yurkovitch, 2008; Pembroke, 1994). It is used here with the former meaning.

As previously noted, older people are much more likely to kill themselves when they attempt to do so; it is clear that when older people decide to end their life, they are very determined to succeed. Hawton and Harriss (2006), in their follow-up study of older people who had attempted suicide, found extremely high levels of intent to die: 65.1% were in the high to very high range of suicide intent scores, and 19.5% scored for moderate intent, across both sexes. By the end of the 20-year follow up period, 30 (4.5% of those traced) had died by either definite or probable (open verdict) suicide – a much higher rate than that for the general population. The majority had died within five years of the initial suicide attempt; those at highest risk were male and aged 60–69 when they first attempted suicide.

The characteristics of older people identified as having deliberately self-harmed are identical to those who do take their own lives: physical ill health, isolation and relationship problems feature highly, and (as Chan and colleagues (2007) put it) 'hopelessness', or depression.

However, not all those who deliberately harm themselves want to die. One study of older people referred to a specialist self-harm unit (Dennis, Molloy, Andrews et al, 2007) sought specifically to explore their reasons. Only half said they had harmed themselves in a deliberate attempt to end their life – although 60% were either ambivalent about their attempted suicide or actively regretted that they were still alive.

Their most common motives for self-harming were to 'gain relief from unbearable emotions' (61%), to 'escape from intolerable situations' (53%), and to communicate how desperate they felt to other people (22%). The majority (67%) met the diagnostic criteria for depression, and 72% were isolated and had poor social networks. Physical health problems were also common: 63% had more than one physical illness or health problem, including cardiovascular disease, arthritis and hearing or vision problems.

These motives and factors in their lives indicate plentiful opportunity for intervention to prevent a repeat attempt. Notably, the study found that those who were depressed had higher suicide intent scores than those who were not depressed, and that 'relief from an unbearable state of mind' was their primary motive for the suicide attempt. Dennis and colleagues specifically recommend that older people who self-harm receive expert psychiatric assessment of risk and need, and are specifically assessed for presence of depression. They also highlight the need for better recognition of depression in primary care.

This recommendation, for specialist psychiatric assessment and follow-up following any suicide bid by an older person, is repeated throughout the research. Any older person who tries to kill him or herself should be seen as at very high risk of making another attempt (Hawton & Harriss, 2006; Chan et al, 2007).

Depression and suicide

As highlighted above, depression features repeatedly in the research into suicide among older people. This is not surprising, given the common association between depression and the other main factors leading to suicide. Hirsch and colleagues (Hirsch et al, 2009) sought specifically to distinguish depression from physical health factors in suicide. Their study of nearly 2,000 older primary care patients found that 'happiness' – positive mental health – broke the link between physical health problems and suicidal feelings: there was an association between physical health problems and suicidal thoughts, but those with positive mental health despite their physical ill health were less likely to feel suicidal.

One in four people aged over 65 suffer from depression: 22% of older men and 28% of older women. Of these, half are considered likely to meet the threshold for diagnosis of severe depression (Age Concern, 2008). Two in five older people in care homes have depression. Yet, as a recent Age Concern (2008) report comments, they are all too often 'undiagnosed, untreated and at risk' of suicide, physical ill health and premature death.

Risk factors for depression are very similar to those for suicide. The primary risk factors for depression are money worries, stressful life events, bereavement, social isolation and loneliness (Age Concern, 2008) – factors that are common across the age groups but are more prevalent among older people. Older people also have fewer resources to do anything about them (they cannot, for example, earn more to deal with financial problems; they are inevitably more exposed to bereavement; physical frailty will limit their ability to stay socially active and engaged with their communities), and face greater obstacles in attempting to do so – not least of which, as Beeston (2006) argues, is age discrimination and social exclusion.

Other research (Dennis, Baillon, Brugha *et al*, 2007) confirms significant associations between depression and lack of social support, being widowed, poor self-rated general health, and physical disabilities. A recent study in Ireland identified a clear association between loneliness and depression among older people in the community (Golden *et al*, 2009). This study, of nearly 1,300 older people living in Dublin, found that over a third (35%) were lonely and 34% had very little in the way of social networks and support. However, a third of those with good social networks also described themselves as lonely. Poor well-being, depression and hopelessness were associated with loneliness and poor social networks; loneliness was strongly associated with depression, in particular in those who were widowed.

Black and minority ethnic people

Research into suicide risk and the specific factors affecting the mental health and well-being of older people from black and minority ethnic (BME) communities is sparse, as is research into effective care and treatment (Sharif *et al*, 2008). This lack of research evidence to support policy and practice is highlighted in a 2008 'mapping' review of the literature published by the Social Care Institute for Excellence (SCIE) (Sharif *et al*, 2008).

The review concludes:

> *'Depression in BME communities is poorly understood and recognised by health and social care professionals, and the potential for treatment or other intervention to make improvements is therefore not made available to those who might benefit.'*

What evidence there is finds that key economic and social factors associated with depression (and therefore suicide) are particularly common among BME older people – poverty, poor housing, and inadequate access to transport, for example, but also the added factors specific to immigrant populations. The experience of migration and loss of contact with the extended family makes them even more at risk. The report also highlights barriers to accessing treatment. They include the cultural insensitivity of services: older people from BME communities often 'somatise' their symptoms (describe or express their mental health problems in physical health terms), and use of culturally inappropriate diagnostic tools and interventions. Older people from BME communities may also lack knowledge about available health and social care services, and be reluctant to seek professional help because of social stigma (mental health is severely stigmatised in some BME communities). Thus BME older people commonly experience a 'triple whammy' of discrimination on grounds of old age, race and mental illness.

An earlier SCIE review of best practice in assessing the mental health needs of older people (Moriarty, 2005) similarly concluded that data on incidence and effective interventions are contradictory and inconclusive. In the absence of such information, SCIE recommends that social care practitioners take a proactive approach to ensuring culturally appropriate service provision, working with their clients and local BME communities. They should, for example:

- find out the older person's preferred language, and arrange for a professional interpreter to be present, rather than relying on families and friends to interpret
- make sure that the older person and their family have all the information they need in a format they can understand
- find out about the person's culture and religious beliefs, and contact people from their local community about particular cultural needs and local sources of support (while maintaining confidentiality)
- make sure the local community knows about services available
- offer mainstream services – don't assume they will be unacceptable to BME older people – but discuss how they might be made culturally acceptable
- talk to local service providers about what they can do to make their services more culturally sensitive and acceptable, and monitor and review services clients are receiving.

What can be done?

Interventions aimed at tackling suicide and self-harm among older people can take place at a number of levels (Beeston, 2006). This includes identifying 'at risk' groups and individuals, and reducing access to means, although there is some debate about the effectiveness of the latter. Interventions may also vary depending on the service setting. Given the high numbers of older people who have contact with their GP in the months prior to taking their own life, it might be argued that primary care is an important setting to provide interventions but these are likely to be different from those provided in secondary services to older people who have already attempted to take their own life.

However, tackling suicide and self-harm among older people also means tackling the primary causes, and the primary causes would appear to be social factors commonly present in older people's lives and the depression with which these negative factors are all too frequently linked (Age Concern, 2008). According to Age Concern (2008), only half of those older people who do discuss their mental health with their GP are diagnosed and receive treatment – some 15% of all older people with clinical depression – and just 6% are referred for specialist mental health care. Only half of older people in care homes who are diagnosed with depression receive any kind of treatment at all.

Antidepressant medication has been shown to be effective in reducing risk of suicide among depressed older people. One review (Barbui et al, 2009) compared findings from eight studies of suicide and attempted suicide among depressed people who were or were not taking antidepressant SSRIs. Taking SSRIs actively protected older people from suicide, but increased suicide risk among young people.

However, some older people may not want to take antidepressants (Wagner et al, 2005). Alternatives, such as talking treatments and complementary therapies, are rarely offered (Age Concern, 2008). The government-funded Improving Access to Psychological Therapies (IAPT) programme, which aims to improve access to talking treatments, was initially established only for working age adults, although it has recently been explicitly opened up to older people (Department of Health, 2009a). New guidance from the Department of Health (2009a) states clearly that people should not be denied access to the new IAPT services on grounds of age and calls on IAPT services to take active steps to reach out to older people, and to ensure interventions and approaches are accessible, available and age-appropriate for older people.

Medication and talking treatments will not deal with the underlying factors of social isolation and what can be broadly described as social exclusion that are known to impact on older people's mental health and well-being. Older people interviewed for the national enquiry into mental health and well-being in later life conducted by Age Concern with the Mental Health Foundation (2006; 2007) described the negative effects on their mental well-being of suddenly finding themselves no longer considered active, equal citizens. They spoke of the importance to their mental well-being of participation in activities such as volunteering and of social networks and maintaining social and family contacts. They also described the constraints placed on their mobility and social participation by physical ill health, disability and poverty, as well as lack of transport and local amenities.

This picture is reinforced in the literature. For example, a small-scale, qualitative study of older people who attempted suicide (Crocker et al, 2006), instead of focusing on risk factors, asked older people who had recently attempted suicide what had led them to try to end their lives. The 15 participants described issues that were not related to the main risk factors identified in the quantitative research, or felt they were irrelevant. Rather, they spoke of a feeling of losing control over their life, or feeling invisible or disconnected from other people and from society, and of feeling that life had become a struggle that became too much for them as they grew older. Other studies emphasise the importance of social engagement and activity as a protection against depression (for example, McMunn et al, 2009; Isaac et al, 2009).

The final report from the national inquiry into older people's mental health and well-being (Age Concern, 2007) set out a long list of actions needed. In addition to improvements in the identification and treatment of depression, the report calls for actions more broadly across all relevant agencies to promote social inclusion and access to services, to challenge age discrimination, and to support older people in maintaining and developing social networks and support.

Most recently, the Department of Health has published a consultation document setting out its mental health strategy for the next 10 years (the final report was due in October 2009). *New Horizons* (Department of Health, 2009b) takes a life-span approach, with a strong focus on preventive, public health interventions to reduce risk of and rates of mental ill health.

These include tackling age discrimination and the social stigma attached to old age, enabling older people to stay actively engaged with their social networks and communities, including involvement in public services planning and provision, and improved health and social care and support services for high-risk, isolated and physically ill and disabled older people, and those in care homes. Improved identification and treatment of depression in primary care and use of social prescribing – where a GP can refer a patient to a social activity group, or link them with a volunteering or self-help group or network – are also highlighted.

Conclusions

What can be concluded from this brief review of the research and related issues is that suicide among older people is a pressing concern – or should be; that whatever we do to prevent depression will also prevent suicide, because depression is the key factor in older people deciding to end their lives, and that depression is not an inevitable feature of growing old – both depression and suicide are preventable. There are things that we, as a society and in our health and social care services, can do to make a difference. And there are things that older people themselves can do, and we can enable them to do, to make a difference. Enabling and supporting the continuing engagement and participation of older people in socially active roles, and valuing their contributions, will of itself promote and protect their mental health and well-being and reduce suicide risk.

References

Age Concern (2007) *Improving Services and Support for Older People with Mental Health Problems*. London: Age Concern.

Age Concern (2008) *Undiagnosed, Untreated, at Risk: The experiences of older people with depression*. London: Age Concern.

Age Concern/Mental Health Foundation (2006) *Promoting Mental Health and Well-being in Later Life: A first report from the UK inquiry into mental health and well-being in later life*. London: Age Concern/Mental Health Foundation.

Barbui C, Esposito E & Cipriani A (2009) Selective serotonin reuptake inhibitors and risk of suicide: a systematic review of observational studies. *Canadian Medical Association Journal* **180** (3) 291–297.

Beeston D (2006) *Older People and Suicide*. Birmingham/Stoke-on-Trent: CSIP West Midlands/Staffordshire University.

Chan J, Draper B & Banerjee S (2007) Deliberate self-harm in older adults: a review of the literature from 1995 to 2004. *International Journal of Geriatric Psychiatry* **22** 720–732.

Crocker L, Clare L & Evans K (2006) Giving up or finding a solution? The experience of attempted suicide in later life. *Aging & Mental Health* **10** (6) 638–647.

Dennis M, Baillon S, Brugha T, Stewart R, Meltzer H & Lindesay J (2007) The spectrum of suicidal ideation in Great Britain: comparisons across a 16–74 years age range. *Psychological Medicine* **37** (6) 795–805.

Dennis M, Molloy C, Andrews H & Friedman T (2007) A study of self-harm in older people: mental disorder, social factors and motives. *Aging & Mental Health* **11** (5) 520–525.

Department of Health (2009a) *Improving Access to Psychological Therapies. Older people: positive practice guide*. London: Department of Health.

Department of Health (2009b) *New Horizons: Towards a shared vision for mental health*. *Consultation*. London: Department of Health.

Department of Health (2002) *National Suicide Prevention Strategy for England*. London: Department of Health.

Golden J, Conroy RM, Bruce I, Denihan A, Greene E, Kirby M & Lawlor BA (2009) Loneliness, social support networks, mood and wellbeing in community-dwelling elderly. *International Journal of Geriatric Psychiatry* **24** (7) 694–700.

Harwood D, Hawton K, Hope T, Jacoby R & Harriss L (2006) Life problems and physical illness as risk factors for suicide in older people: a descriptive and case-control study. *Psychological Medicine* **36** (9) 1265–1274.

Haw C, Harwood D, & Hawton K (2009) Dementia and suicidal behavior: a review of the literature. *International Psychogeriatrics* **21** (3) 440–453.

Hawton K & Harriss L (2006) Deliberate self-harm in people aged 60 years and over: characteristics and outcome of a 20-year cohort. *International Journal of Geriatric Psychiatry* **21** 572–581.

Hirsch JK, Duberstein PR & Unutzer J (2009) Chronic medical problems and distressful thoughts of suicide in primary care patients: mitigating role of happiness. *International Journal of Geriatric Psychiatry* **24** (7) 671–679.

Isaac V, Stewart R, Artero S, Ancelin ML & Ritchie K (2009) Social activity and improvement in depressive symptoms in older people: a prospective community cohort study. *The American Journal of Geriatric Psychiatry* **17** (8) 688–696.

Karvonen K, Rasanen P, Hakko H, Timonen M, Meyer-Rochow VB, Sarkioja T & Koponen HJ (2008) Suicide after hospitalization in the elderly: a population based study of suicides in Northern Finland between 1988–2003. *International Journal of Geriatric Psychiatry* **23** (2) 135–141.

Mangnall J & Yurkovitch E (2008) A literature review of deliberate self-harm. *Perspectives in Psychiatric Care* **44** (3) 175–184.

McMunn A, Nazroo J, Wahrendorf M, Breeze E & Zaninotto P (2009) Participation in socially productive activities, reciprocity and wellbeing in later life: baselines results in England. *Ageing & Society* **20** (5) 765–782.

Moriarty J (2005) *Update for SCIE Best Practice Guide on Assessing the Mental Health Needs of Older People*. London: SCIE.

NHMDU (2008) *National Suicide Prevention Strategy for England: Annual report on progress 2008*. London: NMHDU.

Pembroke L (Ed) (1994) *Self-Harm: Perspectives from personal experience*. London: Survivors Speak Out.

Scocco P, Fantoni G, Rapattoni M, de Girolamo G & Pavan L (2009) Death ideas, suicidal thoughts and plans among nursing home residents. *Journal of Geriatric Psychiatry and Neurology* **22** (2) 141–148.

Sharif N, Brown W & Rutter D (2008) *The Extent and Impact of Depression on BME Older People and the Acceptability, Accessibility and Effectiveness of Social Care Provision. Systematic map report 03*. London: SCIE.

Tadros G & Salib E (2007) Elderly suicide in primary care. *International Journal of Geriatric Psychiatry* **22** (8) 750–756.

Tadros G & Saleb E (2000) Age and methods of fatal self harm (FSH): is there a link? *International Journal of Geriatric Psychiatry* **15** 848–852.

Wagner A, Byritsky A, Russo JE, Craske MG, Sherbourne CD, Stein MB & Roy-Byrne PP (2005) Beliefs about psychotropic medication and psychotherapy among primary care patients with anxiety disorders. *Depression and Anxiety* **21** (3) 99–105.

Chapter 10

Involving families, carers and friends of older people with mental health problems

Drew Lindon

Carers – the national picture

'The notion of mental illness affecting "every family in the land" is no cliché, just the truth.'
(Katona, 2005)

The Princess Royal Trust for Carers (2009) defines a carer as:

'someone of any age who provides unpaid support to family or friends who could not manage without this help. This could be caring for a relative, partner or friend who is ill, frail, disabled or has mental health or substance misuse problems.'

This is distinguished from a paid care worker, in that the carer gives up their time through necessity (mostly, but not always, voluntarily), and are not paid in kind for the work they do.

1.5 million people care for someone with a mental illness in the UK (NCCSDO, 2002). That is one in every 40 people (Shift, 2009), or one in four of the UK's six million carers (Carers UK, 2009). Older carers disproportionately provide intensive care and dementia care, and over 20% of the UK's six million carers are aged 65 and over. Most older carers support a spouse or very elderly parent (Office of National Statistics, 2004; Maher & Green, 2002; Carers UK, 2004). Caring for someone with a mental illness can be a positive, rewarding experience. But it can also harm the carer's mental and physical health, financial situation and life chances.

What do mental health carers do?
Carers of older people experiencing mental health problems often take on a similar range of tasks, including:

- **advocacy** – help with correspondence, and liaising with professionals
- **aid with administering medicines**
- **domestic tasks** – shopping, cleaning, cooking and so on

- **emotional support** – listening, reassurance, motivation, and 'keeping an eye' on someone whose safety may be at risk if left alone
- **physical support** – including personal care if the person cared for is unable to undertake these tasks themselves (such as in advanced stages of dementia)
- **offering financial support** – purchasing shopping, providing 'bed and board'.

These tasks will obviously vary depending on the condition of the person being cared for, and its severity and development. However, with this degree of caring responsibilities, it is unsurprising that many carers are unable to remain in full or part-time employment, and face financial hardship or even poverty as a result (Moriarty, 2005).

The challenges of mental health caring

All carers of people with long-term conditions can find their own health affected due to the pressures of care. But there are also challenges specific to looking after an older person with a mental illness, be this an organic or functional condition (see Lindon, 2008). Mental health carers often report:

- the **unpredictability of caring** for someone with a fluctuating mental health problem, and how this impacts on planning for the future (Tihanyi & Cormac, 2006)
- the **emotional impact of seeing a loved one's personality and capabilities change**, often quickly and abruptly (Moriarty, 2005)
- the **stigma** of mental illness, making it more difficult to ask for and get help (SCIE, 2006a)
- **lack of information**, often as a result of poorly applied confidentiality rules by mental health staff (Pinfold *et al*, 2005)
- the **fear of a loved one's suicide** (Cormac, 2005)
- the **lack of specialised respite** and/or 'sitting services' appropriate for mental health carers and the people they care for (Moriarty, 2005).

These challenges can affect carers' own physical and mental health and well-being. For example, *'a third of people who provide unpaid care for an older person with dementia have depression'* (Age Concern, 2006). Likewise, many carers for older people are themselves older (partners, for example) and 'so are likely to experience physical health problems' themselves (Moriarty, 2005).

Increasing numbers of people will face these challenges in the near future. Currently, around 75% of older people with moderate to severe dementia living in the community have a family carer (SCIE, 2006a). However, the number of older people with mental health problems in the UK is likely to *'increase by a third over the next 15 years to 4.3 million, or one in every 15 people'* (Age Concern, 2006). Moreover, the burden of care and support is increasingly falling on families and friends in the UK. This is a result of a number of factors: an ageing population (leading to greater needs for care, including incidence of dementia-related conditions); the continuing shift from inpatient to community care for mental health service users; and the tightening of local eligibility criteria for social care services.

National policy

In response to these challenges, a number of national charities have emerged that work to exclusively support carers. These include The Princess Royal Trust for Carers, Crossroads Care and Carers UK. The UK government has also recognised the challenges that carers face, and key pieces of legislation and policy affecting carers are listed in **table 1**.

Table 1: Key legislation and policy affecting carers in the UK		
Document	Applicable to country	Some key components for carers
Living Well with Dementia – A National Dementia Strategy	England	Important provisions for carers include: ■ **Objective 4:** piloting 'dementia advisers' to facilitate access to care, support and advice for people with dementia and carers ■ **Objective 6:** improving care for people at home, while providing more support to their carers (including respite) ■ **Objective 7:** ensure the aims of the national carers strategy are applied equally to carers of those with dementia
Mental Health Act (2007) (amends 1983 Act)	England and Wales	If carer is the nearest relative, they have the: ■ right to request advocacy visits for the person cared for ■ right to request a Mental Health Act assessment of the person cared for (if the person has been seen by the carer in the last 14 days) ■ right to be informed of the patient's detention, and their right to discharge the patient, before application under Section 2.
Mental Capacity Act (2005) and Adults with Incapacity (Scotland) Act (2000)	England, Wales and Scotland	■ carers have a right to be consulted by professionals assessing a person's capacity ■ carers have a key role in helping make decisions with and for individuals who lack capacity.
Carers (Equal Opportunities) Act (2004)	England and Wales	■ local authorities have a duty to inform carers of their right to a Carers Assessment; previously carers needed to actively request this assessment ■ carers' needs and desires for work, life-long learning and leisure should be considered when they are assessed.
Mental Health (Amendment) (Northern Ireland) Order (2004)	Northern Ireland	If carer is the nearest relative, they have the: ■ right to request a Mental Health Order (MHO) Assessment of the person cared for ■ right to be informed of the patient's detention, and their right to discharge the patient, before application for a MHO Assessment.
Mental Health (Care and Treatment) (Scotland) Act (2003)	Scotland	Carers have the right to be given general information about the condition of the person cared for, though not specific information if the service user does not consent. If the carer is the named person, they have the: ■ right to request a needs assessment of the person cared for ■ if the carer is the named person, right to appeal on behalf of service user against detention in conditions of excessive security ■ if the carer is the named person, they must be consulted before an emergency or short-term detention certificate is issued for the person they care for.

Community Care and Health (Scotland) Act (2002)	Scotland	■ carers giving regular and substantial care (including young carers under 16) are entitled to a carers' assessment independent of the person they care for ■ local authorities have a duty to inform carers of their right to an assessment.
Carers and Disabled Children Act (2000)	England and Wales	■ carers have a right to an assessment of their own needs ■ carers have a right to receive services to support themselves ■ carers have the right to claim Carers Allowance benefit.
National Service Framework for Older People (2001)	England	Standard 7 outlines that a comprehensive support service for older people should provide support for carers, which would include: ■ short-term breaks ■ information (including explaining the diagnosis), advice and practical help ■ counselling services. (The importance of carers was reiterated in the 2005 service development guide for the NSF for older people's mental health services, Everybody's Business (Department of Health, 2005))
National Service Framework for Mental Health (1999)	England	Under Standard 6, all individuals who provide regular and substantial care for a person on the Care Programme Approach should: ■ have an assessment of their caring, physical and mental health needs, repeated on at least an annual basis ■ have their own written care plan (if they are assessed as eligible for support), which is given to them and implemented in discussion with them.

The government has also released a draft 10-year strategy for mental health in England called *New Horizons*, which addresses all ages, and is currently cut for consultation.

Most relevant is the government's national carers strategy *Carers at the Heart of 21st-century Families and Communities* (Department of Health, 2008), which offers commitments to support carers across the UK (though these apply mostly to England and Wales). These include:

■ additional funding for **flexible carers breaks**
■ future **reform of carers benefit**
■ **expansion of training** for staff on working with carers (Department of Health, 2008).

Overall, the strategy aims to elevate the needs of carers *'to the centre of family policy'* over the next 10 years (Department of Health, 2008). But as a whole it largely fails to take forward progress made on supporting carers within older people's mental health services. Indeed, mental health carers are barely mentioned by the strategy. That said, its broader initiatives are likely to have positive impacts for carers looking after older people with mental health problems. For example, *'teams within adult mental health and substance misuse services will be particularly targeted'* for training and awareness work around working with carers (Department of Health, 2008). If implemented positively, this should better support both young and adult carers within these families.

Indeed, the current direction of development for the social care system should become conducive to better support for carers, if not a lessening of their responsibilities. Statutory social care is undergoing a radical shift, following government reports such as *Our Health, Our Care, Our Say* (Department of Health, 2006) and *Putting People First* (Department of Health, 2007). With statutory services increasingly working to a personalised 'independent living' model, rather than offering institutional or more traditional community care services, carers become more visible in this holistic framework. In turn, carers should increasingly become recipients of newer means of delivering social care, including direct payments and personal budgets. However, increasing costs of social care may lead to the provision of more care at home and a greater burden on carers. This issue will continue to provoke heated debate, as demonstrated by the reponses to the government's green paper on the new care and support system (see Department of Health, 2009).

Engaging with carers: the benefits and best practice

Professionals and carers

By engaging with carers, there have been great improvements in working with carers across health and social care. Yet there is still a long way to go, especially for carers of older people with mental health needs.

Many would also argue that mental health services continue to operate as a very risk-averse system (Royal College of Psychiatrists, 2008). Given the risks that some people with mental health problems pose to themselves and others, this is understandable and most often justifiable. However, this culture contributes to poor working relationships with carers, especially when coupled with some practitioners' obstructive approach to families and friends (SCIE, 2006a). While structural improvements in health and social care may improve support for carers, changing attitudes among many staff is equally important.

One clear means to improve support for carers of older people with mental health conditions (and other carers) is for commissioners, policy makers and frontline practitioners to appreciate the benefits of supporting and involving them, via training, awareness-raising and external resources. Moreover, there are excellent approaches to working with carers that can make this process as easy and successful as possible, with positive impacts on service delivery and treatment outcomes. We will examine both the benefits and approaches in turn.

The benefits of supporting and involving carers

1. Improves outcomes for service users

Carers are '*an integral part of the patient's support system*' (Shooter *et al*, 2005), and are usually in contact with the older person far more than support staff. Carers are also likely to know the older person and how their condition affects them personally in far more depth than professionals (SCIE, 2006a). So for the best care outcomes, we need to understand mental health care as a collaborative effort between professionals, service users and carers (Age Concern, 2006).

2. Improves carers' well-being and ability to cope

Without timely and consistent aid, many carers fall ill from the pressures of care, become unable to care any longer and require greater support themselves. Indeed, carers '*suffer physically, mentally, socially and financially – and may become patients in their own turn if not properly supported*' (Shooter, 2005).

So supporting carers helps safeguard their own health and well-being. Not only should this be a moral imperative, but also a practical one for patient-centred services; service users' well-being can suffer if carers become too ill to support them. As a result, supporting carers' own health, as well as empowering them to make informed choices about the level of care they can provide (see Pinfold & Corry, 2003), is also a path to ensuring consistent support for services users themselves.

3. Strengthens health and social care system

Supporting and involving carers is in the long-term interests of the UK's health and social care system. If we consider the replacement value of their caring work, the UK's six million carers are estimated to save the country up to £87 billion per year (Carers UK, 2007). This saving could increase with better support for carers.

Conversely, a lack of commitment to carers support will lead to greater demands on the mental health system in the long term through (a) under-supported service users and (b) under-supported carers becoming seriously unwell. Hence, meeting carers' support needs before they reach crisis point will reduce future demands on mental health (and other) services, leading to long-term savings.

Best practice when working with carers

Partners in care

Supporting carers makes both moral and economic sense. But how can we translate these aims into consistent and sustainable practice?

For all work with carers, the guiding principle is that carers should be **partners in care**. Indeed, the carers strategy's key vision is that *'carers will be respected as expert care partners and will have access to the integrated and personalised services they need to support them in their caring role'* (Department of Health, 2008). Carers are experts in their own experience (SCIE, 2006b), and deserve to be recognised as partners in care by local commissioners and frontline practitioners.

A 'partner' in care is also an individual; a carer's needs do not necessarily reflect the service user's level of needs. Depending on the caring responsibilities taken on, resilience and coping strategies, and the informal support received, carers may have a very low level of needs when caring for someone with high needs, or vice versa. Consequently, when working with carers as partners, their support should reflect their needs as far as possible, without assumptions based on the needs of the service user (Department of Health, 2008).

The three Is – Identify, Inform and Involve

With this guiding principle in mind, a consistent approach to supporting carers of older people with mental health problems becomes clearer. There are three key elements to successful work with carers; identifying, informing and involving.

Identify carers

Health and social care services should routinely identify carers when someone first accesses mental health services (Audit Commission, 2004). Indeed, this should be best practice within all health and social care settings, including GP surgeries and hospital services (see The Princess Royal Trust for Carers & Royal College of General Practitioners, 2008). Asking a service user if anyone helps care for them should be part of consistent practice when a service user is on the Care Programme Approach

(CPA) (as above) or as part of the Single Assessment Process (SAP) (Department of Health, 2001). However, anecdotal reports from carers support services suggest that too often older people with mental health problems are not asked – particularly when they are being treated for functional mental health problems such as schizophrenia.

Instead, services need to ensure that there is 'no wrong door' to support, as advocated by the Social Exclusion Task Force's *Families at Risk Review* (2007; Department of Health, 2008). Whatever way carers or the person cared for enter services, via GPs, referrals from voluntary agencies, or elsewhere, carers should be identified and offered a personalised package of support (Department of Health, 2008).

There are two main paths to this goal. First, services for older people's mental health must increasingly 'think family' in their organisational culture. Support should *'be tailored to the family's needs, build on the family's strengths and address the whole family, not just individual members'* (Department of Health, 2008). This is particularly important in the case of young carers under 18, who are often overlooked by mental health services (SCIE, 2008). Second, such a culture shift must be instigated and reinforced by consistent primary care trust, NHS trust and social services policy and commissioning arrangements to ensure staff are themselves trained and supported to engage with carers.

There are supportive steps towards this goal nationally. For England and Wales, the Department of Health is developing a common assessment framework (CAF) for adults, *'to share relevant information between agencies and encourage close working'* between statutory agencies as well as with the third sector (Department of Health, 2008). Among other examples, Northamptonshire NHS Healthcare Trust and the West London Mental Health Trust have been developing comprehensive carer policies. Similarly, there are a number of best practice models on joint working, such as Carers in Hertfordshire's Primary Care Toolkit, or the GP Action Guide from The Royal College of GPs and The Princess Royal Trust for Carers (The Princess Royal Trust for Carers & Royal College of General Practitioners, 2008).

Inform and support carers

Carers *'should be able to expect clear, concise, relevant information about their rights and the … support they can get, without asking for it'* (Audit Commission, 2004). Once identified, carers are legally entitled to an assessment of their own needs, which will include discussion of the carer's work and leisure goals (Audit Commission, 2004). This should lead to a carer's care plan developed in partnership between the carer and the responsible professional from mental health services, such as a social worker. The care plan will identify what support, services and information the carer may require as a result of their caring role. This is likely to include:

- **specific information on the diagnosis** (if the service user consents to share this with the carer) (SCIE, 2006a); general information on mental health conditions and the operation of mental health law should be provided if a service user wishes personal details to remain confidential
- **information about the medication and treatment offered, including any side effects**
- **referrals and/or signposting** to external services, such as counselling, carer support groups, and local carer organisations
- **training and information on how to support yourself** as a carer
- **advice on benefits and housing**
- support for the carer to **return to work**, such as provision of home help to the person cared for (Audit Commission, 2004)

■ **respite breaks** to enable the carer to recuperate (Audit Commission, 2004).

This care plan should be reviewed at least annually and if the caring situation changes dramatically (for example, if the service user enters a care home). Direct payments or a personalised budget for the carer should be considered.

What carers want may vary depending upon the caring situation. Carers of older adults who are new to caring (for example, a son whose father has developed dementia) are more likely to need 'start-up' information – what the condition is, what this means for them now and in future, and where to get help. Carers who have looked after someone with a long-standing mental health problem for years tend to prefer ongoing advocacy and emotional support. However, regardless of what else carers receive, empathy, understanding and reassurance from professionals will go far in building a good working relationship.

Involve carers

When looking after an older person with a mental health problem, as far as possible, carers should be:

■ **always included on the service user's care plan by professionals** (as per CPA and SAP guidance), and where possible ensure they are consulted in developing the plan (Audit Commission, 2004).

■ **included in consultations at the hospital discharge process** (the extent depending upon whether the carer is the nearest relative/named person, and the person they care for has given consent) (Audit Commission, 2004).

■ **involved in training and selection of mental health staff locally** – this helps ensure new and existing staff are aware of how to work with carers, and promotes carers' ownership and commitment to the services they help shape.

Challenges and solutions

These are clear aims, but there are equally apparent challenges to delivering better support to these carers. Health and social care provision for older people across local areas can often be unclear, with varying statutory responsibilities and services available across catchment areas. Predictably, this can lead to poor transitions for some service users between adult and older people's mental health services. This can undermine attempts to offer unified support to service users and their carers. Likewise, different definitions of 'carer' may be used in adjacent teams (which can limit carers' access to services), as well as (mis)understandings by health and social care staff on the differences between unpaid informal carers and paid care workers. National initiatives such as the carers strategy can force the issue and offer more resources for cash-strapped services, but local recognition of carers is also needed, along with a local commitment to enact changes.

In addition to internal factors like organisational inertia and resource scarcity in statutory and voluntary organisations, there are external challenges in working with carers such as outreach issues. Certainly, some carers are as equally indifferent to receiving support as some service users, particularly older couples who *'see caring for each other as a natural part … of being together in sickness and in health'* Department of Health, 2008). Indeed, while some carers complain that they only receive help in a crisis despite repeated requests for preventative measures, other carers are reluctant to ask for help and may only approach services in a crisis, making it more difficult for help to be successful (Moriarty, 2005). Improving outreach services to proactively locate both vulnerable older people and their carers must be a core aim of coherent local outreach and carer strategies (SCIE, 2006a).

The views of carers and service users may also conflict, particularly in terms of information sharing. Involving the carer does not have to be at the cost of the service users' privacy or rights. But some carers may want more information about the service user's condition than the older person consents to share (SCIE, 2006a).

Finally, there remains the risk that in some families, carers' actions may be unintentionally or even actively harmful to the older person (Age Concern, 2006). These are legitimate concerns, and it is vital to have effective risk management frameworks to address such dangers (SCIE, 2006). However, this remains the exception rather than the rule for carers of older people. In most circumstances, carers are a valuable asset to the treatment of the person cared for, and can substantially improve the chances of recovery, depending on the service user's circumstances (Age Concern, 2006).

Improving and expanding carer support

Local commissioners can ensure that these aims are achieved and the challenges met by the following:

- Improving mental health professionals' training by including awareness-raising on carers, including involving carers in training as outlined above. This would involve appreciation of how differences in cultural perceptions of mental health and caring can affect services' identification and support of carers from a variety of cultural backgrounds (Department of Health, 2001). A key component of training will be handling information sharing conflicts between service users and carers as identified above. One part of the solution is for discussions about the extent that carers can be involved in an individual's care planning, to be undertaken as soon as possible in the care treatment process. These will include clarifying **what** information the service user is happy for the professional to share, **with whom** and under **what circumstances**. This will help minimise confidentiality conflicts, which often occur between what carers feel they need to know and service users wish them to know. By the same token, carers have an equal right to confidentiality of their own personal information.

Case study: Partners in Care

Partners in Care was a joint campaign between The Royal College of Psychiatrists and The Princess Royal Trust for Carers from January 2004 to June 2005. This produced the *Partners in Care Handbook* (Cormac, 2005), offering a wealth of resources for psychiatrists and other mental health professionals about working effectively with carers, as well as information for carers themselves. This includes a set of leaflets giving information on specific conditions (including Alzheimer's disease), confidentiality and caring, and questions that professionals should ask carers to help support them. See www.partnersincare.co.uk for resources and full details.

- Inspecting health and social care services for how they reach and provide for mental health carers. This may require expansion of the current national indicator 135 for measuring local government performance (carers receiving needs assessment or review and a specific carer's service, or advice and information), which forms part of social services monitoring, to ensure all types of carers are adequately supported locally (Department of Health, 2008).

- Working in close partnership with third sector organisations who support carers (SCIE, 2006b), such as carers' centres, the local Alzheimer's Society, Age Concern and other groups offering support, such as churches and religious societies (Shoard, 2005).

- Commissioning services to support carers specifically, and empowering carers to be vital partners in the commissioning and service development process (Burns et al, 2000). An effective roster of services is likely to include 'information, advocacy, self-help and peer support groups for older people with mental health problems and their carers', as well as flexible home care and respite services (Age Concern, 2006). There are pitfalls. In areas lucky enough to have health funding for mental health carers services, this is increasingly restricted to work with carers looking after a person on CPA. However, carers of people not on CPA can nevertheless have high support needs themselves. A more inclusive approach to commissioning needs to be adopted, bearing in mind the benefits of supporting carers. Indeed, there are innovative models being implemented across the UK. For example, mental health carers support workers from carers centres in Northamptonshire, Gloucestershire and Winchester are embedded as staff members within local community mental health teams.

Case study: Carers Network Westminster

Carers Network Westminster employs a part-time carers support and development worker (older mental health) funded by the Bridge House Trust. This post is focused on supporting carers of older people with functional mental health problems, but also supports carers of older people with dementia. The worker offers advocacy, information and advice to carers, via appointments and home visits. The project worker also runs two support groups available to these clients, one for carers for older people (mixed group), and the other specifically for carers of older people with mental health problems.

The worker offers outreach work, running two carers surgeries a month at community mental health teams (CMHTs) in the north and south of the borough. These offer a drop-in for advice and information for carers, as well as raising awareness of carers' issues with CMHT staff. In addition to working with other health and social care services, the worker also liaises closely with Admiral Nurses services in the borough.

The road ahead

We all need to shift our thinking about health and social care. We need to realise that mental health care on a purely 'patient-centred' basis makes less and less sense as increasingly personalised services shift further into the community. Health and social care professionals can deliver these changes by working holistically with an older person's wider support network, including carers. This is not without significant challenges. But while many carers may not have the knowledge to treat a person medically, their knowledge of the person they care for, and their desire and ability to support them may be unsurpassed. Supporting carers consistently will help both service users and carers, keep families together and give carers the chance to make informed choices about the level of care they can safely provide.

References

Age Concern (2006) *Improving Services and Support for Older People with Mental Health Problems* [online]. London: Age Concern. Available at: http://www.mhilli.org/documents/Inquiryfinalreport-FULLREPORT.pdf (accessed February 2009).

Audit Commission (2004) *Support for Carers of Older People: Independence and well-being 5* [online]. London: The Audit Commission. Available at: http://www.wales.nhs.uk/documents/OlderPeople_5_Report.pdf (accessed February 2009).

Burns A, Dening T & Baldwin R (2000) Care of older people – mental health problems. *British Medical Journal* **322** 789–791.

Carers UK (2004) *In Poor Health: The impact of caring on health*. London: Carers UK.

Carers UK (2007) *Carers save UK £87bn per year media release* [online]. Available at: www.carersuk.org/Newsandcampaigns/News/1190237139 (accessed February 2009).

Carers UK (2009) *10 Facts about Carers* [online]. Available at: www.carersuk.org/Newsandcampaigns/Mediacentre/Tenfactsaboutcaring (accessed February 2009).

Cormac I (2005) An introduction to working in partnership with carers. In: *Partners in Care Handbook* (CD). London: Royal College of Psychiatrists.

Department of Health (2001) *National Service Framework for Older People*. London: Department of Health.

Department of Health (2005) *Everybody's Business*. London: Department of Health.

Department of Health (2006) *Our Health, Our Care, Our Say*. London: Department of Health.

Department of Health (2007) *Putting People First: A shared vision and commitment to the transformation of adult social care*. London: Department of Health.

Department of Health (2008) *Carers at the Heart of 21st Century Families and Communities*. London: Department of Health.

Department of Health (2009) *Shaping the Future of Care Together* [online] Available at: http://careandsupport.direct.gov.uk/ (accessed August 2009).

Katona C (2005) Caring for Richard. In: *Partners in Care Handbook*. London: Royal College of Psychiatrists.

Lindon D (2008) *Five Key Facts about Mental Health Carers* [online]. London: The Princess Royal Trust for Carers. Available at: www.carers.org/articles/key-facts-and-asks-for-mental-health-carers,2776,CA.html (February 2009).

Maher J & Green H (2002) *Carers 2000*. London: Office of National Statistics.

Moriarty J (2005) *Update for SCIE Best Practice Guide on Assessing the Mental Health Needs of Older People*. London: Social Care Workforce Unit & King's College London.

National Co-ordinating Centre for NHS Service Delivery and Organisation (2002) *Services to Support Carers of People with Mental Health Problems*, briefing paper. London: NCCSDO.

Office of National Statistics (2004) *Focus on Older People*. London: Office of National Statistics.

Pinfold V & Corry P (2003) *Under Pressure – The impact of caring on people supporting family members or friends with mental health problems*. Kingston: Rethink.

Pinfold V, Farmer P, Rapaport J, Bellringer S, Huxley P, Murray J, Banerjee S, Slade M, Kuipers E, Bhugra D & Waitere S (2005) *Positive and Inclusive? Effective ways for professionals to involve carers in information sharing* [online]. London: NCCSDO. Available at: http://www.sdo.nihr.ac.uk/files/project/54-final-report.pdf (accessed February 2009).

Royal College of Psychiatrists (2008) *Rethinking Risk to Others in Mental Health Services* [online]. London: Royal College of Psychiatrists. Available at: http://www.rcpsych.ac.uk/files/pdfversion/CR150.pdf (accessed February 2009).

Shift (2009) *1 in 6 people will currently be experiencing problems with their mental health* [online]. Available at: www.shift.org.uk/ (accessed February 2009).

Shoard M (2005) Caring for carers. *Church of England Newspaper*, 9 December.

Shooter M (2005) Who cares for the carers. In: *Partners in Care Handbook*. London: Royal College of Psychiatrists.

Shooter M, Hollins S & Tihanyi P (2005) Foreword. In: *Partners in Care Handbook*. London: Royal College of Psychiatrists.

Social Care Institute for Excellence (2006a) *SCIE Practice Guide 2: Assessing the mental health needs of older people – assessing the needs of carers* [online]. Available at: www.scie.org.uk/publications/practiceguides/practiceguide02/carers/index.asp (accessed February 2009).

Social Care Institute for Excellence (2006b) *Working Together: Carer participation in England, Wales and Northern Ireland: a summary* [online]. London: SCIE. Available at: http://www.scie.org.uk/publications/positionpapers/pp05.pdf (accessed February 2009).

Social Care Institute for Excellence (2008) *Research Briefing 23: Stress and resilience factors in parents with mental health problems and their children*. London: SCIE.

Social Exclusion Task Force (2007) *Families at Risk Review*. London: Social Exclusion Taskforce.

Tihanyi P & Cormac I (2006) Meeting the mental and physical healthcare needs of carers. *Advances in Psychiatric Treatment* **12** 165.

The Princess Royal Trust for Carers (2009) *Who is a Carer?* [online] Available at: www.carers.org/who-is-a-carer,118,GP.html (accessed February 2009).

The Princess Royal Trust for Carers & The Royal College of General Practitioners (2008) *Supporting Carers: An action guide for general practitioners and their teams* [online]. Available at: www.carers.org/professionals/adult-carers/articles/carers-in-practice-rcgp,1792,PR.html (accessed February 2009).

Chapter 11
Integrating health and social care

Jane Gilliard

Introduction

Delivering services to older people with mental health problems cuts across many organisational boundaries. Joining the services up and integrating the commissioning of such services is critical to ensuring such services are effective and efficient. This fact has increasingly been recognised in policy developments.

This chapter briefly reviews policy developments since 2000 and considers the important issue of leadership in older people's mental health services. It then considers the 'shifting sands' of current developments in the wider health and social care context, the impact of these developments and some examples of creative and innovative practice.

Two 'health warnings':

■ The chapter is located within the context of policy development in England only. The devolved governments of the United Kingdom have their own policy initiatives, working to different timescales.
■ The historical context pre-dates 2000, but we have chosen to use the turn of the millennium as a point in time from which we can consider the current position.

The policy context

There has been a regular stream of reports on older people's mental health, including dementia, since the start of the new millennium. Each has made its own contribution to moving the agenda forward, though some have arguably had greater impact and made a bigger difference than others. At the same time, there has been a succession of reports and policy initiatives in the wider health and social care arena, meaning that changes in the development and delivery of older people's mental health have to be seen against an ever-changing backcloth. Some of these changes are radical and fundamental, for example, the move towards empowering service users and offering choice and control. Others have happened at local level and have begun to spread more widely, for example, the move to establish peer support in the form of Alzheimer's cafés. This all sits within the context of clinical advances and research findings, and campaigning and pressure to create a greater awareness of dementia and other mental problems in later life.

It's hard to trace back to the foundations of this move to promote greater awareness and more emphasis on mental health, rather than on mental illness. Arguably, a good place to start is with the publication in 1999 of the *National Service Framework for Mental Health* (Department of Health, 1999). This document explicitly excluded people over the age of 65.

> 'This National Service Framework focuses on the mental health needs of working age adults up to 65 … the needs of older people with mental health problems are being reviewed as part of the development of a National Service Framework for older people, which should be published in spring 2000.' (Introduction)

This created a sense of disquiet in some, who would have preferred to see the needs of all those with mental health difficulties addressed in one document, and at the same time a sense of impatience at having to wait a further period of time for a National Service Framework that would address the needs of older people, and which, in fact, was not published until March 2001.

The following year, the Audit Commission published the first of two reports on the findings of its work to uncover the state of services for people with dementia (Audit Commission, 2000) and led to its recommendations for action that needed to be taken to improve the experiences of patients and service users. They recommended, inter alia, that:

- commissioners in health and local authorities should take the lead in setting out strategic goals and priorities, in conjunction with users and carers, professionals, service managers and other groups such as independent service providers
- a comprehensive strategy should include a policy on the involvement of users and carers in assessments and decisions about their care
- health and social services should share the responsibility for supporting older people with mental health problems.

Two years later the Audit Commission reported again on what had happened in the intervening time (Audit Commission, 2002). They concluded:

> 'In many areas, health and social care agencies have expressed their commitment to work together to support older people with mental health problems in their own homes or, when this is no longer appropriate, in suitable alternative accommodation. Auditors found many examples where agencies had succeeded in achieving this for older people in their areas. However, they also found that older people and their carers, in very similar circumstances, could receive quite different responses – sometimes even within the same area.' (Section 7)

Again they included among their recommendations that 'health and social care agencies should boost team working by promoting closer working, joint assessment and care management, shared case files and compatible IT systems'. In many places this remains to be achieved in full in 2008.

In 2001, the Department of Health published the *National Service Framework* (NSF) *for Older People* (Department of Health, 2001). Standard 7 aimed 'to promote good mental health in older people and to treat and support those older people with dementia and depression'. Some felt this didn't go far enough in addressing the wider needs of all older people with mental health problems, but it did provide a focus and raise the profile of mental health problems in later life. It proposed that the core team members of a specialist mental health service for older people should include:

- consultant psychiatrist specialising in mental health problems in old age
- community mental health nurses
- clinical psychologists
- occupational therapists
- social workers.

Furthermore, it proposed that a *'core team member should act as a care co-ordinator for each older person referred to the specialist mental health service throughout his or her contact with the service'*. (p105)

The recommended actions were laid against both the NHS and local councils to:

- review the local system of mental health services for older people including mental health promotion, early detection and diagnosis, assessment, care and treatment planning, and access to specialist services
- review the current arrangements for the management of depression and dementia, and agree and implement local protocols across primary care and specialist services, including social care
- review the current arrangements for the management of dementia in younger people.

One of the major differences that impaired the successful delivery of changes in the wake of the NSF for Older People was the lack of resources. Investment and targets had been attached to the NSF for Mental Health, but changes in the operational style of the Department of Health between the publications of the two NSFs meant that there was no resource attached to the NSF for Older People and there were milestones but no targets.

Advances were made in service developments at local level, but partnership working across health and social care was often bedevilled by practical detail. Shared understandings, a common language, compatible IT systems, different terms and conditions of employment, issues of ownership, personality clashes, all could get in the way of partnership working that felt real and that made a difference to the lives of those on the receiving end of services. This can be compounded where the geographical boundaries of health trusts and local authorities are not co terminous.

In 2003 the national directors for older people and for mental health hosted a summit meeting to consider the issue of delivering integrated services to older people with mental health problems. This led to a collaboration between two service improvement teams – the Health and Social Care Change Agent Team and the National Institute for Mental Health in England – to provide implementation support to older people's mental health (OPMH) services. This is now the Care Services Improvement Partnership's Mental Health in Later Life Programme (www.olderpeoplesmentalhealth.csip.org.uk).

Continuing concern to raise the profile of the needs of older people with mental health problems, and feedback from the field about the difficulties of commissioning integrated services, led to the publication in 2005 of *Everybody's Business – Integrated mental health services for older adults: a service development guide* (Department of Health, 2005). This was accompanied by commissioning guidance, and six key messages for commissioners.

Everybody's Business was not new policy. It aimed to improve practice at the front line by drawing together existing resources and signposting good practice examples. With reference to integrated health and social care services, *Everybody's Business* addressed the challenges for commissioning:

> *'Effective commissioning of OPMH services demands that partners across health and social care economies, including the independent sector, voluntary sector, users and carers, have an agreed vision for future services and a strategy to implement it.'* (p21)

The document went on to give advice and examples of how this might be achieved:

> *'There are various ways in which systems can work together to secure a broad range of services to meet local population needs. These include:*
> - *single agency purchasing arrangements*
> - *joint or multi-agency purchasing arrangements*
> - *partnering arrangements, for instance using Section 31 Health Act Flexibilities with pooled budgets and agreed lead responsibilities and*
> - *integrated services, involving restructuring of existing service provision.'* (p22)

The publication also addressed the integration of community mental health teams (pp44–46). It advocated:

> - *'easy accessibility, based on shared information systems, so that speaking to one duty person from the team through a designated line will trigger the appropriate response from any member of the team. Information and advice should be available 24-hours per day*
> - *some provision for home-based crisis support 24-hours per day; this may be as part of a younger adult mental health service or generic older people's service*
> - *a broad skill mix across health and social care, so that the outcome of the individual's whole-person assessment can result in a combined health and social care plan*
> - *information on services available and on legal and financial matters*
> - *a key worker system to ensure continuity of support for service users and carers.'*

It also described how the team should operate – through regular meetings, clear professional and managerial leadership and accountability, and supported by jointly agreed policies – and the minimum staffing of such a team.

In 2006, the National Institute for Health and Clinical Excellence published the first joint guideline with the Social Care Institute for Excellence (NICE, 2006). *Dementia: Supporting people with dementia and their carers in health and social care*. This guideline made a number of recommendations to improve the quality of life and service experience of people with dementia and their carers. In relation to the integration of services, in particular, it recommended:

- health and social care managers should co-ordinate and integrate working across all agencies involved in the treatment and care of people with dementia and their carers, including jointly agreeing written policies and procedures. Joint planning should include local service users and carers in order to highlight and address problems specific to each locality.
- care managers and care co-ordinators should ensure the co-ordinated delivery of health and social care services for people with dementia. This should involve:

- combined care plan agreed by health and social services that takes into account the changing needs of the person with dementia and his or her carers
- assignment of named health and/or social care staff to operate the care plan
- endorsement of the care plan by the person with dementia and/or carers
- formal reviews of the care plan, at a frequency agreed between professionals involved and the person with dementia and/or carers and recorded in the notes.

All these documents were received with enthusiasm from commissioners and providers who were looking for the guidance to support creative ways to deliver quality care and support to older people with mental health needs. But they only seemed to make a small difference – they took the issue further up the agenda an inch at a time. The next major publication, which has arguably been influential in taking the issue to the top of the agenda, was the report of the National Audit Office (NAO), *Improving Services and Support for People with Dementia*, published in July 2007 (NAO, 2007). Although this report focuses on dementia, it should be considered that dementia is one element of those services that are provided by older people's mental health services and teams.

The NAO report found that, although the number of integrated community mental health teams (CMHTs) had improved since the *Forget-me-Not 2* report (Audit Commission, 2002), coverage was still patchy with only 56% of CMHTs who responded to the survey saying that they were integrated. Such teams did well on providing a single point of access, but less well on providing access to specialist skills, and nearly one-quarter did not have a defined care pathway for dementia (p33).

The report went on to highlight the difference that successful joint working could make to the lives of people with dementia, and to cost efficiencies in services.

> *'Sixty-four per cent of teams felt that better joint funding and 77% that better joint working would result in either modest or major financial savings.'* (p40)

But it also noted that *'initiatives to bring together health and social care locally, for example the development of joint "care trusts" or the use of Section 31 of the Health Act (1999) to set up joint services, have had limited success to date in integrating older people's mental health services'*.

It further noted that the new Local Area Agreements and Joint Strategic Needs Assessments provided an opportunity to increase the priority given to older people's mental health services. Local Area Agreements are made between central and local government in a local area, aiming to achieve local solutions that meet local needs, while also contributing to national priorities (see, for example, http://www.communities.gov.uk/localgovernment/performanceframeworkpartnerships/localareaagreements/). The Department of Health has published a commissioning framework for health and well-being (Department of Health, 2007a), which *'develops the idea that bringing together partners using Local Area Agreements will help to promote health, well-being and independence, by using contracts, pooling budgets and using the flexibilities of direct payments and practice-based commissioning'*. Joint Strategic Needs Assessments are compiled by primary care trusts and local authorities to address the health and well-being of their population (see http://www.dh.gov.uk/en/Publicationsandstatistics/Publications/PublicationsPolicyAndGuidance/dh_081097).

In August 2007 Ivan Lewis, the care services minister, announced the first ever National Dementia Strategy for England, which would focus on three key areas:

- raising awareness
- early diagnosis and intervention
- improving the quality of care, especially in the general hospital, in a person's own home and in care homes.

At the time of writing, a draft dementia strategy, *Transforming the Quality of Dementia Care – Consultation on a national dementia strategy* (Department of Health, 2008a), has been published and is currently out for consultation. Among the 15 recommendations for transforming services and support for people with dementia, there is much reference to whole systems working. Perhaps the most important of these in terms of integrating services is the call for a joint commissioning strategy (Recommendation 9, pages 42–45) *'based on a Joint Strategic Needs Assessment that specifies the quality outcomes required'*. This should *'feed into operational plans and budget cycles of PCTs and local authorities … and be informed by the world-class commissioning framework'* (see http://www.dh.gov.uk/en/Managingyourorganisation/Commissioning/Worldclasscommissioning/index.htm).

Ownership and leadership

One of the key issues that has bedevilled the commissioning of older people's mental health services has been a lack of ownership and leadership. It doesn't fit neatly. In some places, the commissioning of OPMH services lies with mental health; in others it sits with older people's services. In a very few places there are specific older people's mental health commissioners.

Where OPMH is under the umbrella of wider mental health commissioning and provision, there are fears that it is marginalised in favour of services for adults of working age, where there are greater resources, more targets and, possibly, a greater fear of the headlines when things go wrong. This causes concern for many who perceive this as a form of institutional ageism.

Where OPMH sits with older people's services, there are fears that the needs of services users are misunderstood, that they are excluded from service provision and their needs are not fully recognised. Many of the services delivered to older people with mental health problems are generic social care services, for example, home care, day care and housing support.

Furthermore, the division of leadership responsibility between health and social care, and between mental health and older people's services leads to confusion over assessment processes. Within mental health, service users are usually subject to the Care Programme Approach. In social care, the Single Assessment Process is more common. These two assessment processes have several common factors – taking account of the views of service users; assessing the needs of carers; providing a multidisciplinary and multi-agency framework. *Everybody's Business* addressed the tension that might underlie confusion between the two:

> *'If the older person's first contact is with mainstream or non-specialist services, the overview and current summary record should be passed to the specialist mental health service when they are referred. Mental health specialists should add to, not repeat this information, and feed it into*

their assessment and care planning processes. Similarly, information gained from specialist service involvement should be fed back into the SAP.' (Department of Health, 2005)

Professor Susan Benbow has commented:

'It should not be an "either, or" but must be both. OPMH is part of mental health (and that must be valued and respected) but has to work across all the places where older adults with mental health problems may be found, and therefore has to relate to, work within and work with older people's services, acute hospitals and the whole of residential and nursing care. To see it as one or the other is to deny the challenge of working across both service areas.' (Benbow, 2006)

What is important is that there is a nominated lead commissioner for each locality. People with dementia and their carers tell us that they don't mind whether their service is delivered by health or by social care, and in fact they often don't know. The important things for them are that the service meets their needs, that it is of good quality and that any transition is managed without any gaps. Similarly, they are often unaware of the assessment process that has been used. All they want is a single common assessment that is shared across services so that they are not required to tell their story several times over.

Joint working should mean more than health and social care. It should take account of other local authority corporate functions like housing, leisure, lifelong learning and transport together with the emergency services, the voluntary and independent sectors. Work undertaken by the Health and Social Care Change Agent Team between 2001 and 2004 to address the issue of delayed discharges (sometimes referred to in the media by the provocative term 'bed blocking'), for example, demonstrated that bottlenecks in one part of the system were often caused by difficulties in another part of the system. A discharge might be delayed because of insufficient care home placements of the right type, or by the lack of availability of appropriate domiciliary care. Their experience demonstrated the importance of taking a whole systems approach to planning care and support for older people with mental health problems.

Commissioning plans, service developments and service delivery should include the voices of service users and carers. In the case of people with dementia, this is often challenging. The Care Services Improvement Partnership has produced a very helpful toolkit to help guide commissioners and providers in including older people with mental health problems (http://www.olderpeoplesmentalhealth.csip.org.uk/service-user-and-carer-engagement-tool.html).

There remains much ageism within mental health services and mental health-ism in older people's services. This is unhelpful. As the noted ecologist and educationalist, Satish Kumar, has commented *'Let all isms become wasms!'* (Kumar, 2007). There has been much misunderstanding about what is meant by age equality in relation to older people's mental services. Some have argued that, if we are to be inclusive and if services are to be based on need and not age, we might not need an older people's mental health service at all. To address this, Phil Minshull, on behalf of the Care Services Improvement Partnership, has written a very useful guidance note (see http://www.olderpeoplesmentalhealth.csip.org.uk/silo/files/age-equality-guidance-note-pdf.pdf).

The NHS next stage review and transforming social care

As noted above, the reports and policy initiatives that have emerged in the field of older people's mental health services since 2000 are set against a backcloth of changes in health and social care. The current review of the National Health Service, *High Quality Care for All – NHS next stage review final report* (Department of Health, 2008b) will have implications for the delivery of health care, including OPMH. Similarly, the government's white paper *Our Health, Our Care, Our Say: A new direction for community services* (Department of Health, 2006) will change the landscape for the delivery of social care by putting more power and choice in the hands of the service user.

In July 2007 Lord Darzi was asked to lead the NHS next stage review. His interim report, published in October 2007 (Department of Health, 2007b), set out a *'vision for a world class National Health Service that is fair, personal, effective and safe'*. The review has been led locally by clinicians in each NHS region. They have developed improved models of care for their regions to ensure that the NHS is up-to-date with the latest clinical developments and is able to meet changing needs and expectations. Full information about the next stage review can be found at http://www.ournhs.nhs.uk/. Some regions addressed dementia as a specific issue; others located within one of the major topic areas being addressed, for example, under long-term conditions. Work is ongoing to implement changes in the way in which health care is delivered as a result of this review.

The white paper, which set out a new direction and plans for the transformation of social care (Department of Health, 2006) was further supported by a ministerial concordat, *Putting People First: A shared vision and commitment to the transformation of adult social care* (Department of Health, 2007c). This established the collaboration between central and local government, the sector's professional leadership, providers and the regulator. It set out the shared aims and values, which will guide the transformation of adult social care. Among its key elements was:

> *'Agreed and shared outcomes which should ensure people, irrespective of illness or disability, are supported to:*
> - *live independently*
> - *stay healthy and recover quickly from illness*
> - *exercise maximum control over their own life and where appropriate the lives of their family members*
> - *sustain a family unit which avoids children being required to take on inappropriate caring roles*
> - *participate as active and equal citizens, both economically and socially*
> - *have the best possible quality of life, irrespective of illness or disability*
> - *retain maximum dignity and respect.'* (pp3–4)

Both reports supported the notion of the personalisation of adult social care services, putting the service user in control of the assessment of their needs and the commissioning and purchasing of support services. This is also referred to as self-directed support. Work has only just started to test out what this new way of working will mean for older people with mental health needs.

Some local authorities have established a means of enabling their residents to assess their needs, before responding to say whether they are eligible for services (see, for example, http://www.kent.gov.uk/SocialCare/adults-and-older-people/self-assessment/).

The word 'personalisation' may mean different things to different people, but there is general agreement that it includes the notions of self-directed support and personal budgets. The philosophy is one of putting the service user at the centre with greater choice and more control about the services they receive, including being given the money to buy the services themselves, known as direct payments. Where users are reluctant to take on the responsibility of managing the budget for their care and support, as well as the employment of their care assistants, it is possible to have an individual budget – a notional sum, which is managed on behalf of the service user by the local authority although the user retains the right to say how they would like the money to be spent. It is still possible for service users to say that they would prefer to remain with the former system, where the local authority retains control of the money and the choice of service.

This work is still in its infancy. People with physical disability and learning disability have been among the first to take advantage of this new way of thinking and working. Older people are more reluctant, and local authorities perceive it to be much harder to revise their ways of working to make self-directed support a reality for older people. How much more is this the case for people with dementia?

The Older People's Programme, the Centre for Policy on Ageing and Helen Sanderson Associates are undertaking a project called Practicalities and Possibilities to test out the personalisation agenda in nine localities. Early findings from this project suggest that involving older people is often not well developed; there are concerns about the structures and resources required to make this a reality, and achieving attitudinal change is arguably more fundamental than the required systems change.

Early intervention and preventative services are an important part of the personalisation agenda. There have been several pilot schemes, including the Partnerships for Older People (POPP) pilots run by the Department of Health and LinkAge Plus run by the Department of Work and Pensions. Details of the POPP programme can be found at www.changeagentteam.org.uk/popp. Some of the POPP pilots were specific to older people with mental health problems – see, for example, Leeds, Bradford, Camden and Southwark on the aforementioned website.

There are some tensions and perverse incentives in the personalisation agenda, both in terms of self-directed support and early interventions. The Fair Access to Care Services system, whereby users are only able to access services if their requirements fulfil certain criteria – and this often means that they are assessed as having substantial or critical needs – can create barriers to earlier support. A further tension can be created between access to healthcare, which is free and social care services, for which users are assessed to pay. In the case of older people's mental health needs, the distinction between whether a service is required for health reasons or social care reasons is often blurred and indistinct, leaving users and carers further confused.

Other initiatives, which are proving popular involve peer support – people with dementia supporting each other. Among these are support groups for people with dementia (see, for example, Cheston et al, 2003) and the development of Alzheimer's cafés. The Bradford POPP pilot programme involved the establishing and evaluation of such support services.

Conclusion

This chapter has only allowed a brief overview of a complex development of policy initiatives, which have impacted on the commissioning and delivery of older people's mental health services. It provides a time-limited and location-specific view – English policy developments since 2000.

Different terminology is used to describe the way that services might be linked to provide a more coherent picture – integrated, co-located, joint working, whole systems. We are recognising that integrated services means more than health and social care – it also involves housing, the voluntary and independent sectors, other local authority corporate functions like leisure and lifelong learning, and the emergency services.

Integrating services is challenging. There are obstacles created by the systems, by personalities, by geographical boundaries, by a lack of leadership and ownership.

But at the end of the day, older people who are living with mental health problems and their carers tell us that they don't mind where their service comes from. The important thing for them is that they receive the right service at the right time in the right place.

References

Audit Commission (2000) *Forget-Me-Not*. London: Audit Commission.

Audit Commission (2002) *Forget-Me-Not 2*. London: Audit Commission.

Benbow S (2006) *Internal Report on the CSIP Older People's Mental Health Programme* (unpublished).

Cheston R, Jones K & Gilliard J (2003) Remembering and forgetting: group work with people with dementia. In: T Adams & J Manthorpe (Eds) *Dementia Care*. London: Arnold Publishers.

Department of Health (1999) *National Service Framework for Mental Health*. London: Department of Health.

Department of Health (2001) *National Service Framework for Older People*. London: Department of Health.

Department of Health (2005) *Everybody's Business – Integrated mental health services for older adults: a service development guide*. London: Department of Health.

Department of Health (2006) *Our Health, Our Care, Our Say: A new direction for community services*. London: Department of Health.

Department of Health (2007a) *The Commissioning Framework for Health and Well-Being*. London: Department of Health.

Department of Health (2007b) *Our NHS, Our Future: NHS next stage review*. London: Department of Health.

Department of Health (2007c) *Putting People First: A shared vision and commitment to the transformation of adult social care*. London: Department of Health.

Department of Health (2008a) *Transforming the Quality of Dementia Care – Consultation on a National Dementia Strategy*. London: Department of Health.

Department of Health (2008b) *High Quality Care for All – NHS next stage review final report*. London: Department of Health.

Kumar S (2007) *Spiritual Compass – The three qualities of life*. Totnes: Green Books.

National Audit Office (2007) *Improving Services and Support for People with Dementia*. London: NAO.

National Institute for Health and Clinical Excellence (2006) *Dementia: Supporting people with dementia and their carers in health and social care*. London: NICE.

Websites

www.olderpeoplesmentalhealth.csip.org.uk (accessed December 2008).

http://www.communities.gov.uk/localgovernment/performanceframeworkpartnerships/localareaagreements/ (accessed December 2008).

http://www.dh.gov.uk/en/Publicationsandstatistics/Publications/PublicationsPolicyAndGuidance/dh_081097 (accessed December 2008).

http://www.dh.gov.uk/en/Managingyourorganisation/Commissioning/Worldclasscommissioning/index.htm (accessed December 2008).

http://www.olderpeoplesmentalhealth.csip.org.uk/service-user-and-carer-engagement-tool.html (accessed December 2008).

http://www.olderpeoplesmentalhealth.csip.org.uk/silo/files/age-equality-guidance-note-pdf.pdf (accessed December 2008).

http://www.ournhs.nhs.uk/ (accessed December 2008).

http://www.kent.gov.uk/SocialCare/adults-and-older-people/self-assessment/ (accessed December 2008).

www.changeagentteam.org.uk/popp (accessed December 2008).

Note

The Dementia Strategy has been published in the time between writing this chapter and the publication of the handbook. For the latest information on the Dementia Strategy please see: www.dh.gov.k/en/SocialCare/Deliveringadultsocialcare/Olderpeople/NationalDementiaStrategy/DH_083362.

Chapter 12

Person-centred care and recovery

Kevin Sole and Lynne Read

Introduction

Recovery is becoming well known as a guiding principle for mental health services, which has evolved from the lived experience of people who use services. It is a concept that has attracted considerable enthusiasm and hope in an area often characterised by disillusionment and defeat. It is supported in several key policy documents, including:

- *The Expert Patient* (Department of Health, 2001a)
- *Our Health, Our Care, Our Say* (Department of Health, 2006)
- *Commissioning Framework for Health and Well-being* (Department of Health, 2007)

However, the term recovery is all too misleading within some service areas, especially within the field of older people with dementia, where person-centred care has grown to be the underpinning practice of choice for several years and is supported in policy documents including:

- *National Service Framework* (NSF) *for Older People* (Department of Health, 2001b)
- National Institute for Health and Clinical Excellence (NICE) clinical guidelines – *Dementia: Supporting people with dementia and their carers in health and social care* (NICE, 2006)

There are shared themes that have emerged from both practices, which impart the aim of empowerment and wellness. This chapter sets out to give some clarity around the two frameworks and give the reader an understanding of how recovery and person-centred care can work in association with one another and complement older people's mental health services, particularly in relation to caring for people with dementia.

What is recovery?

In the work undertaken by Anthony (1993) recovery is described as:

'a deeply personal, unique process of changing one's attitudes, values, feelings, goals, skills and roles. It is a way of living a satisfying, hopeful and contributing life, even with the limitations caused by illness. Recovery involves the development of new meaning and purpose in one's life as one grows beyond the catastrophic effects of mental illness...'

According to the National Institute for Mental Health in England (NIMHE, 2005):

'Recovery has a number of different meanings within the mental health and substance misuse communities. There is no one definition of the term acceptable to all parties involved.'

NIMHE described recovery to include the following meanings:

1. a return to a state of wellness (eg. following an episode of depression)
2. achievement of a personally acceptable quality of life (eg. following an episode of psychosis)
3. a process or period of recovering (eg. following trauma)
4. a process of gaining or restoring something (eg. one's sobriety)
5. an act of obtaining usable resources from apparently unusable sources (eg. in prolonged psychosis where the experience itself has intrinsic personal value)
6. to recover optimum quality of life and have satisfaction with life in disconnected circumstances (eg. dementia).

NIMHE went on to suggest that *'taken together, these six meanings suggest a broad vision of recovery that involves a process of changing one's orientation and behaviour from a negative focus on a troubling event, condition or circumstance, to the positive restoration, rebuilding, reclaiming or taking control of one's life'*.

It is important to understand that the term recovery does not automatically mean to make well or cure as in medical recovery.

Davidson *et al* (2006) suggest the following.

■ Recovery is about building a meaningful and satisfying life, as defined by the person themselves, whether or not there are ongoing or recurring symptoms or problems.

■ Recovery represents a movement away from pathology, illness and symptoms to health, strengths and wellness.

■ Hope is central to recovery and can be enhanced by each person seeing how they can have more active control over their lives ('agency') and by seeing how others have found a way forward.

■ Self-management is encouraged and facilitated. The processes of self-management are similar, but what works may be very different for each individual. No 'one size fits all'.

■ The helping relationship between clinicians and service users moves away from being expert/ service user to being 'coaches' or 'partners' on a journey of discovery. Clinicians are there to be 'on tap, not on top'.

■ People do not recover in isolation. Recovery is closely associated with social inclusion and being able to take on meaningful and satisfying social roles within local communities, rather than in segregated services.

■ Recovery is about discovering – or rediscovering – a sense of personal identity, separate from illness or disability.

■ The language used and the stories and meanings that are constructed have great significance as mediators of the recovery process. These shared meanings either support a sense of hope and possibility, or invite pessimism and chronicity.

■ The development of recovery-based services emphasises the personal qualities of staff as much as their formal qualifications. It seeks to cultivate their capacity for hope, creativity, care, compassion, realism and resilience.

■ Family and other supporters are often crucial to recovery and they should be included as partners wherever possible. However, peer support is central for many people in their recovery.

There have always been negative connotations associated with mental illness and for some the characteristics of having a mental illness can cast a shadow over all aspects of personhood and individuality. The label can cause a person to lose a sense of being, lose optimism of a positive future and thus give up.

This is best demonstrated by Jacobson and Curtis (2000). They suggested that '*sometimes a person can feel very small in comparison to their illness (the circle on the left.) The illness holds them captive and they feel swallowed up by it*'. See **box 1** below.

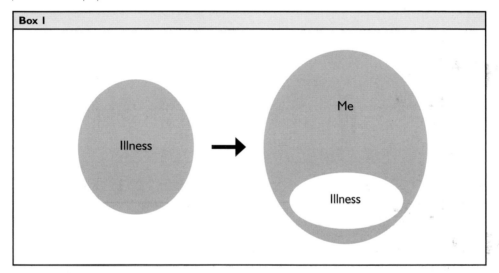

Box 1

Jacobson and Curtis further suggest a move to recovery that '*involves moving from the mental illness being the most important part of one's life to being a person who simply has a mental illness (the circle on the right)*'.

The circle on the right would be in line with a strengths-based approach to recovery. The strengths-based approach focuses on the ways in which people 'survive' and manage their mental illness, and the resources that they draw upon to do this. The approach '*involves looking at people with mental health problems with fresh eyes and noticing appreciatively qualities which were previously seen as only peripheral to the recovery journey*' (McCormack, 2007). McCormack goes on to say that '*taking a strengths-based approach involves moving away from a focus on deficits and therefore represents a paradigm shift. Assumptions on "treatment" are challenged and the role of the service user is transformed from passive recipient of treatment into active collaborator or indeed director of their own recovery*'.

One NHS mental health trust that has tried to embed a recovery approach into its services is South West London and St George's Mental Health NHS Trust. According to their strategic document *Promoting Recovery and Facilitating Social Inclusion* (2007):

'Recovery requires that we move beyond "cure" to thinking about how we can help people to make the most of their lives. If we are to do this then we must put the individual at the centre and think not about "the service user in our services" but instead about "the person in their life" and the impact – for good or ill – that services have their journey through this life.'

Associate Professor Larry Davidson of Yale University (2006) developed 'building blocks' to recovery in which he said, *'Recovery-oriented care identifies and builds upon each individual's assets, strengths, and areas of health and competence to support the person in achieving a sense of mastery over his or her condition while regaining a meaningful, constructive, sense of membership in the broader community'*.

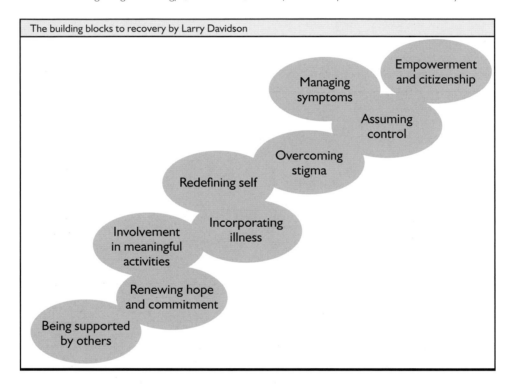

The building blocks to recovery by Larry Davidson

Summary

So in summary, we are aware of how easy it is for people with mental health problems to become nothing other than a service user or to become an illness, such as 'the manic depressive' or 'the schizophrenic', ceasing to be a person or a valued citizen. Recovery, on the other hand, allows people with a mental health problem to believe in themselves and be positive about their future. It is about finding an identity where mental illness is only one element of a person's life, allowing the individual to retain a positive sense of self, where they are in control of their illness and their life at their pace, allowing for self-determination and engagement within a meaningful and valued life.

Mental health recovery is about the individual process of overcoming the negative impact of a mental illness despite its continued presence. Recovery is the progression by which an individual recovers their self-esteem, identity, self-worth, dreams, pride, choice, dignity and a meaningful life.

What is person-centred care?

For those people whose illnesses are likely to worsen over time as with dementia, this does not prohibit the possibility of supporting the person to live as meaningful and valued a life as possible, for as long as possible and to celebrate what they have achieved in their life. Such practice would not only be in line with the principles of recovery, but also the principles underpinning person-centred care.

According to Brooker (2007), *'person-centred care has its origins in the work of Carl Rogers'* who was a leading psychologist and founder of the humanistic approach in psychology. However, it was the late Professor Tom Kitwood who first used the term 'person-centred' in relation to people with dementia.

According to Kitwood (1997) *'the underlying principle of person-centred care is that the person is respected as a fellow human being who happens to have some special needs'*.

Kitwood used the term 'person-centred' in the context of dementia care to bring together ideas and ways of working with the lived experience of people with dementia that emphasised communication and relationships.

According to Brooker (2004) there are four essential elements to person-centred care.

1. Valuing people with dementia and those who care for them, promoting their citizenship rights and entitlements regardless of age or cognitive impairment.

2. Treating people as individuals; appreciating that all people with dementia have a unique history and personality, physical and mental health and economic resources and that these will affect their response to neurological impairment.

3. Looking at the world from the perspective of the people with dementia; recognising that each person's experience has its own psychological validity, that people with dementia act from this perspective and that empathy with this perspective has its own therapeutic potential.

4. Recognising that all human life including that of people with dementia is grounded in relationships and that people with dementia need an enriched social environment that both compensates for their impairment and fosters opportunities for personal growth.

There has in recent years been an inundation of interest in person-centred care, which aims to maintain the personhood of older people. Kitwood (1997) describes personhood as, *'a standing or status that is bestowed upon one human being, by others, in the context of relationship and social being. It implies recognition, respect and trust'*.

Various research suggests that 'personhood' is about:

■   having social relationships
■   having identity
■   being respected and acknowledged
■   being able to act

- having feelings acknowledged
- having a sense of belonging.

As an example of applying person-centred care in practice, McCormack (2004) summarises it in relationship to the nursing role:

> 'The nurse as a facilitator of an individual's "personhood" and 'the need for nurses to move beyond a focus on technical competence and requires nurses to engage in authentic humanistic caring practices that embrace all forms of knowing and acting, in order to promote choice and partnership in care and decision-making.'

To support this, and develop a sense of comparative well-being there are four key elements suggested by Tom Kitwood (1997). These are:

- personal worth – we must feel wanted by somebody
- agency – we can have an effect on the world around us (we can make things happen and make choices)
- social confidence – we can trust the people we are with
- hope – we must always feel things can be better.

Personhood and personal worth are elements of being that everyone would aspire to, regardless of what disease labels they have attached to them. A person with dementia needs to feel respected and valued for who they are now, as well as who they were in the past.

Such practice would ensure that we treat each person with dementia as a unique individual, with their own very different experiences of life, their own needs and feelings and their own likes and dislikes.

Person-centred care respects the person as an individual and arranges care according to individual need. The aim of person-centred care therefore is to ensure that the person is an equal partner with the professional and that the person is treated with respect, courtesy and dignity at all times.

Kitwood (1997) suggests that in practice, the following values, skills and knowledge need to be evident in person-centred care:

- the importance of life history/identity eg. systematically gathering, maintaining and using a detailed personal profile about the person with the person and their family
- implementation of a collaborative care plan that encompasses full use of the person's strengths and abilities
- the importance of promoting positive health/minimum medication/well-being
- encouraging inclusion in all aspects of the care environment
- identify opportunities to enhance well-being by working imaginatively to unlock each individual's potential for engaging in and benefiting from activity
- validation of a person's experience and feelings
- understand and explore 'challenging behaviour' as an expression of a meaningful message of some kind
- to view all actions and utterances as potentially meaningful messages of some kind and not just symptoms of all illness

- to recognise the contribution of families and significant others, and to engage them in choices, activity, care and decisions
- proactively address staff needs/support issues promptly
- to recognise power and equality in relationships and environment
- meaningful and regular activity and occupation
- provide holistic care that is empowering and includes personal choice
- it is fundamental that the person is supported to maintain positive relationships with their families and friends
- maintenance of links outside the hospital ward within the community.

Summary

In summary, 'person-centred care' is user-focused. It promotes independence and self-support as much as possible, rather than dependency and a lack of control. It involves service users choosing and participating in developing their own care and support, but more so, person-centred care is about accentuating the positives and minimising the negatives, promoting well-being and focusing upon the perspective and experience of the individual. It is about seeing the person as a unique individual in a unique context and taking into account the individual preferences and expectations at every step.

With this in mind, it is no wonder that it has been incorporated into modern UK mental health policy with the main focus being on personalised care, giving people greater personal choice and empowering people to personalise their care ensuring greater quality of life and independence.

Links between person-centred care and recovery

The links between recovery and person-centred care are unmistakable according to Adams and Grieder (2004), who suggest that the ideas of recovery and wellness, *'embody what it means to be person-centred, they simultaneously address process and outcome. The concern is not only with the impact of services but also with the importance of the experience for the individual'*.

The recovery approach has its roots in the experiences of service users having involvement and control over their lives, which in itself is person-centred. Both approaches focus upon goals and not problems; they cultivate hope and value strengths. They both operate from a respecting culture, and creating an environment that supports and enables rather than dominates and takes control.

Both are concerned with developing and maintaining a connection with meaningful activities and purpose, further allowing people to have their own voice. Moreover, both support people to work out what they wish to do – their dreams and aspirations, and how they wish to work towards them.

Table 1 lists some of the common themes throughout both approaches and demonstrates the links, with a particular focus on caring for people with dementia.

Table 1: Themes throughout recovery and person-centred care	
Recovery	Person-centred care (PCC)
Pursuit of health and wellness.	A positive social environment to enable the person with dementia to experience relative well-being
A shift of emphasis from pathology and morbidity to health and strengths.	Enabling – it is all too easy to focus on the disability and loss associated with cognitive impairment. We need to recognise the strengths and abilities of people with dementia and ensure opportunities exist for them to be utilised.
Hope and belief in positive change.	Health and social care staff should aim to promote and maintain the independence, including mobility, of people with dementia. Care plans should address activities of daily living that maximise independent activity, enhance function, adapt and develop skills, and minimise the need for support.
Empowerment through information and support.	Empowerment through information and support.
Meaning and spiritual purpose of distress.	Understanding the person as a whole being including a cultural, spiritual and religious context.
Service supports reconceived as mentoring, not supervisory.	Enabling the person to function at an optimum level.
Identity explored as a cultural issue.	Uniqueness – regardless of illness, all people are unique and this must be acknowledged for people, including those with dementia.
Social inclusion (housing, work, education, leisure).	Enabling the person to participate in every day life and allowing the person to remain in an environment of their choice.
Personal wisdom.	Personhood – this refers to the recognition of a sense of self, who we are and what place we hold in the world around us. Personhood is an intrinsic part of PCC and places an emphasis on the positive effects of daily interaction with other people. PCC teaches the recognition of well-being and ill-being of personhood.
Creative risk taking replacing overcautious risk assessment.	Older people should be involved in decisions about their care, and empowered to determine the level of risk they are prepared to take.
Personal recovery focuses on collaboration, partnership working and self-directed care.	The importance of relationships and interactions with others to the person, including those with dementia, and the potential of these for promoting well-being.
The recovery approach recognises that service users often feel powerless or disenfranchised, that these feelings can interfere with initiation and maintenance of mental health and medical care, and that the best results come when service users feel that treatment decisions are made in ways that suit their cultural, spiritual, and personal ideals.	Recognising and understanding the individuality of people with dementia regardless of age or cognitive impairment, with their unique personality and life experiences, and how this affects their reaction to the dementia. Looking at the world from the perspective of the person with dementia.
The recovery approach focuses on wellness and resilience and encourages service users to participate actively in their care, particularly by enabling them to help define the goals of psychopharmacologic and psychosocial treatments.	Service users should have the opportunity to make informed decisions about their care and treatment in partnership with their health and social care professionals.

Choice and control for people.	Within dementia care people should continue to have the opportunity to make informed decisions about those aspects of their care and personal lives for which they retain capacity.
An approach that positively values different cultural understandings.	Treating people as individuals.
Recovery emphasises a person's capacity to have hope and lead a meaningful life.	The importance of the perspective of the person with dementia.
Recovery is based on the core belief that adopting recovery as a guiding purpose for mental health services favours hope and creativity over disillusionment and defeat.	Service users, carers and staff are supported, remain positive and hopeful, and avoid becoming cynical and defeatist (sometimes called 'therapeutic nihilism'). Recovery for people in later stages of dementia means supporting them to have as much control over their situation as possible.
Recovery is the process of regaining active control over one's life. This may involve discovering (or rediscovering) a positive sense of self, accepting and coping with the reality of any ongoing distress or disability.	NHS and social care services treat older people as individuals and enable them to make choices about their own care.

Conclusion

Whether people suffer from the effects of mental illness or dementia, they face the challenge of rebuilding, or where possible retaining a valued and satisfying life. We hope that in this chapter we have been able to dispel some of the myths that recovery does not apply to people with dementia.

Recovery and person-centred care can work together to put the service users at the heart of our services. Both are strengthened by empowerment and hope, making possible the opportunity to reach an optimum level of functioning that is significant and meaningful to the individual.

As we have heard earlier, person-centred care is based upon the work of radical psychologist Carl Rogers, who argued against the traditional model that put the professional in the role of 'expert'.

The 'professionals as expert' notion is still in existence today among many mental health professionals. If we are to achieve real recovery and person-centred care, it will require a shift in attitudes among practitioners and clinicians. It will require practices that recognise that it is the service user's life and well-being at stake and that the service user needs to be in control of this.

So with this in mind, we ask you to reflect on your own individual practice and services and ask to what extent are they really person-centred or recovery focused?

On conducting our literature search for this chapter, we came across the following poem written by a service user, which we would like to leave you with.

I've finally decided,
With some inner will,
That I'm too busy,
To be mentally ill,
I take my meds,

And try to think,
Sitting and talking,
With the shrink,
I am so busy,
I don't have time,
To think about it,
All the time.
I'm so busy,
Be assured,
I won't even noticed,
If I am cured.

Dylan Abraham

References

Anthony WA (1993) Recovery from mental illness: the guiding vision of the mental health service system in the 1990s. *Psychosocial Rehabilitation Journal* **16** (4) 11–23.

Adams N & Grieder D (2004) *Treatment Planning for Person-Centred Care: The road to mental health and addiction recovery: Mapping the journey for individuals, families and providers.* London: Academic Press.

Brooker D (2004) What is person-centred care in dementia? *Reviews in Clinical Gerontology* **13** (3) 215–222.

Brooker D (2007) *Person-centred Dementia Care: Making services better.* London: Jessica Kingsley Publishers.

Davidson L, O'Connell M, Tondora J et al (2006) The 10 top concerns about recovery encountered in mental health system transformation. *Psychiatric Services* **57** 640–645.

Department of Health (2001a) *The Expert Patient: A new approach to chronic disease management for the 21st century.* London: Department of Health.

Department of Health (2001b) *National Service Framework for Older People.* London: Department of Health.

Department of Health (2006) *Our Health, Our Care, Our Say.* London: Department of Health.

Department of Health (2007) *Commissioning Framework for Health and Well-being.* London: Department of Health.

Jacobson N & Curtis L (2000) Recovery as policy in mental health services: strategies emerging from the states. *Psychiatric Rehabilitation Journal* **23** (4) 333–341.

Kitwood TM (1997) *Dementia Reconsidered: The person comes first.* Buckingham: Open University Press.

McCormack B (2004) Person-centeredness in gerontological nursing: an overview of the literature. *Journal of Clinical Nursing* **13** (supp 1) 31–38.

McCormack J (2007) *Recovery and Strengths Based Practice.* SRN Discussion Paper Series. Report No.6. Glasgow: Scottish Recovery Network.

National Institute for Mental Health in England (2005) *NIMHE Guiding Statement on Recovery.* London: NIMHE.

National Institute for Health and Clinical Excellence (2006) *Dementia: Supporting people with dementia and their carers in health and social care. NICE clinical guidance 42.* London: NICE.

Shepherd G, Boardman J & Slade M (2008) *Making Recovery a Reality* (2008) London: Sainsbury Centre for Mental Health.

South West London and St George's Mental Health Trust (2007) *Promoting Recovery and Facilitating Social Inclusion: A strategy for practice and implementation plan. Recovery and social inclusion strategy.* London: South West London and St George's Mental Health Trust.

Chapter 13

Involving older people in service planning, development and evaluation

David Crepaz-Keay and Lisa Haywood

Service user involvement in mental health services has become established practice. Virtually unheard of 25 years ago and the preserve of radicals and a handful of activists as recently as the late 80s, it now forms part of NHS foundation trusts' prospectuses and primary care trusts' commissioning criteria, as well as good practice in local authorities. Regulators look for it and governments praise it as an important lever for service improvement.

One of the consequences of the passage of time is that the radical activists of the 80s are becoming the users of older age services today. This is not a generation that will just stand in line and be grateful for what they are given; this is no longer a 'mustn't grumble' group. The service users of today's older age services have years of campaigning and plenty of views to express and voice to make them known.

Older people with mental health problems also face three particular barriers in mental health services as well as in society as a whole.

■ **Direct discrimination** is unequal treatment on grounds of age such as an upper age limit on certain services.
■ **Indirect discrimination** can be seen in apparently neutral practices that disadvantage older people such as when it is assumed that older adults can be treated identically to younger adults without taking older people's needs and preferences into account.
■ **Ageism** promotes negative stereotypes and prejudice towards older people based on assumptions about them as a group, such as the assumption that mental health problems are an inevitable part of ageing.

All of these require the introduction and implementation of specific strategies to counteract them.

The principles of service user empowerment to achieve this are the same across the age ranges. Effective involvement must include participation in:

■ the individual's personal care
■ the planning and design of services
■ strategic longer-term policy-making.

This chapter looks at these three in turn, illustrated with examples.

Involving people in their own care

This is undoubtedly the poor relation of the service user involvement family. Most aspects of the mental health system could be significantly improved by more constructively involving people in their own care. Evidence from other branches of medicine suggests that treatment plans are more likely to be adhered to and effective if people are involved in them, so it seems reasonable to assume that mental health care would be the same. At the most extreme end of failed services, people seeking and being denied help is a common feature in reports into serious incidents involving people with a psychiatric diagnosis. One of the key problems is the common belief among professionals that people with a psychiatric diagnosis inevitably lack insight into their condition.

The NHS Plan 2000 and the *National Service Framework for Older People* introduced the Single Assessment Process (SAP), which was viewed as a multidisciplinary approach to care management of the individual older person. This could include the framework of the Care Programme Approach (CPA) for people with severe and enduring mental health needs. Guidelines (2006) from the Social Care Institute for Excellence (SCIE) emphasise that this is *'the basis for the development of a personal care plan ... and is the pivotal mechanism which aims to ensure that older people receive appropriate, effective and timely responses to their health and social care needs. This requires a rigorous adherence to the system of assessment, care co-ordination and review and the active involvement of the older person at every stage of the process'.*

Since the introduction of the *National Service Framework for Older People* introduced person-centred care as an expectation (Department of Health, 2001a), there is a policy expectation that older people are treated as individuals who can be involved in decisions about their own care. As defined by law in the Mental Capacity Act (2005), the practitioner must start with the assumption that the older person has the capacity to make decisions for themselves, unless and until that assumption is proved wrong. Ideally, from the start there needs to be a statement of the person's needs, expectations, abilities and goals in their own words. Communication is recognised to be an essential part of user involvement, but older patients who wish to be involved in decisions regarding their care may be prevented from doing so by cognitive impairments, frailty, very poor health, language difficulties, or a lack of confidence when faced with health and social care staff. In this case, it would be good practice to involve a professional advocate to represent their interests. Families and carers are often thought to be the natural advocates, however, sometimes the emotional, practical and financial complexities of family life will cause significant conflict of interest.

During the needs assessment process, there are a number of issues for people with mental health problems, including learning opportunities, meaningful daily activities (including employment opportunities for older people who may want them) and sexuality that are well known to play a significant role in the improvement of health, emotional security and mental well-being.

Recovery

The concept of recovery was introduced by the Department of Health (2001b) to increase expectations about what people with a psychiatric diagnosis could expect to achieve. 'Recovery' does not imply 'cure', but builds on the personal strengths and resilience of an individual *'to recover optimum quality of life and have satisfaction with life in disconnected circumstances. Recovery is about the development of coping skills, and about social inclusion, making it possible for people to have quality of life and a degree of independence and choice, even those with the most enduring and disabling conditions'* (SCIE, 2006). The principles of recovery are standard in care assessments for adults, however, Age Concern and the Audit Commission have identified unfairness in services due to the divisions between 'adults of working age' and older people (Audit Commission, 2006).

A recent study (King & Knapp, 2006) found that although newer atypical antipsychotic medications are potentially more effective and have fewer undesirable side effects, older patients are less likely to be prescribed these. Antipsychotics are also reportedly being prescribed 'off licence' to older people (Burstow, 2008) for a range of purposes beyond their licensed antipsychotic use. For every five-year difference in age, the probability of being prescribed an atypical antipsychotic decreases by 15%. Medication is a big issue with this age group and this is exacerbated by the limited provision of psychologists – and thus psychological therapies – for older people (Tucker *et al*, 2007).

In relation to social care, information and promotion of direct payments are also rarely discussed as part of the care plan, although they are clearly a powerful tool in promoting independence and were identified by older people as an important means to ensure that they, rather than service providers, were in control. Support in managing the financial and administrative demands was identified as crucial in making direct payments work for older people (Joseph Rowntree Foundation, 2008). Research into the individualised budgets pilot programme identified reduced benefit of individualised budgets for older people and lower satisfaction and psychological well-being among older people receiving individual budgets. It is not clear whether this is likely to change as generations of people get more used to self-employment and managing their own budgets in their working lives (IBSEN, 2008).

'It is like a magic door opening. It's meant that, well, I'm living a life now.' (Mrs Young)

Specialist training for non-mental health staff such as GPs, other health professionals, unqualified staff, and their managers is critical to develop a more appropriate and effective service. A report from the Mental Health Foundation concluded that (staff) would benefit from a more comprehensive and ongoing approach, which would assist them in recognising possible mental health problems and in promoting mental well-being, which would result in better care and improved health outcomes. (Mental Health Foundation, 2007). This should include mental health awareness training, recognition of mental health problems, communication skills, risk management, person-centred care, which would include the expressed wishes of many older people for human contact and social interaction and of intergenerational work. Staff also need to have a range of information available to older people to enable them to make informed decisions. These must include practical links to advocates and welfare rights advisers, information on medication and their side effects, guidance to a range of community facilities etc.

A baby boomer service user's point of view

When I look at mental health services for older people I see an even more medicated paternalistic approach that seems to make an automatic assumption about my reduced capacity in decision-making. The worst case nightmare scenario sees a future in a bleak, smelly back ward full of people with totally different needs – Alzheimer's, depression, acute psychosis, anxiety – all lumped in together. Staffing in this service scenario is based on control and management not recovery – because why bother when we're old and have no future?

> If I needed services in my older age, I would want a flexible range of services delivered in response to my expressed needs and wishes – this range would include CBT (without waiting six months), home visiting, good physical health checkups, interesting and stimulating activities.
>
> I have worked all my life and brought up a daughter single-handed. I have been very disciplined in overcoming my personal problems and working out my own strategies for good mental health. It is essential that I would have the full and total respect for my choices in my care.
>
> We need staff who consider recovery not just care as the default position.
>
> (Haywood, quoted in Williamson, 2008)

Involving service users in planning and developing the services they are using

This is probably where service user involvement properly began. Where involving people in their own care is, in theory at least, simply a part of the clinical process, involving people in developing the services they use requires a structural shift in organisational form and a mind shift in everyone involved.

Even amongst service users, the move from wanting more control over how someone is treated to how services need to develop is a leap of thinking that most don't bother with. The vast majority of people using mental health services use them and then get on with their life. This is the biggest untapped resource in service user involvement and requires little effort to improve marginally and a lot of imagination to change completely.

As with personal care, involvement of older service users in planning and delivering services and longer-term strategic policy should use the same principles and values as with other adults, of respect, valuing and support.

A discussion paper based on literature, both academic and policy-related, plus interviews conducted with senior and middle managers in eight organisations found that:

> 'despite a stated belief that older people should be able to access the same services as those under 65 years, often older people's teams did not know about services, such as assertive outreach, which were managed by the adult teams. There was also a generally held view that there were fewer services for older people and that they tended to be less well staffed. Low levels of resources for identification and early intervention work was highlighted as having led to high levels of unmet need, particularly for older people with anxiety and depression.' (Beecham et al, 2008)

This view was mirrored in a report by Age Concern, drawing on a range of research and other sources that said:

> 'Adult mental health teams have better access to occupational therapy, occupational therapy assistants, day centres in the community, psychotherapy services. A patient with chronic schizophrenia [was] transferred to us from the adult services [where he] was getting an occupational therapy assistant visiting once or twice a week, a community psychiatric nurse visiting weekly and a consultant visiting every two weeks. Once transferred, the consultant and community psychiatric nurse will visit [once a] month, if you are lucky.' (Age Concern, 2007: p36; 2006)

Good practice over the years offers some well-established practical guidelines for making sure that the views of older people are incorporated into planning services in both the short and long term to ensure these inequalities are effectively overcome. These include:

- clarity about the purpose of involving service users
- working with them to agree the way they are involved, listening and taking account of what people identify as being important
- making sure service users can make informed choices about how to be involved
- overcoming physical and environmental barriers of access, safety and transport such as wheelchair access, hearing, transport, visual and hearing impairments
- overcoming barriers of procedures and practices that exclude service users by identifying a contact person who can explain the agenda in advance, by providing a glossary of terms, by making sure the service users have papers well in advance etc
- developing opportunities to include groups that are 'rarely heard' and those with communication barriers
- setting up audit and monitoring systems to make sure involvement can be formally assessed
- reporting back to service users about how their contribution was used
- developing different ways of accessing users' views other than inviting them to meetings such as focus groups
- remembering that older people can contribute to the whole of the agenda not just user issues
- applying the principle that people should be paid for their involvement, while understanding that some older people may be on means tested benefits that could be put at risk by payments.

A practical example

In an arena such as a residential home, these guidelines could be implemented in a range of ways. Key to successful involvement is simply 'asking'. Start with asking the residents what areas they might be interested in being involved in eg. monitoring services, recruiting staff, being involved in developing and running social and therapeutic activities etc. This could be done in a group setting or in individual meetings and a realistic assessment of the input required from a range of options should be discussed with residents.

The practitioner also needs to ask how they might like to be involved or what residents think is the most effective way of being involved. Options in monitoring, evaluating and consultation on services, for example, could include questionnaires, focus groups, newsletters, customer satisfaction surveys, regular resident meetings etc. Whatever the method, it is essential that residents are fully informed about purpose of the activity; the status of their views (decision-making/advice etc) and how and when feedback on their input will be made.

It is also important that the 'asking' is done in an appropriate fashion. In particular, communication with people with dementia must be sensitive to their needs.

Meaningful involvement in recruiting staff also requires input from staff. Time must be allocated to train service users about the processes, the purpose of the job, the context of the post in the organisation etc. Again there must be clarity about the status of the input. Is it to give a perspective? Does the vote of the resident have equal status to the manager? There are also issues about payment for taking part in this formal service activity.

As with adults, there is a group of people who are housebound or otherwise not engaged in organisations such as day centres and their views largely go unheard. There are several imaginative ways to overcome these barriers as evidenced below:

> Wakefield health and social care agencies actively involved members of the Age Concern Service Users Action Forum in planning and consultative groups, but were aware that the voices of frail, housebound older people were unheard. The Talk-Back project teamed trained volunteer 'partners' with frail older people. Together they complete a diary of the user's views and needs, enabling systematic feedback to service planners and providers.

> In Kirby, a project group of older people and professionals was set up. The team worked in pairs. They visited people in their own homes and in informal groups and clubs. The older person took the lead in conversations while the professional took notes. They asked people about their experiences of services and their quality of life. Review meetings were held to reflect on what had been learned and to assess the impact of policies and services (or the lack of them) on the lives of older people. The team considered what needed to change to improve their lives. The team prepared a report and made presentations to a wide range of agencies (including housing, leisure, transport, local traders, the local MP and British Gas). An action plan was developed and the team continued to oversee putting it into practice.
>
> (Thornton & Tozer, 1994)

Involving people in the broader strategic environment

This is what people generally mean by service user involvement and covers a vast range from involvement in local planning groups to national policy initiatives. It's also the most complicated and controversial area, but the key questions remain a useful guide to getting it right. The point of involvement will vary with each initiative but service users are readily drawn to national initiatives for a variety of reasons, not least of which is the opportunity to send strong messages, about what and how services feel, to those ultimately responsible for them. There is no doubt that even the most senior policy maker or practitioner can be moved by being brought into personal contact with service users who are at the receiving end of their decisions. But the question of 'who should be involved?' is one of the most troubling parts of this higher level. Throughout the 1990s, there were strong national groups of service users with sizeable active memberships, but even then they often felt uneasy about being seen as representatives of broader service user views. In their absence, national organisations have looked to individuals to fill this gap. Sometimes self-styled champions, sometimes experts by experience, they often put great weight on the views of very few people. For some positions of this type, organisations now go through a serious recruitment process, even for unpaid roles. A recruitment process forces the recruiter to think about the role and type of person they're looking for; it gives them an opportunity to create a transparent process; they can even involve service users in the recruitment process.

The lack of the consistent commitment to the provision of high quality services for older people at policy-making level is evident:

> *'Amongst the service issues of low staffing levels, lack of training and lack of leadership, it was also noted that there was a lack of clarity at strategic health authority level about where responsibility*

for older people's mental health services lay, and that the lack of targets for this area of work meant that it risked being neglected' (Mental Health Foundation, 2007).

Policy makers need also to focus more on prevention, health promotion and early intervention through integrated commissioning arrangements between health and social care and integrated provision of services.

The National Service Framework (NSF) for Older People (Department of Health, 2001a) includes clear reference to the importance of involvement of older people in the planning and implementation of health and social care developments. The vehicle for taking the NSF forward is designated as the local implementation team (LIT) made up of representatives from local primary care trusts, hospital trusts, social services departments, borough councils, the private sector, voluntary organisations and older people and carer representatives.

It is essential that these strategic planning bodies do not depend on one or two 'representatives' attending the LIT even when adhering to the guidelines above. This would fail to take into account that 'old age' can last for over 30 years; the complexity of the combinations of diagnoses of dementia/depression/psychosis etc or different cultural needs and so on. It is essential that a range of tools, materials and resources to provide effective feedback and involvement are developed according to the needs of the particular geographical area.

Involving 'seldom heard' groups

Some groups of people who have been particularly marginalised or excluded need extra support to ensure effective engagement. SCIE has produced a useful guide and position paper on this topic (Robson *et al*, 2009, SCIE, 2007).

'Seldom heard' groups include:

- people from black and minority ethnic (BME) communities
- lesbian, gay, bisexual and transgender people
- people who are isolated at home
- people with communication difficulties
- people with dementia (see next section)
- people who do not wish to engage with services despite having health and social care needs
- homeless people
- refugees and asylum seekers.

Looking at service users from BME communities as an example, a recent study by Jayasree Kalathil from the National Survivor User Network (2008) identified a number of barriers to involvement including:

Barriers to involvement

- Experience of coercive and punitive care within psychiatric services. Discriminatory experiences discourage people from participating in user involvement initiatives, unless there is willingness and space to explore these difficult and emotional journeys.

- Many people from black and minority ethnic communities find it difficult to have even their basic needs met, which may hamper their ability to be involved.
- Experience of racism within user involvement initiatives and user groups. The pressure to separate identities of race and ethnicity from that of a service user/survivor is felt as threatening and thwarting.
- Race and class combine to create exclusionary practices within user groups and involvement initiatives.
- The stigma within communities and racial stereotypes of mental distress make people want to disassociate with mental health initiatives.
- Lack of role in setting the agenda and decision-making. Often involvement of black and minority ethnic service users/survivors seem to be tokenistic, tick-box exercises.

Although this work was specific to mental health service users from BME groups and not aimed at any particular age group, many of these also apply to other disadvantaged groups and some of the solutions identified in the box below as applicable more widely.

Enabling effective user involvement from black and minority ethnic communities

- Link work to change mental health services with broader race and rights based initiatives like education, forensic services, citizenship rights, social inclusion, employment, income generation etc.
- Build relationships between mainstream groups and black and minority ethnic groups, between communities and between professionals and service users/survivors.
- Enable professionals from black and minority ethnic communities to think about race related issues in their practice.
- Actively seek out groups and organisations working locally, highlight their work and endeavour to support and sustain them.
- Support local organisations to develop autonomy and access sustainable resources.

Involving those who are most disadvantaged may be more difficult and time consuming, but mechanisms that work for them are likely to improve involvement for all.

Involving people with dementia – different rules apply?

Unlike mental health services for people with 'functional' mental health problems, up until recently involving people with dementia in stating the type of care, treatment, and services has been relatively undeveloped. This can be explained for a number of reasons including:

- dementia being seen as an illness of old age with little attention paid to it at policy level, and a lack of investment, therefore, in developing user involvement
- the organic, progressive nature of dementia, combined with late or no diagnosis, meaning that it was usually quite difficult or too late to get people's views
- a relatively strong, well developed carers' movement who, partly because of the nature of dementia, often spoke on behalf of people with dementia, as well as in respect of their own issues.

Over the last 10 years or so, however, more and more people have been receiving an early diagnosis, and there have been some improvements in treatments to slow down the rate of memory loss, resulting in people retaining their cognitive faculties for longer. This has led to a significant increase in directly involving people with dementia in research and other initiatives, to find out what their views and experiences are, both of the dementia itself, as well as the care and support they receive, or what they would like to receive.

The work of Harris and Stein (1998), for example, was particularly important in identifying how social interactions that people with dementia experienced could impact on their sense of self, as well as different types of coping strategies that people with dementia developed. Another example of this was the 2001 research report, *Tell Me the Truth* (Mental Health Foundation, 2001). The research looked at the effect of being told of their diagnosis of dementia from the perspective of 24 people who had dementia. Most recently, the Alzheimer's Society published *Dementia – Out of the shadows*, a research project exploring the views and experience of people with dementia before, during and after receiving a diagnosis, different ways they had adjusted and coped, and the effect of stigma (Alzheimer's Society, 2008).

Running in parallel with these initiatives have been developments involving people with dementia with a more overtly campaigning aspect to them. This can be seen with the establishment of the national dementia groups such as the Scottish Dementia Working Group (supported by Alzheimer Scotland) and the Living With Dementia programme in England (supported by the Alzheimer's Society). Members of the Living with Dementia programme and others with dementia have, for example:

- given presentations and raising public awareness
- organised a unique UK wide convention of people with dementia
- contributing articles and letters to the Alzheimer's Society *Living with Dementia* monthly magazine
- lobbied MPs and commented on government legislation
- been interviewed by national press and television
- recruited and inducted new staff at the Alzheimer's Society
- run the website for people with dementia – Alzheimer's Forum
- developed information for other people with dementia and their families
- participated in the national consultative body, the Living with Dementia working group.

Perhaps of greatest note is the involvement of people with dementia in the development of the national dementia strategy for England, *Living Well with Dementia* (Department of Health, 2009). The strategy involved people with dementia in the various working groups that contributed to its development. It contains personal stories and a substantial number of quotes from people with dementia, and includes a specific recommendation/objective emphasising the importance of peer support and learning networks.

These developments suggest that the involvement of people with dementia is beginning to mirror a similar stage of involvement for other people with mental health problems. Certainly, a recent interview with a prominent campaigner who has dementia, Peter Ashley, focuses on a number of issues that other service user movements have had to deal with, such as support, training and paying people with dementia for their participation (Ashley & Savitch, 2009). The challenge of involving people with dementia from 'seldom heard' groups, such as people from BME communities, is an issue that has also had to be tackled by the other service user movements. The publication in 2007 of *Strengthening the Involvement of People with Dementia* by the former Care Services Improvement Partnership

(Department of Health, 2007) also contains many commonalities with service user involvement elsewhere.

However, it is also important to recognise areas where there are likely to be important differences. These include the following:

■ Language and terminology – defining dementia as an illness, disease or condition is far less problematic for many people with dementia (of whatever type) than, for example, defining schizophrenia as an illness for people with that diagnosis. 'People with dementia' is a common term, whereas 'people with schizophrenia' is not. Conversely, 'mental health problems' and 'service user' are terms that are far less common among people with dementia and some actively resist what they see as an incorrect or stigmatising association with the concept of mental health problems.

■ Communication – because of the progressive, irreversible affects of dementia, especially on people's communication and cognitive faculties, as well as memory loss, particular attention has to be paid to communication issues when involving dementia. This applies just as much to involving people in the care they receive as individuals through to their involvement in designing and evaluating services and strategic planning. Non-verbal communication and use of picture symbols may be very important to use, particularly in more advanced stages of dementia. The University of Stirling has developed a visual framework to help people with a communication difficulty understand and respond more effectively, called Talking Mats (Murphy *et al*, 2007).

■ Carers – the families and friends of people with dementia have long played a very active role in the care of people with dementia and for many this has been a considerable burden and source of distress. Because of the absence of an effective cure or treatments for dementia the experience of many carers has been that health and social care services have provided little support or help until perhaps only the very later stages of dementia. This contrasts with the experience of people with functional mental health problems where mental health services are likely to be more active in working with service users and their carers, although at times there may be differences between the views of carers and services (and service users). For this reason, and because of the nature of dementia itself, carers have often spoken on behalf of people with dementia, as well as representing their own issues. Some carers may therefore need support and reassurance to enable them to gradually step back from the role of speaking on behalf of people with dementia, where the provision of care and other initiatives specifically focusing on directly involving people with dementia are being implemented. Clearly the experience of carers is an extremely important one for services to take into account and they will continue to play a crucial role in supporting people with dementia but it remains important that services can differentiate between the carers' agenda and the views of people with dementia.

■ Recovery – the concept of recovery, whereby a service user is supported to regain as much control over their mental health problems as possible, is clearly much more challenging when applied to a progressive, terminal condition like dementia. In the absence of an effective cure or treatment, enormous care and sensitivity must be utilised if using the language of 'recovery' when involving people with dementia in their own care, or designing new services.

Conclusion

Underlying all these different activities and processes that could be called service user involvement is a belief, supported by evidence that it is the right thing to do. But to shift from this belief to making it happen in a meaningful way requires time, patience and understanding, support, and above all, resources, including money. Too many service user initiatives have failed because they are not adequately resourced. At the moment, it seems everybody wants service user involvement but not everyone is so keen to pay for it. This is likely to become a more pressing issue as contracts to provide services become more demanding and the money shrinks.

If service user involvement is to succeed it's not that different from anything else:

- be clear about what it is intended to do
- don't confuse consultation with involvement
- 'quick and cheap' is likely to cost more in the long run
- check out what expertise is available locally (for example, established service user groups) before looking further afield.

References

Age Concern (2006) *Promoting Mental Health and Well-being in Later Life*. London: Age Concern.

Age Concern (2007) *Improving Services and Support for Older People with Mental Health Problems*. London: Age Concern.

Alzheimer's Society (2008) *Dementia – Out of the shadows*. London: Alzheimer's Society.

Ashley P & Savitch N (2009) Valuing the contribution of people with dementia. *Journal of Dementia Care* **17** (3) 16–19.

Audit Commission (2006) *Living Well in Later Life*. London: Audit Commission.

Beecham J, Knapp M, Fernández J-L, Huxley P, Mangalore R, McCrone P, Snell T, Winter B & Wittenberg R (2008) *Age Discrimination in Mental Health Services*. London: Personal Social Services Research Unit.

Burstow P (2008) *Keep Taking the Medicine 4: The inappropriate medication of older people in care* [online]. Available at: http://www.paulburstow.org.uk/resources/sites/217.160.173.25-3edc7f82c67eb0.46705678/Keep+Taking+the+Medicine+4.pdf (accessed June 2009).

Department of Health (2001a) *National Service Framework for Older People introduced person-centred care as an expectation*. London: Department of Health.

Department of Health (2001b) *The Journey to Recovery – The government's vision for mental health care*. London: Department of Health.

Department of Health (2007) *Strengthening the Involvement of People with Dementia*. London: Department of Health.

Department of Health (2009) *Living Well with Dementia*. London: Department of Health.

Harris P & Stein G (1998) *Insider's Perspective: Defining and Preserving the Self in Dementia*. Paper presented at the 51st Annual Scientific Meeting of the Gerontological Society of America, Philadelphia.

Individual Budgets Evaluation Network (IBSEN) (2008) *Evaluation of the Individual Budgets Pilot Programme: Final report*. York: Social Policy Research Unit, University of York.

Joseph Rowntree Foundation (2008) *Making Direct Payments Work for Older People*. London: Joseph Rowntree Foundation.

Kalathil J (2008) *Dancing to Our Own Tunes: Reassessing black and minority ethnic mental health service user involvement*. London: National Service User Network & Catch-a-Fiya.

King D & Knapp M (2006) Patterns of, and factors associated with atypical and typical antipsychotic prescribing by general practitioners in the UK during the 1990s. *Journal of Mental Health* **15** (3) 269–278.

Mental Health Foundation (2001) *Tell Me the Truth*. London: Mental Health Foundation.

Mental Health Foundation (2007) *Better Prepared to Care*. London: Mental Health Foundation.

Murphy J, Gray CM & Cox S (2007) *Using Talking Mats to Help People with Dementia to Communicate*. London: Joseph Rowntree Foundation.

Robson P, Sampson A, Dime N, Hernandez L & Litherland R (2009) *Seldom Heard – Developing inclusive participation in social care*. SCIE position paper 10. London: SCIE.

Social Care Institute for Excellence (2006) *SCIE Practice Guide: Assessing the mental health needs of older people*. London: SCIE.

Social Care Institute for Excellence (2007) *SCIE Guide 17: The participation of adult service users, including older people, in developing social care*. London: SCIE

Thornton P & Tozer R (1994) *Involving Older People in Community Care Planning: A review of initiatives*. York: Social Policy Research Unit, University of York.

Tucker S, Baldwin R, Hughes J, Benbow S & Barker A (2007) Old age mental health services in England: implementing the National Service Framework for Older People. *International Journal of Geriatric Psychiatry* **22** 211–217.

Williamson T (2008) Baby boomers in transition. *Working with Older People* **12** (3) 15–18.

Chapter 14

Housing: the backdrop to good mental health and well-being in later life

Jane Minter

Introduction

'Good housing is basic to mental health and well-being and can play an important role in improving the well-being of older people with mental health problems.' So says the *UK Inquiry into Mental Health and Well-being in Later Life*. (Lee, 2007) Yet housing can often be overlooked in debates about mental health in older age.

Housing is increasingly being seen as an important ingredient in meeting people's health and social care needs and is being recognised as such in debates about the future of health and social care. The focus on 'care close to home', developed as part of the Department of Health's review of health and social care services (Department of Health, 2006; 2008c) is beginning to focus public policy on the importance of the home in later life. This, it can be argued, is followed through in the recent Darzi review with a clear focus on care outside hospitals, though the focus on housing, and home is perhaps less prominent in the report (Darzi, 2008).

The more recent public services agenda on the 'personalisation' of services means a new vision for social care that focuses on the development of 'universal services' and a culture of 're-enablement'. (Department of Health, 2008b) This means, too, that where and how people live should become as important as the care they are likely to receive. In this debate, many policy makers and commentators are now arguing that the debate about the future of social care must include housing.

A much more positive agenda, too, is developing for housing and older people. Publication of the government's strategy for housing in an ageing society in 2008 (Department of Communities and Local Government, 2008) has put housing issues for older people higher on the political agenda. There are a number of recommendations, which aim to meet the housing challenges of our ageing society in the report and the subsequent implementation programme.

Yet, so much more still needs to be done to make the strategic and operational links with housing, care and mental health in later life. Only by doing this can we ensure that services can be put in place that meet the housing needs of older people and help to improve their mental health and well-being.

This chapter looks at older people's housing circumstances and what older people say about their housing, current housing policy, provision and practice with a focus on mental health, and makes some suggestions about what more needs to be done.

Where do people live and what do they say about their home?

The majority of older people want to stay in their own homes in the community for as long as they can and do so well into later life (Tinker et al, 1999.) However, there are still too many older people living in poor and inconvenient homes. 2.1 million households with at least one person aged over 60 are living in non-decent homes (ie. 28% of this age group) (Department for Communities and Local Government, 2007).

Many older people also live alone. In 2006, 61% of women aged over 75 lived alone as did 32% of men in this age group (Office for National Statistics, 2006.) With the growth in the older population, there are increasing concerns about meeting care and health needs in the community. The direction of travel in health and social care policy is about supporting well-being and about providing care and support outside hospitals and in the community. Housing is seen to play an increasingly important role in meeting older people's health and care needs. Thus the home and the environment need to be recognised as playing a more central role. How important is where you live to your well-being?

Studies of what older people want also show the inter-relatedness of different aspects of ageing. Older people see healthy ageing as adapting to physical change, engaging in relationships, maintaining independence, having adequate money, fulfilling desires and keeping busy (Age Concern & Mental Health Foundation, 2006). Jo Moriarty gives a useful example about this interrelationship focusing on the role of housing (Moriarty, 2005). Supporting people financially to purchase adaptations and to make their home more comfortable can counteract the emotional effects of their decline in physical health, for example.

It is the quality of housing (repairs and adaptations) and the support offered (home care, specialist housing such as sheltered housing and extra care housing) that enable older people, who wish to, to continue to live comfortably at home in the community. While there have not been many studies that identify what older people with mental health needs say about their housing, research shows that there are strong links between housing quality and mental health (Blackman & Harvey, 2001). As an example, older people living in poor quality housing are at greater risk of experiencing depression (Stewart et al, 2002).

In the research for the *UK Inquiry into Mental Health and Well-being in Later Life* (Seymour & Gale, 2004), older people with mental health needs said they wanted supportive housing options and technologies to support their links with their family and their communities. This is about supporting people to stay at home or in homely places in the community. It is also about options. No one model of housing or one housing solution will be the answer. Older people with mental health needs are diverse and so their housing solutions will also be.

Factors to be considered in improving housing and housing choices for older people with mental health problems

A host of studies, over the years, have shown the interrelationship between housing, health and well-being (Housing Corporation, 2006). Strong links have also been established between housing quality and mental health (Blackman & Harvey, 2001). A person's home is central to their quality of life. The state of their housing, its location and how appropriate, comfortable and secure it is as people age are important as the foundation for a good quality of life.

Thirty per cent of all households are already headed by someone over retirement age (ONS, 2002) and we know that our population is ageing. This is a significant number of people and older people will make up 48% of the increase in households to 2026. (Department of Communities and Local Government, 2008). The current population of older people in 2006 was 9.6 million rising to 12.7 million in 2021.

The UK Inquiry into Mental Health in Later Life identified that in the next 15 years there will be 4.3 million older people with mental health problems – one in every 15 people. This includes 3.5 million older people with symptoms of depression, one million older people with dementia, and around 91,000 older people with schizophrenia (Lee, 2007). With the ageing population, housing options – both mainstream and specialist – for older people with a range of diverse mental health problems must be addressed.

There are many housing factors that need to be considered:

- Many older people live in poor housing in bad repair. A high proportion of older people own their own homes (Department of Communities and Local Government, 2008).
- Approximately 5% of the older population live in specialist or supportive housing and there are shortages of provision in parts of the country (Department of Communities and Local Government, 2008).
- There is a real need for housing adaptations. Around a quarter of a million people aged 65 and over need specially adapted accommodation because of a medical condition or disability and 130,000 of them report living in homes that do not meet their needs (Department of Communities and Local Government, 2008).

Factors affecting the housing needs for people with mental health problems include:

- People with functional mental health issues are living into older age. The Royal College of Psychiatrists has highlighted the lack of attention given to older people who enter old age with enduring or relapsing mental illness. Such people are moving from services for people of working age to services for older people, and are often poorly served by both (Royal College of Psychiatrists, 2005).
- There are a small but significant number of older people who are homeless and experiencing functional mental health problems. Many people with mental health problems will have lived on the streets or in homeless hostels (Crane & Warnes, 1997) so finding the right housing and support solution is a crucial and yet a neglected area in public policy.
- Given increases in populations, there will be real issues about supporting people with dementia

and depression in later life whether in their own homes or in supported housing. For example, in the consultation about the forthcoming (at the time of writing) dementia strategy it was stated that *'Dementia costs the UK economy £17 billion a year and in the next 30 years the number of people in the UK with dementia will double to 1.4 million'* (Department of Health, 2008a).

Policies, provision and practice

The housing needs of older people with mental health problems are not a priority for public policy. Yet housing for older people plays a significant role in health and social care. Sheltered and extra care housing have developed over the years to meet the needs of older people for housing with support and care. There has been a growing market in extra care housing often seen as an alternative to residential care. Alongside this specialist provision, the development of home improvement agencies in many parts of the country has focused on supporting older people in their own home with repairs, improvements and adaptations.

Sheltered housing is typically housing with an emergency alarm system and on-site support through a resident warden, though in some cases, this is provided by non-resident staff. It does not provide care, though some of its occupants will have a care service provided from elsewhere. Originally developed for rent by local councils and housing associations, there is also a growing number of schemes offering sheltered housing for sale in the public and private sector. Sheltered housing has played a key role in offering older people a place to 'live life to the full' and many older people have benefited from the appropriate housing and sense of community that it offers. Indeed, sheltered housing, over the years, has contributed enormously to good mental health and well-being and the prevention of isolation for older people.

Extra care housing generally offers people a full tenancy with 24-hour flexible on-site care. Extra care housing has become a key development in recent years responding to the needs of frailer older people and supported through a programme of funding from the Department of Health and the Housing Corporation. In 2008, the government announced an extra £83 million for extra care housing. There are also schemes developing in the private sector offering assistive living and this can include larger retirement communities that offer a range of facilities and care on-site.

Studies have shown that extra care housing can offer a supportive environment for people with dementia, especially with good local links with health and social care (Vallelly *et al*, 2006). This counters arguments that older people with dementia need, necessarily, to live in a residential care environment. The research was undertaken in partnership with the University of the West of England and found:

- extra care housing has a role to play in maintaining the health and well-being of older people with dementia
- with the right support, older people with dementia are able to live independently in extra care housing for nearly as long as those without cognitive impairment
- older people and their families choose extra care housing because it meets their aspiration better than other options
- friends and relatives are more likely to remain part of the informal support networks compared to other forms of residential care provision.

Oak House: Providing extra care housing for older people with dementia

Oak House is a specialist housing scheme with 38 flats and an 'extra care' cluster of nine flats for people with dementia. The scheme employs an activities co-ordinator and offers facilities such as lounges, a hair salon, a laundry, a guest room and assisted bathing with a Jacuzzi bath. Also available are freshly cooked lunches and day services three days a week, with one day reserved for people with special needs including people with dementia. The communal garden is designed to suit different moods and activities and incorporates a circuit for walking that discourages disorientation. District nurses are available and a local GP visits weekly. The scheme also has good links with the local mental health services.

Housing 21, which keeps annual statistics on the care and well-being of its residents, identified in 2007 the following profile of its residents in terms of their mental health. A small but significant and rising group of people in their specialist housing have mental health problems including dementia. Housing 21 provides specialist training and advice for its staff on dementia and mental health issues through its centre of excellence – Housing 21 Dementia Voice – so as to support older people with dementia and mental health issues living in its schemes. It also offers a range of specialist housing and care services specifically focused on supporting people with dementia.

	Sheltered	Extra care
Diagnosed or suspected dementia	8.4%	17.7%
Drug and alcohol problems	2.6%	2.5%
Diagnosed or suspected depression	10.0%	15.7%
Other mental health problems	1.7%	5.9%
	22.7%	41.8%

Housing 21, 2008

Social isolation is identified as a strong risk factor for poor mental health (Lee, 2007). A recent study by Evans and Vallelly (2007) of Housing 21's extra care housing also showed how the development of personal relationships and social networks contributes to well-being in extra care. A number of features of extra care that are seen to be key to this are the provision of activities and facilities, the design of the built environment, the continued involvement of the family, connections to the wider community and the 'culture' of promoting dignity, which has been an important driver in housing and care solutions like extra care.

Home improvement agencies (HIAs) help vulnerable and older people to maintain their independence. For over 20 years, HIAs have been meeting older and vulnerable people's needs for repairs improvements and adaptations. They have also offered handyperson services to support older people with small jobs that can make a big difference to people's lives (Adams, 2006). The importance of the home to health and well-being has been clearly identified by the Department of Health in a number of reports about health and well-being, *'If people are to be supported to live at home in greater numbers we need to make sure that local housing stock is suitable in terms of condition and adaptability'* (Department of Health, 2005).

Many HIAs have worked with older people with dementia and mental health problems to enable them to stay at home. Foundations, the national body that co-ordinates the agency movement provides good practice guidance on supporting people with mental health needs including dementia (Foundations, 2006).

A useful website that provides information about the housing and care market for older people as well as access to key reports and other information is http://www.housingcare.org/.

More recently **assistive technologies** have developed to support older people at home and in housing environments, including people with mental health problems and dementia. These technologies offer personal monitoring options such as telehealth and telecare and also enabling technologies such as the 'smart house' technologies that support people with daily activities and with orientation.

Research has identified that technology works well when they meet users' preferences and fit the environment in which they are used or installed (Lansley *et al*, 2004). Government has set aside funds for demonstrator projects looking at how technologies can support people with long-term care needs in the community. Projects have been agreed in Kent, Cornwall and Newham. The Department of Health has also developed a web resource, which included information on these projects, which are subject to an evaluation, and on other issues in this developing field. See http://www.wsdactionnetwork.org.uk/.

Technological advances can mean new ways to enable people to feel safe and secure and engaged at home, particularly people with dementia or other mental health problems. Examples of simple enabling technologies include:

- bed occupancy sensors
- cooker monitoring
- intelligent taps
- lighting controls
- door entry/exit monitoring sensors
- verbal messaging units.

There have been a number of research projects looking at pilot projects in this field (Beech & Roberts, 2008) and there is a website dedicated to technology issues for people with dementia at http://www.atdementia.org.uk/.

Lastly, there are a number of projects around the country that support **older homeless people** many of whom have mental health problems. According to the UK Coalition on Older Homelessness, there is still more that needs to be done to offer people the right housing solutions. Work has been undertaken to bring together organisations concerned with provision for homeless people and those concerned with provision for older people to look at how they can work together to provide better services and offer training and support. See http://www.olderhomelessness.org.uk/.

Current government policy on housing for older people is set out in the government's housing strategy for an ageing society, *Lifetime Homes, Lifetime Neighbourhoods* (Department of Communities and Local Government, 2008). This report draws attention to the range of provision for older people, though it is quite light on issues for older people with mental health needs.

In terms of general government housing policies, key priorities at present are the shortage of affordable housing for families and the impact of the credit crunch on housing. However, the above report does give focus to our ageing population and the need for, *'more older people to live in high quality, warm environments that are suited to their needs – homes that help to make life easier, and to turn the challenges of ageing into opportunities'* – (extract from foreword by the Prime Minister, Gordon Brown).

Key proposals in this report include:

- the development of local and national advice and information on housing options
- proposals for lifetime homes and the development of lifetime neighbourhoods so that people do not have to move just because they grow old and their needs change
- local support services to help people to stay at home including more funding for handyperson services and for disabled facilities grants that support adaptations
- the recognition of the role of specialist housing, including sheltered housing and extra care and a commitment to setting up an innovations panel looking to the future of specialist housing.

The report does recognise the *'growing need for specialised housing for the growing numbers of older people with special needs, such as learning disabilities and mental health problems'*. It also recognises that some groups of older people face additional barriers to making the right choice for themselves, including those with mental health problems, and identifies that Supporting People funds have been used effectively in some areas to support older people with mental health needs. It also identifies the housing needs and support issues for the growing number of people with dementia but there are still some gaps in the solutions it aims to achieve for these groups. It is to be hoped that the latest dementia strategy will make greater play of the key role that housing can and should play.

So while there are some positive developments with regard to housing issues for older people there is still much more to do in linking older people's mental health issues with older people's housing issues and meet the expectation behind the statement made at the beginning of this chapter from the UK Inquiry into Mental Health in Later Life. As a reminder it said, *'Good housing is basic to mental health and well-being and can play an important role in improving the well-being of older people with mental health problems'* (Lee, 2007).

What else needs to be done?

Despite there being a climate to join up policies and new strategies and plans taking shape in health, social care and housing affecting older people, there are several key issues housing and mental health in later life that must remain high on the change agenda in order to support good mental health and well-being in later life.

- Although there is a much greater recognition of housing in health and care it can still often be an afterthought. Housing pays a distinct role in meeting health and mental health targets. The importance of good housing to good mental health and well-being needs to be actively promoted, given more prominence and more active consideration in all developing strategies and plans that focus on health and care.

■ When developing general housing policy, both policy makers and practitioners must not ignore the fact that older people make up 30% of all households now and our population is ageing. Older people's housing can no longer be seen as a marginal issue and, as all housing policies must consider older people, so they must not ignore the specific needs of older people with diverse mental health problems.

■ This means that local and national housing strategies for older people need to be developed and reviewed so as to support the well-being agenda and respond to the needs of older people with mental health problems in both general and specialist housing provision. Too many local and national strategies continue to ignore mental health issues in later life.

■ There needs to be a greater emphasis on enabling people to stay in comfort in their homes and to link to their communities. This means ensuring that new housing meets quality standards including lifetime homes (accessible and easily adaptable). It also means ensuring that existing housing is improved to meet these standards and that there is recognition that older people, particularly those with mental health problems and dementia, require a range of support services to repair, improve and adapt their homes and to take part in community.

■ Recognising the needs of older people for support to live independently will also mean focusing on new forms of supported housing including sheltered housing, extra care and specialist housing, and services for people with mental health needs. There are still not enough housing choices and options, especially for the growing number of older homeowners who would consider purchasing suitable housing if it were available. Diversity of provision is needed for a diversity of needs.

■ There will be a need to offer better delivery of home care and practical support services so that older people are supported to stay at home and be part of their communities. This will require housing and care providers to recognise and respond to the mental health needs of their existing residents and service users and to develop and enhance provision that focuses on well-being. To do so there is a real need for more:
   □ specialist training and support for staff
   □ partnerships with housing providers, commissioners and other local agencies to offer practical services and activities
   □ better ways to engage older people in relationships in their communities and neighbourhoods, for example, housing providers need to facilitate a range of practical support services and activities to enhance older people's well-being living in their housing and in the community.

■ With the growth in interest in technology at government level, some work on how enabling technology should develop to enhance well-being and housing choices for people with mental health problems would be timely. Some technology is already used in specialist housing built into the fabric of the building or using wireless systems. Smart technologies and telecare products can also support older people to stay at home so increasing their housing choices. The increasing use of wireless and communications technologies will also play a key role in supporting the development of information systems, support systems and issues of security and safety, which all help to deliver choice in housing.

■ Lastly, in the review of provision for long-term care (HM Government, 2008), which is focused on dignity and well-being as well as funding, there needs to be a move away from institutional models of provision to more housing-based solutions, including for those groups still on the margins, such as older homeless people and older people with enduring mental health problems.

References

Adams S (2006) *Small Things Matter: The key role of handyperson services.* Nottingham: Care and Repair England.

Age Concern & Mental Health Foundation (2006) *Promoting Mental Health and Well-being in Later Life.* London: Age Concern & Mental Health Foundation.

Beech R & Roberts D (2008) *Assistive Technology and Older People.* Research brief. London: Social Care Institute of Excellence.

Blackman T & Harvey J (2001) Housing renewal and mental health: a case study. *Journal of Mental Health* **10** (5) 571–583.

Crane M & Warnes AM (1997) *Homeless Truths: Challenging the myths about older homeless people.* London: Help the Aged and Crisis.

Darzi A (2008) *High Quality Care for All: NHS next stage review final report.* London: Department of Health.

Department of Communities and Local Government (2007) *Housing in England 2005/06.* London: The Stationery Office.

Department of Communities and Local Government (2008) *Lifetime Homes, Lifetime Neighbourhoods: A national strategy for housing in an ageing society.* London: Department for Communities and Local Government.

Department of Health (2005) *Independence, Well-being and Choice.* London: Department of Health.

Department of Health (2006) *Your Health, Your Care, Your Say.* London: Department of Health.

Department of Health (2008a) *Transforming the Quality of Dementia Care Consultation on a National Dementia Strategy.* London: Department of Health.

Department of Health (2008b) *Putting People First– Working to make it happen: adult social care workforce strategy.* London: Department of Health.

Department of Health (2008c) *Delivering Care Close to Home: Meeting the challenge.* London: Department of Health.

Evans S & Vallelly S (2007) *Promoting Social Well-being in Extra Care Housing.* York: Joseph Rowntree Foundation.

Foundations (2006) *Providing Services to those with Age Related Mental Health Needs.* Glossop: Foundations.

HM Government (2008) *The Case for Change – Why England needs a new care and support system.* London: HM Government.

Housing 21 (2008) *Care and Well-being Survey – summary findings.* London: Housing 21.

Housing Corporation (2006) *Good Housing and Good Health Sector Study.* London: Housing Corporation/CSIP.

Lansley P, McCreadie C & Tinker A (2004) Can adapting the homes of older people and providing assistive technology pay its way? *Age and Ageing* **33** (6) 571–576.

Lee M (2007) *Improving Services and Support for Older People with Mental Health Problems.* The second report from the UK enquiry into mental health in later life. London: Age Concern England.

Moriarty J (2005) *Update for SCIE Best Practice Guide on Assessing the Mental Health Needs of Older People.* London: King's College London.

Office of National Statistics (2002) *Living in Britain – 2001* [online]. Available at: http://www.statistics.gov.uk/lib2001/about.html (accessed March 2009).

Office of National Statistics (2006) *General Household Survey.* London: Office of National Statistics.

Royal College of Psychiatrists (2005) *Caring for People who Enter Old Age with Enduring or Relapsing Mental Illness. Council Report CR110.* London: Royal College of Psychiatrists.

Seymour L & Gale E (2004) *Literature and Policy Review for the Joint Inquiry into Mental Health and Well-being in Later Life.* London: Mentality.

Stewart R, Prince M, Harwood R, Whitley R & Mann A (2002) Quality of accommodation and risk of depression in later life: an analysis of prospective data from the Gospel Oak Project. *International Journal of Geriatric Psychiatry* **17** (12) 1091–1098.

Tinker A, Wright F, McCreadie C, Askham J, Hancock R & Holmans A (1999) With Respect to Old Age: Long-term care – rights and responsibilities. Research. *Volume 2: Alternative Models of Care for Older People, a report for the Royal Commission on the Funding of Long-term Care.* London: The Stationery Office.

Vallelly S, Evans S, Fear T & Means R (2006*) Opening Doors to Independence.* London: Housing 21.

Chapter 15

Dignity in care of older people with mental health problems

Lesley Carter

Introduction

This chapter is about promoting dignity and dignified care for older people with mental health problems. It particularly focuses on care settings such as hospitals or care homes but many of the staff behaviours described, and ways of improving practice could also apply to staff working with older people living in their own homes.

There are examples of bad practice, and a section that gives a simple approach to making a service improvement within a care setting. The chapter gives an opportunity for you to reflect on the kind of dignified care that is delivered in their own area of work. It will encourage this personal reflection to question your own attitudes and those of the people with whom you work.

What is dignity?

One might define dignity as meaning 'worthiness'. To feel dignified is to feel that you are worthy in yourself – you are of value. It implies that you have something of significance that you can give others. It means that you feel that you yourself are of sufficient value that your presence in the lives of others makes a significant difference. It also implies that you enjoy being with others in a way that makes a meaningful connection.

Unravelling words often associated with dignity may help to clarify and understand what dignity really means. 'Dignity', 'respect', and 'compassion' are words that seem to work with each other.

- **Dignity** is about treating others as you would wish to be treated, in a calm and courteous manner, being seen as worthy, and treated with respect.
- **Compassion** is often described as a profound human emotion prompted by the pain of others – a sorrow for the sufferings of others with a desire to help. Interestingly all major religions consider compassion a virtue.
- **Respect** is often described as a sense of worth or excellence of the person, a personal quality or ability, a courteous regard for an individual's feeling.

Most of us as individuals would recognise these positive traits and would be sure that we demonstrate them in our everyday lives. So why in care organisations do we find it so hard to treat the individuals in our care with the dignity, respect and compassion they deserve?

Regrettably, many citizens will have experienced how not being treated with dignity feels like; it is difficult to articulate those feelings into words. Words that are often used to describe a loss of dignity are feelings of vulnerability, unimportant, second class, don't matter, a burden, useless, old, disabled. One sure fact is that not being treated with dignity is subjective and will feel different to everybody in every different situation. Individuals who are constantly treated like they no longer matter will act and feel like they no longer matter. How service users perceive themselves is important, and is a powerful motivator that supports feelings of dignity.

Respecting dignity in practice

'Dignity in practice' refers to the delivery of care, by anyone, in any care setting. 'Dignity in care' describes a positive experience of care delivery, which supports and promotes individuals, never undermining an individual's self-respect. The setting where care is delivered must provide an environment to assist people to maintain their autonomy, their own control, their choices and promote a positive experience, enabling the person to live a quality of life that could be reasonably expected by anyone within our society – a humane society.

Fortunately for some of us, the experience of not being treated with dignity will be fleeting, for example, we may be in a situation with a temporary loss of control, or being temporarily dependent on someone else to meet our needs. Some individuals, when facing a situation with a temporary reliance on others may have the ability and confidence to challenge their loss of dignity and be sufficiently empowered to confront the situation and have the wherewithal to be able to articulate or confidently explain to others how their actions have contributed to their feelings of a loss of dignity.

The sad reality is that many older individuals who, because of illness and reduced capabilities, do not have the ability to reply or ask for what they need. They are left feeling uncomfortable, alone, embarrassed and uncared for. Undoubtedly, they will be the most vulnerable members of our society, those who rely on others for their basic human needs and on someone else to ensure that their dignity is maintained.

What is dignity from a societal perspective?

Incorporating dignity into everything we do should be an expected part of society life and organisational culture; we as humans should be able to demonstrate dignity and respect as a matter of course in all aspects of our everyday life. Sadly, in many communities and organisations this is not the reality. We know dignity is about compassion and respect, but there is a need to address the other wider societal issues of dignity – those of age discrimination and abuse – to challenge inequalities and stigma within communities and organisations, and work towards rekindling the importance of dignity in communities and organisations. For this to be successful, a wide reaching change in culture will need to take place. This will include acknowledging and making direct challenges to tackle the deep-rooted issues of ageism and discrimination that seem to begin to develop from childhood, and continue throughout our lifetime. To make a change, society and individuals need to have the confidence to challenge age discrimination and promote respect for elders from birth. Giving that challenge to communities and individuals may help raise the awareness of dignity and respect and can help to promote a positive community attitude, which in turn will encourage intergenerational community work and citizenship, bridging the gap between young and old in communities.

Dignity in organisations

We know that promoting dignity is a matter that organisations feel passionately about; clear statements are made about what people can expect from services and communities, which respect dignity. In health and social care organisations and other care services, such as residential and home care, professionals and carers constantly make assessments, write statements and complete care plans that should have a strong focus on treating people with dignity, but in the context of care delivery. What does 'respecting dignity' really mean, and moreover, is it carried through? Nurses, doctors and allied health professionals have a professional duty to respect a patient's dignity, and it should be standard good practice for other staff such as nursing assistants and non-professionally aligned staff working in care homes. To support this The Royal College of Nursing has launched a campaign called Dignity at the Heart of Everything We Do. The campaign will champion patient dignity by giving practical tools to nurses that will ensure compassionate care and challenge poor practice where it exists.

Communication skills are also imperative and organisations must provide support and training to ensure that communication skills are acceptable. Dignity is often threatened by a lack of communication and this could lead to care staff speaking to adults like children, either because of assumed or actual lack of mental capacity. Addressing a person as they would wish and speaking respectfully will promote self-esteem. With the diverse population of the care workforce, service users, and carers it is imperative that people can understand each other, not just in speech but with a cultural sensitivity as well. Feeling comfortable and familiar with staff and seeing a recognisable face is very important for people receiving residential care, home care and in hospital wards. Recruitment and retention of staff are key areas that need attention.

The experiences of older people and their carers

Despite all this rhetoric we know that being treated with dignity is not the experience that service users and their carers describe, particularly older people. Considering that the older population is expected to rise dramatically over the next 20 years it is crucial that changes are made and embedded into society now.

Despite a great raft of new initiatives and high level focus on dignity in care, older people continue to tell in their stories, at stakeholder events and focus groups, examples of treatment that show that they are not being treated with dignity, either in hospital, in social care, in GP surgeries, in A&E, in care homes, or even in their own homes.

Listening to stakeholders is a constructive and influential way to engage, assess and make changes to service delivery. Some care staff find service user stories difficult to hear and feel that there is an exaggeration or it's not the whole story. It may not be the full story but it is the experience of the person – the subjective feeling of the experience that is remembered.

Some examples to consider

■ On a mixed medical assessment ward an older woman is lying opposite a man who has his pants off. He had been calling for the toilet for some time and had been incontinent, and then tried to relieve the wetness of his clothes by taking off his trousers. The daughter of the man comes in and is horrified to see her father wandering around his bed area undressed. He was a professional man who always took pride in his appearance. Whose dignity has not been respected?

■ In the GP surgery, a patient who has a hearing loss is trying to talk about her medical condition to the receptionist. The receptionist is getting frustrated and is shouting questions and repeating answers so that everyone else can hear, instead of speaking clearly or communicating in other ways that the patient can understand.

■ Agnes is in A&E because she has fallen over and broken her arm. She is also in the later stages of dementia. In A&E she is put into a hospital gown that is much too big for her and open at the back. She is observed walking down the corridor on the arm of a health care assistant with the back of her gown flapping open and no pants or dressing gown on. Did the health care assistant not notice? Did no other nurse or health professional notice this person walking along the corridor in this condition? The daughter arrives at the A&E department and is mortified at her mother's appearance and experience.

■ Mavis is an inpatient on a ward at visiting time. She is put on a bedpan with the curtains not securely closed – they are open just enough for people who walk past to see in. A health care assistant yells down the ward, 'Mavis, are you done yet?' Is there a culture of dignity on this ward? Who is responsible for the lapse of dignified care?

■ Martha is suffering from depression and living in a care home. One of the symptoms of her depression is a lack of motivation for personal care. Part of her care plan is that staff assist Martha with her personal care. However, the staff are observed talking among themselves over Martha's head while washing and dressing her. There is minimal interaction or encouragement between the staff and Martha. Who or what was the focus of their attentions? How do you think Martha felt?

Other examples include:
■ being medically examined by several people and onlookers with no gown or modesty sheet
■ having a porter shout, when wheeling a patient on a trolley; 'here comes a big one' when going for an x-ray
■ being spoken to as a child, or staff using pet names, such as 'Love' or 'Duck'
■ being fed impatiently by someone who stands over you
■ receiving personal care from a carer who never speaks.

Let's try and unpick a story to see what might be done differently

Burt Jones and his daughter had been caring for his wife Edith at home for 12 years. Edith had a diagnosis of dementia. Edith, for many months, had been physically going downhill. She was having home care and the family were managing well with their support. Food was a real issue and Edith would only eat pureed food, and would only take this if fed by her husband or daughter.

Edith's physical condition deteriorated and Edith needed a hospital admission. The issue of food continued, but this ward supported the practice of protected mealtimes (Department of Health, 2007) and the ward was closed for an hour during each mealtime. Burt was not encouraged to feed his wife and was not allowed on the ward at mealtimes.

Burt watched his wife steadily lose weight. He heard from other people in the ward that Edith would not eat when the staff tried to feed her so Burt brought in pureed food during visiting times. However, by the time he had been on three buses to reach the hospital, the food was cold. Edith didn't like cold food and Burt was unable to heat up the food on the ward, so Edith wouldn't eat it.

Sadly, Edith died after five weeks in hospital, never having returned home. Burt believes that he contributed to the death of his wife. He believes that he allowed his wife to be starved to death and that he should have asked more forcefully to be allowed to feed her at mealtimes. He feels that he should have been able to provide all the care that she needed. What are the issues around this vignette?

There are many issues around this story but the bottom line is that this man felt that he had failed his wife of 50 years because he didn't provide care for her and he allowed her to starve to death in hospital.

When we unpack this story, the ward recognised the difficulties in ensuring that patients receive the correct nutrition and followed best practice guidelines for protected mealtimes. However, the ward didn't encourage long-term carers to come and feed their loved ones. Perhaps the ward staff could have dealt with the relatives with more compassion, recognising the needs of lifetime partners and carers to continue to care when in hospital (Department of Health, 2008) and dealing with those needs sensitively.

Promoting dignity in practice

Dignity is as much about treating others as you yourself would wish to be treated. The next section explains how this dignity can be promoted in practice.

A question of balance

Ensuring a dignified experience, dignity-specific tasks are tricky to describe. Literature searches and academic papers reflect tensions and questions of balance. For example:

- protecting privacy but ensuring the service user does not become isolated
- finding the balance between genuine frailty and dependence, balanced against the need for an older person to feel useful
- getting the balance between delivery targets and ensuring flexible, personalised care.

All of these will help to make certain that dignity and respect is a shared challenge owned by everyone so that respecting dignity will become habit.

Organisational culture

Delivering good quality health and social care that meets the needs of the person is understandably a complex business. Care delivery usually needs to meet several targets simultaneously. For example, the criteria set down by inspectorate organisations, delivering national and organisational policy directives, being mindful of good practice guidelines, as well as operating under time pressures. However, these are not excuses for delivering poor care or sub-standard services. Commissioners can be instrumental in driving up standards by making sure that there are clauses in contracts that are specific about the expectations of providing dignified care, giving a clear message that dignified and respectful treatment must be at the centre of all care delivery. This is a clear responsibility of all those who commission, provide and deliver services.

Improving dignity in a care delivery setting can be complicated as it involves not only the people who work directly in that setting but all those other professional and support staff, and members of the public, who come into contact with service users, in fact, anyone who comes into contact with service users in the care setting where you work.

For example, there would be little point in ensuring that all staff who worked in your ward called all the patients by the name that they had specified but then when the porter came to collect a patient for x-ray he says 'are you ready pet?' If this manner of address offended a particular patient it would be likely that this would be the treatment that they would remember. This example demonstrates that treating people with respect and dignity must become part of the organisational culture.

Sometimes the focus of care providers becomes excessively concerned with implementing policy and the balance between best practice, respect, compassion and sensitivity is lost. Promoting an organisational culture that challenges a lack of dignity, a culture that is owned by everyone, championed by the chief executive and owned by the staff on the shop floor ensures a top down and bottom up approach. Organisations cannot expect their staff to respect the dignity of their patients if staff do not feel that the organisation treats them with respect. Challenging the organisational culture will only be achieved through effective leadership.

Leadership

Effective leadership is key to improving and maintaining the quality of dignified care; leaders have the responsibility to challenge lapses in dignity and promote dignity to grow and develop as part of the organisational culture. Leaders also have the duty to lead by example, to inspire, to treat staff with respect and fairness and ensure that they cultivate positive relationships. An environment that has contented staff who laugh, feel appreciated, have job satisfaction and feel supported are more likely to have a more positive caring attitude towards the people for whom they care. When individuals in our care feel safe both physically and emotionally it leads to their positive feelings of dignity.

Understanding staff issues values, fears and personal growth

We are all patients, in the sense of being people who endure, bear and suffer pain throughout life. Patients look towards health care as they would a mirror, seeking their continued sense of worth (Chochinov, 2007). Equally true is the converse, that when health care staff look at their seriously ill patients they are facing a mirror of their own human frailty and vulnerability. This mirror can awaken their personal fears about suffering at every level, and raises in them all the questions linked to the meaning of life and the role of care.

Care staff need to be aware and carefully examine and question their own attitudes towards the individuals in their care as it may help to address the issue of poor care delivery. It is a personal task that requires individual thought but it is also an organisational responsibility to facilitate and explore, through staff training, clinical supervision and support.

Some issues to consider if you work in health or social care with older people include the following.

■ How I would feel if I was the service user in this situation?
■ Is my attitude affecting the way that this older person behaves?
■ Could my attitude be based on something to do with my own life experiences?
■ Is my behaviour promoting a positive image to the person in my care?

Often powerful support can be given to service users by acknowledging what they are feeling: 'it must be frightening for you', 'I can only imagine how you are feeling', 'it's ok and understandable to feel like this'.

Staff may find it easier to understand, communicate and relate culturally to individuals in their care if they have some understanding of the individual during their life. It helps to look behind the illness – trying to know individuals as they were throughout their life and know some of their life experiences, their beliefs and values. This knowledge will give a greater understanding of the whole person. Having a better understanding of the whole person will lead to being able to better understand and treat the individual with dignity and respect.

The continual learning, support and development of staff will drive standards up and improve the quality and efficiency of care delivery developing alongside a culture of staff having the confidence to challenge negative attitudes towards dignity.

Practical ideas for tackling undignified care

In 2006, the government, in order to address the increased reporting of poor practice and undignified care, as well as to highlight the importance of observing dignity, presented the Dignity Campaign.

The Dignity Campaign lays out national expectations of what constitutes a service that respects dignity. The challenge focuses on 10 different aspects of dignity – the things that matter most to people.

The dignity challenge

1. Have a zero tolerance of all forms of abuse.
2. Support people with the same respect you would want for yourself or a member of your family.
3. Treat each person as an individual by offering a personalised service.
4. Enable people to maintain the maximum level of independence, choice and control.
5. Listen and support people to express their needs and wants.
6. Respect people's right to privacy.
7. Ensure that people feel able to complain without fear of retribution.
8. Engage with family members and carers as care partners.
9. Assist people to maintain confidence and a positive self-esteem.
10. Act to alleviate loneliness and isolation.

The 10 aspects above are paramount to engender positive feelings, as is treating individuals and their significant others holistically. All staff must be encouraged to behave towards patients in a way that promotes dignity during each and every interaction. In the UK there is an increasing emphasis on service users' rights to be treated with dignity and according to the Human Rights Act. Nurses (and other staff) have a professional duty to respect dignity and actively alleviate loneliness and isolation.

The dignity challenge is for everyone – those who provide services, those who receive services and those who commission services, and members of the public – underlining that respecting dignity is everybody's business.

The dignity challenge is about providing high quality care services that respect dignity. The dignity challenge makes a clear statement of what people can expect from a service that respects dignity.

Tools to help improve practice

When we consider dignity themes and what components make a person a unique individual, we will find that looking at someone's past life is vitally important, seeing them as they were. Knowing some of their life experiences and their beliefs and values will help give a greater understanding of the whole person. Having a greater understanding of the whole person will lead to being able to treat that individual in a way that respects their uniqueness and in turn respects their dignity.

Some useful sources of information and tools are as follows.

- On the dignity champions website evidence of good practice can be found at: http://www.dhcarenetworks.org.uk/dignityincare/

- Amanda Waring is an actress who has been a passionate campaigner for older people's rights for the past five years. Following her mother's poor experience of hospital care when she was not treated with dignity, Amanda was inspired to write an award-winning, powerfully emotional film called 'What Do You See?'. The film has been used in dignity training sessions around the world. The film (available as a DVD), in which an older person, acted by Virginia McKenna, eloquently demonstrates not being treated with dignity and powerfully emphasises the importance of caring for, as well as caring about, older people who are receiving care. It also reiterates that it's not just what tasks are performed but it's also about how they are performed. Available at: http://www.amandawaring.com/what-do-you-see

- **Life story books** help to support and inform care staff about who the person is and describe some of their life experiences, giving staff a greater understanding of the real person, their values and their beliefs. Patients, families and care staff can all contribute to the book. Relatives are key in providing information and should be actively encouraged. Life story books help staff to meaningfully engage with individuals with complex needs and can be used to inform care planning to more accurately meet personal needs. It helps to respect wishes and promote dignity. For more information see: http://www.mentalhealthequalities.org.uk/our-work/later-life/communities-of-interest/life-stories/

- **The Let's Respect project** – Let's Respect is a campaign aimed at better meeting the mental health needs of older people. It has focused initially on generic secondary hospital care settings and the three most prevalent presentations – depression, delirium and dementia. There is a Nursing Standard Good Practice guide, PowerPoint presentations and the Let's Respect Resource Box for your work area – filled with information presented in a variety of formats from small case studies in booklet form, to guide books and bookmarks. See: http://www.mentalhealthequalities.org.uk/our-work/later-life/lets-respect

---

Thinking it through

When reading through this chapter and based on some of your own observations and experiences you may feel overwhelmed about how you can address issues where dignity is not being respected in the place that you work. The next section invites you to reflect on your own feelings and behaviour.

Think about what would be the ultimate of loss of dignity for you?
- How would you deal with it?
- What would you say to the staff treating you?
- How could you make sure that this situation does not occur where you work?

Think about care delivery in your area; consider some areas where you feel care delivery does not respect patient's dignity.

Changing practice

Introducing service improvements does not have to be difficult; it's about having the courage to think creatively and try new ideas; understanding that small changes can make big differences to the patient experience. Try and look at the bigger picture and overall patterns, if change is delivered in a methodical and planned way the change should be sustained (Carter, 2008).

Make a detailed plan to address one practice that does not deliver dignified care. Keep the focus on small steps with rapid feedback making sure that the improvement is addressing the need. Quick wins demonstrating small improvements to care will keep staff interested, give a more positive approach to care, and generally improve care delivery.

Eight simple steps to changing practice:

- **acknowledge** the problem
- **tell others** and challenge the problem
- **diagnose** the why, what and when of the problem
- **agree** how to make changes that will improve care delivery
- **test** the improvement – have a trial run and check the difference the improvement has made
- **revisit** the problem and check that improvements have changed the practice for the better
- **implement** the improvement fully and evaluate it in one, three, and six months.

Next steps – improving dignity in care

1. Find your own baseline

- **Monitor experiences** and feedback from people who come into contact with your area.
- **Listen to stories**. Invite former patients, current patients, visitors, and members of the public to a focus group, and ask them what their experiences of dignity have been on your work area.
- **Design a survey** asking questions about experiences of receiving dignified care.

---

2. **Call a staff meeting**

Discuss with staff and other people who work with patients on your area (eg. porters, administrative staff, domestic staff, technicians, doctors, occupational therapists, care assistants etc.) the outcome of the focus group.

3. **Pick out a task identified in the focus group that didn't deliver dignified care**

For example, sometimes staff did not draw the curtains all the way round the bed when delivering personal care, carrying out tests, or having personal conversations.

4. **Check when and if this happens**

One way that this could be done is to observe the ward for a set time – one hour per day for seven days.

5. **Design a checklist of questions**

- Were the curtains routinely closed?
- Who didn't close the curtains: nurses, nursing assistants, doctors, technicians?
- Were there mechanical reasons why the curtains could not be fully closed?
- Were all the curtains there?
- What time of day was it?
- What was the state of the ward (eg. busy, quiet).
- Any other comments.

6. **Do a simple analysis of the results**

- How many times were the curtains not closed completely?
- How many staff were on duty?
- Which staff didn't close the curtains?
- What else was happening on the ward?
- Were all the curtains in good repair?
- Any other comments.

7. **Take some time to reflect**

- From the results decide why this problem is occurring.
- What steps you could take to stop it?
- For the sake of this example let's suppose that staff do try to close the curtains, but the curtains do not mechanically fully close.

Consider how you will present your findings from the steps described above (often called a service audit).

- Write a simple report.
- Suggest some ways that this problem could be resolved.
- In this example, making a minor mechanical alteration to the tracking would allow the curtains to close fully.
- A reminder to staff in a staff meeting about privacy and dignity and careful curtain closing.
- Present your report to your manager.
- Share your findings with staff.
- Tell the people who came to the focus groups.
- Share your findings with other departments.

Conclusion

Dignity will never be a simple matter – there will always be surrounding difficulties and barriers where respecting dignity is challenged and is overlooked, particularly when targets, budgets and other bureaucracy become barriers.

Clearly, leaders, professionals and caregivers must all make every effort to always promote dignity in every circumstance. Unfortunately, there can never be a policy or procedure to cover dignity as every interaction will be unique, as is each individual. But the prevailing message is that 'dignity matters'.

References

Carter L (2008) *Dignity Champions Master Class*. London: CSIP.

Chochinov H (2007) Dignity and the essence of medicine: the a, b, c and d of dignity conserving care. *British Medical Journal* **335** 184–187.

Department of Health (2007) *Hospital Food* [online]. London: Department of Health. Available at: http://www.dh.gov.uk/en/Publicationsandstatistics/Publications/AnnualReports/Browsable/DH_5326824 (accessed June 2009).

Department of Health (2008) *Carers at the Heart of 21st Century Families and Communities: A caring system on your side, a life of your own* [online]. London: Department of Health. Available at: http://www.dh.gov.uk/en/Publicationsandstatistics/Publications/PublicationsPolicyAndGuidance/DH_085345 (accessed June 2009).

Waring A (2005) *What Do You See?* (DVD). Available at: http://www.amandawaring.com/

Chapter 16

Adult protection and risk among older people with mental health problems

Bridget Penhale

Imagine a world in which nothing is the same as it once was. Where everything seems familiar but is not quite right. Like continually seeing things as if through a mirror, a parallel universe in which all is similar but not the same. And you don't know why this has happened, or even quite when. Suddenly, one day it is apparent to you that this has occurred, but quite when or how it happened is not clear. Imagine the questions that arise. Surely this change didn't just happen over night? But if it didn't happen suddenly, then why did you not know about it before? Have you been ill, or away whilst this transformation occurred? Has something also happened to time itself?

Nobody has told you that the world is changing and will be different from now on and yet everyone else is acting as if nothing has happened. At least they still appear comfortable with the world. So of course this means that you cannot discuss this with other people, because you don't know how they will react and what they might say and do to you. Time and space have suddenly, or perhaps gradually, become dislocated and fractured for you and the certainties that were once part of your life are no more. Sometimes it seems like you only have to reach out and touch the mirror and things will be restored. There are days when things are a little less strange and unpredictable and the opaqueness clears. There are other days when it is much worse and it seems like the fog surrounding you will never clear again and things will never be how they once were, when the world around you at least made sense in a way that sometimes seems like a distant memory for you now.

Being lost in time, and adrift in space is very frightening and unsettling. Sometimes it even seems unbearable. So, the world is completely uncertain and may be dangerous and you may need to defend yourself, even physically, to at least protect your being from further attack and uncertainty. And what happens if maybe those other people try and make you do something that you really do not want to do, or even fight back against a perceived threat from you? Do these people, once so close to you know what you are feeling? Can they really understand what it is like for you and are they to be trusted if you tell them what this is like for you and how it is getting worse over time? Is it safe to tell anyone? Can you really feel safe anymore? Who will protect you or how will you obtain protection and keep safe in future?

This chapter focuses on the issues of abuse, adult protection processes, risk and mental health difficulties. It begins with an experiential piece, as seen above, which was developed following discussions over a number of years with older people who were developing dementia-related illnesses and is a compilation of their views and experiences of difficulties, particularly in the earlier stages of their illnesses. It is followed by two case studies, again derived from social work practice, this time from experience of working with older people at risk of abuse and the strategies and interventions used with and for those individuals in their situations. Some of the issues raised by these cases are discussed before a few concluding comments are provided. The chapter ends with an outline of key points and some suggestions for further reading on the topic.

Case studies

The following case studies concerning abuse and older people with mental health problems are derived from social work practice over a number of years. The names of individuals have been altered in order to preserve anonymity.

1. A village milkman in a rural area hears an extreme amount of noise, a terrible argument coming from the cottage where an older couple live. The man is screaming at the woman, it is a strange, almost inhuman noise. It is 5am, in the middle of winter. The milkman is uncertain what to do. After all, it is very early and he does not really know the couple. But he is worried about what he has heard and so he contacts the local health centre as soon as it is open to express his concern and ask someone to provide some help.

The social worker who offers a liaison service to the primary care team is due to visit the health centre that day and is ideally placed to become involved. The doctor contacted the wife that morning following the milkman's report. Mrs Jones said that her husband had had a 'very bad night' but that he was sleeping at that point so she did not want a visit then. She agreed, however, to a visit by a social worker later to check how things were.

The GP suspects that Mr Jones, who is 78 years old, has arterial-sclerotic dementia. This has been developing for some years now, since he had a stroke. Although he made a good recovery physically from the stroke, his blood pressure is still rather high and there is a family history of heart disease in Mr Jones' family. Additionally, it would appear that his mental state has been deteriorating in recent months. Over the last year, his wife has noticed some changes in his personality and his memory appears to be getting worse. He has mood swings, is increasingly irritable and has become very verbally aggressive on several occasions resulting from minor disagreements with his wife and other members of the family. There has been little ongoing support from the primary care team, due to reluctance by the couple to accept this intervention.

The social worker is given this information in the referral she receives from the GP. She visits the couple in their isolated cottage. Mr Jones is still asleep, which allows for some initial discussion with Mrs Jones. Her world is in upheaval, and almost seems to be disintegrating. Her husband has been losing track of time and is now up for long periods at night; he is disturbed by flashbacks from his time as a soldier and at times is convinced he is on a battlefield in France once again. She has tried to settle him down, to get him to go to bed at night, to convince him that all is well and that he is imagining things. This is becoming increasingly difficult.

He has accused her recently of trying to poison him and last night he threatened to kill her. She does not want to lose her husband, her partner of almost 60 years, and yet she has already lost him. To allow him to sleep during the day at least means some respite for her from his demands and his unpredictability but may also make it more likely that he is up at night. Mrs Jones is uncertain about how to deal with this situation and more than a little afraid. If her husband were to be physically violent to her she is not sure how to respond. The couple's oldest son, who lives some distance away, has said that she should defend herself, if not retaliate, but using violence to deal with violence does not seem to be the answer, somehow. She is concerned about her husband's behaviour and its effects and she wants some help with this. Mrs Jones said that this type of situation has never occurred during their married life; he has changed from a loving and devoted father to an argumentative tyrant. Towards the end of the conversation with Mrs Jones, Mr Jones wakes up and comes downstairs. Mr Jones was uncertain about and a little mistrustful of the social worker when they met, but agreed that he had not been well in recent weeks and that his wife would benefit from some assistance with his care.

The social worker who visited the family held a number of discussions with the whole family as part of the assessment, whilst retaining a clear focus on Mr and Mrs Jones as a couple. She also involved the GP in a referral to a local psycho-geriatric assessment unit, which diagnosed Mr Jones as having multi-infarct dementia. Assistance by way of regular support from a community psychiatric nurse (CPN) was initially provided to the couple at home and Mr Jones began to attend a local day centre to provide him with some interests outside the home and some respite for his wife. An offer of future contact with the social worker should the need arise was maintained.

Over a period of time, Mr Jones' condition worsened. Disagreements with his wife again resurfaced and indeed became much more frequent and severe, largely focused on his personal hygiene, or lack of it. One day Mrs Jones lost her temper with her husband over his refusal to wash and they both became physically violent. Fortunately one of their daughters arrived and called for help before either was badly hurt.

The social worker visited quickly and re-assessed the situation. Although it was treated within a framework of elder abuse according to the local authority social services department (SSD) procedures, the situation was recognised as being complex and at crisis point. A punitive approach was not adopted; help was needed, not reprisals or removal. The social worker managed to obtain home care assistance, using specially trained home care assistants, to help Mrs Jones to care for her husband. The CPN changed her focus to trying to help the family reach more understanding about Mr. Jones' illness and assist with managing his behaviour.

Mr Jones remained living at home for several more months. He was admitted to a psychiatric ward for older people based in the district general hospital with a physical, heart related problem following a period when he had been disturbed, extremely disoriented and very aggressive both verbally and physically for a continuous period of some 10 days. Following the inpatient assessment, the multidisciplinary case conference, held in the hospital with Mrs Jones and her family present, recommended that Mr Jones should be admitted to a specialist nursing home. The social worker helped the family to find a place and to obtain help with funding. Mr Jones moved to the home and initially appeared to be settling in well; his family were able to visit often and were happy with the care provided. However, about three months after his admission, Mr Jones had a further stroke from which he never recovered consciousness. He died after several days in a coma.

2. Mavis was 85 years old when a family friend referred her to the local social services department. She lived with her carer, to whom she was not related. Mavis had been a housekeeper to a lady and her unmarried son, Bert, for many years. When the lady died, some 15 years previously, Mavis and Bert continued to share accommodation as they had done for some 30 years. Initially, Mavis continued to act as housekeeper for Bert, who was around 15 years younger than her. Over the past eight years, however, Mavis' health had deteriorated. She had developed severe arthritis, major hearing difficulties and Parkinson's disease. Dementia had also been developing, possibly worsened by a long history of excessive alcohol usage, which she shared with Bert. Bert had thus become Mavis's carer in the last few years; he appeared keen that Mavis should continue to share his accommodation. Mavis was at times fearful of Bert; at others she appeared to be very attached to him.

Following an assessment of need, services were introduced to try and alleviate Mavis' difficulties and to provide some assistance for Bert. However, over a period of months, the service providers involved in the situation developed strong suspicions that Mavis had been and was being abused by Bert: physical; sexual; psychological (verbal) and also very possibly financial abuse were all suspected at different times. Bert always denied acting abusively, although he was seen on occasion to handle Mavis physically in a very rough manner and also at times to verbally chastise her using strong and aggressive language. He claimed, however, that he cared deeply for and about Mavis. Equally, Mavis had not communicated to anyone that she had been subject to abuse from Bert, although at times she had said that she wished to live elsewhere. This was not a consistent statement from Mavis, however, and her statements varied over time. Communication with Mavis was extremely difficult to achieve and sustain given the level of her impairments. Despite concerns about abuse of Mavis, including strategy discussions and a case conference being held within the local adult protection procedures, it was not possible to prove that the situation was overtly harmful to her health and condition. Decisions to increase the amount of care and support received were therefore taken rather than action taken to remove Mavis from the situation.

Over a period of some months as Mavis's needs for care steadily increased, her informal support networks diminished, and more support from both statutory and voluntary agencies became necessary. The support network that developed included: domiciliary (including personal) care; day care for Mavis locally; regular visits by a district nurse; sitting services provided by the local Crossroads group (a voluntary organisation set up to provide support for carers); support for Bert from the local Age Concern project for carers; social work visits; the provision of regular respite care for Mavis in a local hospital for older people with mental health problems and also the provision of some support for Bert, as carer, by a community nurse based at the hospital. This situation continued until Bert was no longer able to care for Mavis at home, even with quite intensive support provided. At this point, Mavis was admitted to the local psycho-geriatric hospital and then to a privately run nursing home on a permanent basis. Mavis was resident in the nursing home for a relatively short period of several months before she died; during this time Bert continued to visit and was involved in her care and received support to do so. The risks to Mavis from the situation were managed by close monitoring by a number of individuals and agencies involved and regular communication between the service providers and social services in order to try and ensure that as far as possible, Mavis' needs and interests were met within the situation.

Issues raised

There are a number of issues that arise when considering this complex area concerning abuse and mental health difficulties in later life. The following aspects are important, although not exhaustive.

Identifying abuse

First, it can be difficult to recognise, or identify situations of abuse, especially if individuals are comparatively isolated or impaired, if external contact is limited and complex situations are involved. Individuals may have low or unclear expectations and may not be certain about what constitutes abuse or neglect or what could be done about a situation. This may mean that situations are either not detected, or not acted on quickly enough in some cases. In the situation with Mr Jones, although the milkman was not sure about what he had heard and whether it was a situation of abuse or not, he contacted the local health centre when it opened to report his concerns and did so appropriately (it's also worth remembering that in other situations, it could be a neighbour or another visitor to the house who notices the first signs that something is not right).

Although many people may think that the majority of abusive situations happen in institutions, it is more likely to occur in the person's own home, in community settings (if living with a relative, for example). As is known from situations relating to domestic violence of younger women, the perpetrator of abuse (or 'abuser') is likely to be known to the person who is abused. Alternatively, as with Mr Jones, it may be the person themself who acts abusively towards their carer or relative, probably due to perceptions arising because of their mental health condition.

In the second case study, the family friend referred Mavis to social services for assistance rather than specifically about abuse, but it was clear at the time of the initial visit by the social worker to the home that the situation was complex and that the relationship between Mavis and Bert was somewhat problematic and that there might be concerns relating to abuse within the situation. These concerns were realised over time although no formal action was ever taken in relation to Bert at any time and an approach was taken to try and offer support and reduce as much stress as possible for him in the absence of complaints from Mavis, rather than to take any more 'punitive' action.

Autonomy and self-determination

Second, in developing responses to such situations, issues of autonomy and self-determination often play a major part. Within situations where individual service users may lack mental capacity, some form of protection may be required, especially if the abuse is severe or potentially life threatening. Issues of consent by individuals to particular forms of intervention and treatment are particularly likely to be of importance here. However, best interests decisions also need to be taken and reviewed on a regular basis within the remit of the Mental Capacity Act and people assisted to take the decisions that they are able to whenever possible. Generally, individuals should consent to the interventions that are proposed; in cases where the person is not able to give informed consent, the principles underpinning the Mental Capacity Act must be used in relation to the decisions that are taken.

Legal interventions

Third, legal interventions in this sphere can be a sensitive and rather complex matter. In England and Wales there are several pieces of legislation that may be used to support and protect older people with mental health difficulties who experience abuse and/or neglect (Scotland and Northern Ireland have their own legislation, which is different to most of what is listed here). Although it is not possible to discuss these in detail here, there are provisions in the following areas:

- Mental Health Acts (1959, 1983, 1995, 2007)
- Sexual Offences Acts (1956, 1967, 1985, 2003)

- Family Law Act (1996) (Part IV: non-molestation and ouster orders)
- Protection from Harassment Act (1997) (protections from stalking and bullying)
- Care Standards Act (2000) (introduction of minimum care standards for services and the POVA list)
- Mental Capacity Act (2005) (which included a specific offence concerning ill-treatment and neglect and introduced Independent Mental Capacity Advocates to assist individuals)
- Safeguarding Vulnerable Groups Act (2006) (vetting procedures of people who work with children or vulnerable adults)

There is also government guidance concerning partnership, or multi-agency working in the area of adult protection/safeguarding adults. In England this is entitled *No Secrets* and in Wales, *In Safe Hands*. Both documents have been subject to a review process during the period 2008–2009.

In terms of possible interventions, it is necessary to consider carefully the extent of any harm that has resulted from the situation of abuse or neglect and to explore the relative risks and consequences that arise from acting or not acting within the situation. For example, Mr Jones was clear that he wished to remain living at home and his wife agreed with this view and was supported to care for her husband at least until a time when his behaviour was so disturbed that he could not be managed at home any longer. Likewise, Mavis continued to live at home and was supported to do so by a range of services until a point was reached where her needs could no longer be met at home and her carer (Bert) was no longer able to cope even with intensive support. At this point, Mavis was no longer to communicate her views about this and did not appear to be distressed by moving away from the home she had shared with Bert. When dealing with an individual who lacks decision-making capacity or where this fluctuates over time, issues of autonomy and who takes a key role in decision-making are likely to be central.

Other interventions and responses

The final issue relates more generally to interventions and responses in situations of abuse. There are, increasingly, resource constraints connected with service provision, and at times difficult choices have to be made concerning both service provision and what is likely to be most effective within situations. Whilst it is important to be realistic about the intervention used, it is essential to remember that this needs to be with the agreement (if not the full participation) of service users, their families and their caregivers. It may also be necessary to distinguish between practical and emotional forms of assistance and support and what might be most successful and acceptable within the situation. In both case scenarios, the individuals and their principal carers received practical support of various types; some of this was undoubtedly more costly than others (for example, the cost of specialised home care staff for Mr Jones, as compared to Crossroads provision or the local Age Concern carer's project for Mavis and Bert). However, in both situations, emotional support was provided by a variety of different individuals and interventions and this required co-ordination to ensure that it was appropriate and not duplicated. What is also apparent from these scenarios is that through the provision of support, the situations could be monitored in a number of different ways and it is likely that this resulted in a reduction in the number of abusive incidents that occurred. Even in Mr Jones' situation, where the presence of other people did not overtly reduce his capacity for aggressive outbursts, having other people present enabled management of these outbursts to be achieved. Moreover, if harsh choices have to be made between different types of intervention that may be used, it may not be possible to exactly tailor responses to need at all times. This may be particularly evident in situations where there are a number of individuals who have been abused and/or neglected, for example, in institutional settings or in situations where the needs of the individual and their carer/family are not congruent or are even in opposition to each other.

Concluding comments

Until now, there is no absolute evidence that the presence of mental health problems in later life, whether these are long-standing in nature or develop in old age, necessarily results in elder abuse. However, cognitive impairments related to mental health difficulties such as those caused by dementia, for example, are clearly an important factor in the development and perpetuation of a number of abusive situations. As is the case with other aspects of elder abuse and neglect, research has been somewhat limited in this area. A number of studies have been based on reports by caregivers, or professionals, are of limited types of abuse or somewhat non-specific mental health difficulties. There are others, which are not methodologically sound. As a body, such studies can hardly be considered to be conclusive. However, they do present findings, which need to be followed up by additional research in order to examine the issue more fully. Such research would also help to establish the validity of the earlier studies that have taken place and to assist in establishing more detail and understanding about the links between mental health problems in later life and situations of abuse and neglect.

Although the exact nature of the links between mental health and abuse and the degree of importance of such conditions within abusive situations are not yet clear, it appears that those individuals with dementia who become aggressive or violent may be at increased risk of abuse. As seen in the initial case study, this may well be within the context of a potentially mutually abusive relationship. The risk of abuse for individuals with dementia appears to be particularly high in the presence of other pre-disposing factors. A history of problematic relationship(s); of substance misuse or psychiatric illness on the part of the carer or of increased vulnerability of the individual, perhaps due to other health conditions seem to be of importance within this multi-factorial context. Although it has not yet been fully established by research, it is likely that these factors of aggression, long-term relationship difficulties and other vulnerabilities, including behaviours that are labelled as 'challenging', and an increased risk of abuse are also similar for other mental health conditions in later life. The research evidence that those individuals who abuse are more likely to have substance abuse, or a history of mental health problems, including personality disorders, is somewhat more convincing and substantial at present.

We do not yet know enough about elder abuse and neglect. More needs to be done to improve recognition of such situations and some of the causes; further research will surely assist in this. For practitioners dealing with such situations, professional and personal standards need to be acknowledged, explored and developed. Work to establish effective systems of public accountability, including developing clear lines of support for individuals and clear expectations of what is required needs to continue. In developing the care plan with the individual and other parties, practitioners need to consider the nature and extent of any cognitive impairment and the extent of decision-making capacity. Additionally, they must bear in mind aspects relating to any planning for safety or protection that might be necessary and the views and degrees of consent by individuals about this. This will also include determining the benefits and costs, financial and otherwise, of particular interventions to ameliorate situations.

Interventions need to be appropriate, and as far as possible, sensitively tailored to meet the needs of the individuals involved. They need to be monitored and reviewed to ensure that they remain appropriate and re-assessments of individuals and their carers should take place as necessary. Education and training must be provided in order to increase awareness, knowledge and understanding about abuse and also about mental health difficulties and, if required, the conjunction between the two areas. This will then act as the framework from which appropriate responses can be developed. To act as the springboard for this, we need more research into this whole area to improve our knowledge and understanding of abuse and neglect and crucially, the extent of the linkage of these to dementia and other mental health problems that occur in later life. Much work in this area is needed in coming years in order to address these most pervasive of problems. The evident commitment to achieving this is not questioned, but energy is needed to translate the commitment into action.

Key points

■ Elder abuse should be the concern of all practitioners who work with older people and their caregivers, including those specialising in the mental health of older people.

■ Mental health practitioners should know about risk factors for abuse and potential factors in causation of and intervention in abusive situations.

■ If there is a history of long-term difficult relationships between individuals, awareness of the possibility of abuse should be raised for and by the practitioner and the practitioner should bear this in mind and ask further questions and/or monitor the situation more closely for possible indicators of abuse and/or neglect.

■ Likewise, if there is a history of psychiatric or substance misuse problems for individuals, particularly for those who are providing care, the practitioner should also be aware of a possibility of abuse, bear this in mind and ask further questions and/or monitor the situation more closely for possible indicators of abuse and/or neglect.

■ In situations of long-term involvement in and care for people with illnesses such as dementia, which may include violent or aggressive behaviour towards caregivers, there should be a raised awareness of the possibility of abuse occurring. This may be mutual, or two-way abuse or it may occur in the context of provocation or retaliation by the individual with cognitive impairment and/or mental health problem. The practitioner should bear this in mind and ask further questions and/or monitor the situation more closely for possible indicators of abuse and/or neglect.

■ Practitioners should know about their local policies and procedures concerning elder abuse (or safeguarding adults) and how to act on them. They should know what to do if they come across situations of abuse within their practice, whom they should report abuse or suspicions of abuse and/or neglect to. They should also be aware of what processes need to be followed to ensure that any needs for safeguarding of the service user are considered as appropriate.

Suggested further reading

Bennett G & Kingston P (1993) *Elder Abuse: Concepts, theories and interventions*. London: Chapman & Hall.

Browne K & Herbert M (1997) *Preventing Family Violence*. Chichester: John Wiley & sons. (chapter on elder abuse)

Department of Health (2000) *No Secrets: The protection of vulnerable adults guidance on the development and implementation of multi-agency policies and procedures*. London: Department of Health.

Penhale B, Parker J & Kingston P (2000) *Elder Abuse: Approaches to working with violence*. Birmingham: Venture Press.

Penhale B & Parker J (2008) *Working with Vulnerable Adults*. London: Routledge.

Pritchard J (1999) (Ed) *Elder Abuse Work: Best practice in Britain and Canada*. London: Jessica Kingsley Publishers.

Chapter 17

Mental health, palliative care for older people and end of life care

Adrian Treloar, Aparna Prasanna and Kapila Ranasinghe

This chapter examines issues involved in the care and treatment for older people with mental health conditions requiring palliative and end of life care. It will cover the following areas:

- mental illnesses requiring palliative and end of life care
- principles of palliative care
- current provision for people dying with dementia
- identifying when palliative care is appropriate for dementia
- key symptoms and problems in palliative care of dementia
- key challenges
- solutions
- good end of life care
- practice examples
- conclusion.

Mental illnesses requiring palliative and end of life care

Dementia as a terminal illnesses

Dementia is a progressive condition with a variety of causes and types. Dementia is associated with progressive loss of brain cells, connections between brain cells and brain tissue. People have often thought that while it causes mental problems it does not cause death. Indeed, it is relatively rare for those who die with dementias to be certified as dying from dementia (NCPC & Alzheimer's Society, 2006). But in fact, patients with dementia have a life expectancy of about 4.5 years from diagnosis (Xie et al, 2008). What happens in dementia is that the progressive loss of mental ability leads to a progressive under-use of physical abilities with consequent decay of those physical functions. In addition, the increasing disability leads to an increase in infections, vascular events, falls etc. Then, finally, an increasing inability to communicate leads to a reduced frequency of treatment, which is provided later as a result of the illness itself. As a result, people with dementia will have more frequent chest infections, strokes, heart attacks, falls and fractures. For each one of these conditions, care will often be slower and less effective, with the result that most people with dementia die, in the context of their advancing illness from those conditions. It is very often the case that the same conditions in someone without dementia do not lead to death and so dementia is very much the cause of death in such circumstances.

It should also be noted that all of the medical conditions described above will often lead to a delirium, and accumulating evidence suggests that delirium does not often fully resolve in those who have a pre-existing dementia (Treloar, 1998). Or in other words, when a person with dementia is treated for a broken hip, there will often be a worsening of that dementia as a result of the trauma of the broken hip and its repair.

For those who do not succumb to such illness, dementia progresses and, in the end, causes death as a result of inability to eat, epileptic fits and the other features of very advanced dementia.

Terminal illness as multiple co-morbid illnesses

Put together, dementia is very clearly a condition that causes death, in its own right, but which does so by being associated with multiple co-morbidities (co-existing conditions), all of which cause frailty. This is important because, as we shall discuss below, the indicators for providing palliation to those with advanced dementia is both the suffering and distress caused by the dementia itself, as well as the likely effects and outcomes of treatments for those who are very physically frail.

Parkinson's disease and other diseases such as Huntingdon's chorea

Parkinson's disease is another illness for which it has become clear that palliative care is highly relevant. As a progressive neurological condition, which is closely associated with dementia, hallucinations and also depression, it too causes a similar combination of physical and mental frailty to that which is seen in dementia. In a joint clinic set up in Greenwich to meet the combined mental and physical health needs of those with advanced Parkinson's disease, it was found that 100% of patients had other major medical co-morbidities, and that 25% of a small sample of 12 patients had three major medical co-morbidities while 58% had two or more such co-morbidities. It is no surprise therefore, that Parkinson's disease has featured large among the neurological conditions for which palliative care is seen as a priority (NCPC, 2007).

In addition to dementia and Parkinson's disease, which are probably the commonest conditions that lead to a progressive loss of ability and brain function, other conditions also cause progressive mental disablement and death. Examples are Huntingdon's Chorea, as well as HIV (which produces an encephalopathy (brain inflammation or dysfunction), and also brain tumours, all of which present similar challenges.

Other mental illness and shortened life

Few people recognise that other mental illnesses such as schizophrenia and depression can also shorten life. In schizophrenia, as well as the excess mortality from suicide, life is also often shortened by obesity, diabetes, high levels of blood lipids (blood fats), as well as from smoking, and accidental death. As a result, the life expectancy of a 20 year old with schizophrenia is reduced by between 10–25 years (Brown et al, 2000; Newcomer & Hennekens, 2007). Depression too is associated with higher mortality in the elderly: just being depressed, being less active and losing weight all cause people to die sooner.

But while other mental illnesses may, at least in part be treated by good psychiatric care, good metabolic and medical care, and social care, dementia (and Parkinson's disease), by its very nature, is an illness that leads to progressive disablement and death. It is the very disease process that leads to a progressive loss of ability and brain function. For these reasons, and the prevalence of dementia among older people, this chapter will concentrate on issues involved in providing good palliative care for people with dementia.

Principles of palliative care as they apply to dementia

Upon its founding, the hospice and palliative care movement saw symptom control and the alleviation of distress as priorities, when cure was no longer possible. Founded and developed upon the experience of dying with cancer, the hospices recognised that when cure was no longer possible, care, dignity and quality of life are hugely important and the success of the hospice movement has been based upon its ability to apply that to individual patients and their families. Indeed, the transformation from suffering with an incurable illness to dying in comfort with one's family is so compelling that the voluntary sector was able to build huge parts of the hospice network in the UK.

Underlying the movement are some very clear ethical positions that fit well with the care of those who have terminal mental illness. Accepting natural death and affirming life are commonly quoted. In those with mental illness, especially those illnesses where the personality of the individual becomes shrouded from those who care for them by reason of the illness, it is crucial that carers can continue to see and reflect the worth of that individual in all the care that they provide.

Dame Cicely Saunders, who founded the hospice movement, based her work on a number of essential principles.

- The patient is a whole person, an interplay of physical, psychological, social and spiritual dimensions. These all have an effect in a single individual and interplay together. So doctors must recognise and respond to psychosocial and spiritual distress, and not just deal with physical disease.
- The family is the unit of care and the family and broader society become centred around the person.
- Symptoms and the process of adaptation to life-threatening illness can be analysed scientifically in the same way that any other illness can, to suggest effective ways of management (Richmond, 2005).

This view of palliative care as an interplay of two ecologies, one internal to the patient and the other comprising their relationships, is expressed, for example, in the concept of total pain. Cicely Saunders insisted that pain in advanced disease is the product of an interaction of physical, psychosocial and spiritual factors, and could only be adequately addressed if all these factors were understood and attended to. In mental health too, we see that while the individual experiences the illness, the solutions and best care also deal with the family and all those who are properly involved in the care of that individual. Even more so, this is the case in those who are dying for reasons connected to a mental illness.

'First do no harm' vs. the Hippocratic oath: justifying palliative treatments

An oft-quoted maxim for medicine is 'first do no harm'. While many think that this maxim came from Hippocrates it turns out that it was not really quoted until around the 18th century. In fact, Hippocrates did not say this and the maxim 'first do no harm' does not work very well in medicine. All treatments have side effects and some treatments are especially damaging. Chemotherapy is a good example of a treatment where, if harm was not done, the patient could not be treated. It demonstrates that, in fact, treatments that harm are legitimate and may be the only way to cure someone. The issue is the purpose of treatment – if the intent and purpose is to help and make better, then treatment is acceptable. If the primary intent is to harm or kill then it is not acceptable. This principle of double effect has, in the past, been used to justify the use of strong analgesics in cancer care. In fact, it turns out that in appropriate doses opiates do not shorten life (George & Regnard, 2007). But on the other hand, some medicines such as antipsychotics are clearly harmful and yet they may be appropriately used in dementia (as elsewhere in palliative care) to alleviate severe distress. Of course, key principles such as beneficence and non-maleficence as well as autonomy must be respected, although it seems that the central purpose for all this must be the alleviation of distress. The principle of double effect (ie. treatment will have side effects, as well as the effect it has on the illness or condition) allows some harm or side effects to achieve a very important purpose (Treloar & Crugel, 2009).

Hippocrates actually said: *'I will prescribe regimens for the good of my patients according to my ability and my judgment and never do harm to anyone'*. So we see that any treatment must be provided for the good of the patient and that if there is a risk of harm from side effects, that risk MUST be outweighed by the expected and intended benefit to the patient of the treatment. This, in a nutshell, encapsulates the concepts of double effect and burdensomeness.

Restorative treatments vs. treatments aimed at distress reduction

Early on in dementia the focus will be upon restorative treatments and treatments that might delay progression. This will include anti-dementia drugs as well as drugs such as blood pressure medicines, aspirin and statins (that lower cholesterol) and might delay the progression of some forms of dementia. In due course, it is hugely to be hoped that drugs that really can modify the progression of Alzheimer's disease will become available.

But as the disease progresses, and disability increases, the focus will move towards a more palliative approach. Given that dementia is an end of life condition that is distressing and disabling, treatments must:

1. limit care to that where the burden of treatment does not outweigh the benefit (Abbey, 2006)
2. aim to alleviate distress
3. see the patient as a whole and balance treatments against their effect upon that whole, rather than a single disease measure.

Severe distress in dementia – pain and mental pain

It is unquestionably the case that dementia can be very distressing for both patient and family. Dementia is frequently associated with psychosis and depression and also with behaviour disturbance. Sometimes the behaviour disturbance arises as a result of fear and poor understanding and sometimes also as an appropriate response to poor care. But often enough distress and agitation is caused by depression or psychosis. Problematically, later on in dementia, it is much harder to tell if someone is psychotic. The patients themselves become unable to report hallucinations or describe abnormal fears and beliefs and even in those who were psychotic earlier in the course of their illness, it may be impossible to tell now if they remain so. But on the other hand, we do know that antipsychotics are effective in dementia, that they reduce behaviour disturbance, and that they appear to reduce distress. But they are also overused (see section on over-use of antipsychotics on page 205).

A useful key to this is to apply the fundamental principles of palliative care. Pain is bad and should be alleviated in the most appropriate way. Physical pain should be alleviated with analgesics of sufficient strength, or by nerve blocks, operations etc. Mental pain is no less important than physical pain and must also be alleviated in the most appropriate way. This may well mean medication appropriately used despite the risks and side effects. Some mental pain is in fact existential or 'soul pain' and requires a proper approach of exploration, understanding and discussion. But if treatment is required, it should be discussed with the family/carers/advocates and agreement reached that the benefit of treatment outweighs the risks. This is discussed further with regard to the specific issue of antipsychotics. All pain requires an approach that understands the physical, psychological, social and spiritual dimensions as they apply to the individual being cared for.

Good practice must ensure that cause of distress is identified: physical pain is missed in dementia
There is good evidence that physical pain is often missed in dementia (Nygaard & Jarland, 2005). Those with dementia are less able to report pain and those who care for people with dementia fail to see distress as being a symptom of physical pain. This is unfortunate and in standard practice probably means that those who are in physical pain get treated with a sedative rather than an analgesic.

Current provision for those dying with dementia

Poor input from specialist palliative care but much more input from community mental health services
Few people who have dementia see a palliative care physician, and in the UK hospices care for, on average, less than one person per year with a primary diagnosis of dementia. It is well recognised that palliative care does not provide an extensive direct clinical service for people with dementia (Hughes *et al*, 2005). This may be because hospices have grown up around cancer care and there is a culture that that is what they do. Alternatively, hospices tend to have open doors and may struggle to cope with those who wander etc. Or perhaps the palliative care needs of those with dementia are not recognised as they ought to be. Or, just possibly, a lot of palliative work is already done by others. Whatever the reason, the *End of Life Care Strategy for England and Wales* (Department of Health, 2008b) recognises the importance of good palliative care for all at the end of life and that there are around 200,000 people in care homes with dementia.

For example, in the district of Greenwich in south east London, there are 15 hospice beds, alongside 900 residential and nursing care beds as well as 35 continuing care beds for elderly people with mental illness. The community mental health team is bigger in terms of doctor numbers and community nurse numbers than the palliative care service. This is a typical picture for the UK and it suggests that a lot of palliative treatments must be based within community mental health services. Hughes *et al*, (2005) suggested that continuing care units for dementia are, in fact, providing two functions. One is to manage and treat those with the most complex and challenging behaviours. The other is to provide palliative care for those with advanced dementia. It may well be that the two functions do not sit well together (dying with dementia alongside a very disturbed and distressed patient at an earlier stage of the illness does not sound ideal) but, in fact, there is good reason to believe that a lot of the care rightly provided by community mental health services is palliative.

Dementia care services do not see their work as palliative
But dementia care or community mental health services do not tend to see their work as palliative. Indeed, little mention of palliative care was made in the draft dementia strategy published in June 2008 (Department of Health, 2008a). If in fact, good palliative care was being provided by staff who did not know they were doing it, that might not matter. But it appears to us that by understanding the principles of palliative care better, the justification for treatment will be greatly improved along with the understanding by professional and family of why they are doing what they are doing. In my clinical

experience, discussing the need for treatment using a palliative model of understanding (especially when giving antipsychotic medicines) is a huge help in reaching agreement as well as avoiding complaints.

Identifying when palliative care is appropriate for dementia
Gold standards question

The Gold Standards Framework (2009) has been established to support better end of life care for a much larger population than that which is currently served by the hospice movement. The GSF aims to:

1. **identify** patients in need of palliative/supportive care towards the end of life
2. **assess their needs**, symptoms, preferences and any issues important to them
3. **plan** care around patients' needs and preferences and enable these to be fulfilled, in particular support patients to live and die where they choose.

In order to prompt better identification of those for whom end of life care is appropriate the GSF has a key question, called the 'surprise question': 'Would you be surprised if this patient were to die in the next 6–12 months?' It is an intuitive question integrating co-morbidity, social and other factors. Of course the trajectory for dementia is slower than other conditions (see **figure 1** for illness trajectories for people with progressive illness) (Murray *et al*, 2005). As a result, predicting death may be more difficult and it is often the case that clinicians will fail to spot and discuss the likelihood that someone will die in the next year.

But even if one could accurately predict the time of death in dementia (which we cannot do) there remains a very real question as to what palliative care is for. Is it there to manage the last days or weeks of life, or is its purpose to alleviate suffering in those who are dying of a terminal illness regardless of whether they are in the final days? Put another way, if someone is not suffering but dying, they may not want or need palliative care. But if they are suffering badly early on in an illness, palliative medicine may have much to offer. Perhaps the central reason for palliation, is a need to palliate.

The GSF also sets out prognostic indicator guidance for dementia and states that being:

- unable to walk without assistance
- urinary and faecal incontinence
- no consistently meaningful verbal communication
- unable to dress without assistance
- Barthel score < 3 (a standard score of physical disability)

plus any one of the following:

- ☐ 10% weight loss in previous six months without other causes, kidney infection (pyelonephritis), urine infection, or a blood protein (albumin) of 25 g/l or less
- ☐ pressure sores eg. stage III/IV, recurrent fevers, reduced oral intake/weight loss, or aspiration pneumonia

merit an assessment and consideration of end of life needs.

These criteria are very much based upon physical ability and do not address the mental health and mental distress needs of dementia and may also have problems. Being unable to dress is an early

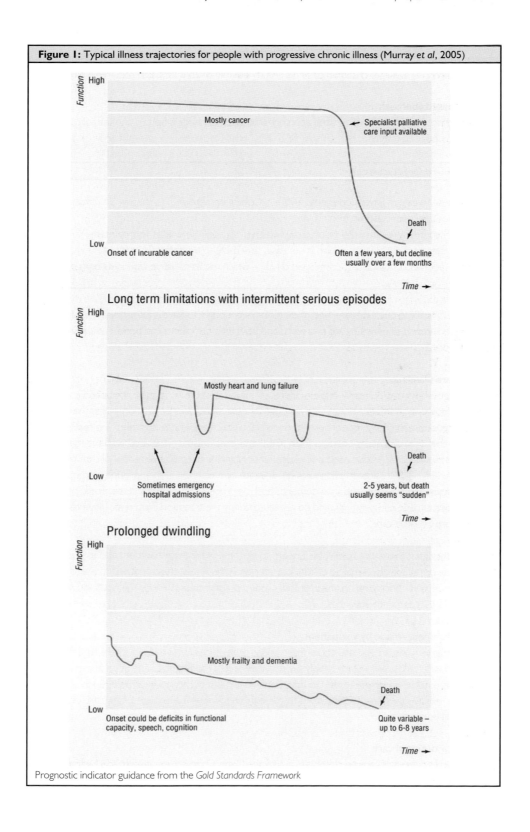

Figure 1: Typical illness trajectories for people with progressive chronic illness (Murray *et al*, 2005)

Mostly cancer

Specialist palliative care input available

Death

Onset of incurable cancer

Often a few years, but decline usually over a few months

Time →

Long term limitations with intermittent serious episodes

Mostly heart and lung failure

Death

Sometimes emergency hospital admissions

2-5 years, but death usually seems "sudden"

Time →

Prolonged dwindling

Mostly frailty and dementia

Death

Onset could be deficits in functional capacity, speech, cognition

Quite variable – up to 6-8 years

Time →

Prognostic indicator guidance from the *Gold Standards Framework* symptom and lacking all meaningful conversation is a late symptom. Moreover, urinary tract infection (UTI) is common at all stages of dementia and a serum albumin of 25 is rare and requires a blood test.

Criterion based approach

It may therefore be that a criterion-based approach that assesses needs is better, and the following criterion may be used instead.

Box 1: Criteria for palliative care

1. Does the patient have moderately severe or severe dementia?
2. Does the patient also have:
   a. severe distress (mental or physical), which is not easily amenable to treatment
   b. severe physical frailty, which is not easily amenable to treatment
   c. another condition (eg. co-morbid cancer), which merits palliative care in its own right?

If the answers to these questions are 'yes', then each patient ought to have a full assessment of need and a focused analysis of why they are distressed and how their symptoms can best be improved and distress reduced.

Advance care planning

When a diagnosis such as dementia is given, there will always be a desire to think about and consider the future. However, dementia brings with it a huge amount of fear and trepidation and in the context of this it is important to give an opportunity to discuss and allay fears where possible. The reality of dementia is that it is a distressing condition, but that the distress is usually managed with the right care, support and medications. As discussed elsewhere, understanding the palliative model of care may well help considerably. A discussion on prognosis and advance care planning is an appropriate component of any major assessment of someone with dementia and is a process that can start at diagnosis, particularly if the diagnosis is made early enough, and be repeated during the transition from restorative care towards more palliative care.

Early on in the illness there will, rightly, be a desire to treat the memory impairment and to work out ways to delay or reduce disease progression. But later on in the illness, treatment will move towards being more focused upon symptom control and a reduction of distress. Various methods allow the planning of care as dementia advances.

Advance statements made by the patient

Advance statements are an opportunity to make broad preferences known about future care and can be very useful. Most will, in fact, simply say that they accept the diagnosis and ask that sensible treatments are made, which are limited to the effect, benefit and burden of treatment. Such statements can be very useful as they enable the patient to guide those towards more appropriate care once capacity has been lost.

Preferred priorities of care

The preferred priorities of care protocols set out by the Marie Curie organisation (NHS National End of Life Care Programme, 2008) enable the person with any diagnosis to set out what their priorities are and where they would like to be cared for during their last illness. Of course, most choose home, but such statements are best to be advisory and not binding as it is hard to predict precisely what needs there will be and it may well be that nursing or residential care provides the best comfort and dignity of care. But these statements go beyond merely stating where to be cared for; they enable requests to be made as to what sort of care, spiritual support and visitors etc. are wanted and at which stage.

Illness contingency planning
Later on, it becomes feasible to think through what treatments are appropriate and what treatments are no longer appropriate (Department of Health, 2008b).

Many people will hope that hospital can be avoided at the end of life but because dying at home is an uncommon event, they may worry that this will not be possible. However, the acquisition of infections as well as the distress of admission via an emergency department all add up to make the stay at home, with GP input option preferable. Several questions can be usefully asked and discussed with carers and advocates that take into account the declining physical functions and increased risk of other illnesses, infections, falls and fractures associated with dementia (**box 2**). Some might feel that these questions do not specifically relate to dementia, but it is good to have some clear plans for all these eventualities, if unnecessary admission to hospital is to be avoided. Of course, some common things occurring towards the end of a dementia illness (such as a broken hip) will almost always still need admission and repair – repair being the best method of alleviating distress. In a sense, this demonstrates that any plan that simply says 'no' to all possible treatments at that stage in dementia may be inappropriate. If the person with dementia lacks mental capacity, the care and treatment must be in the person's best interests, in accordance with the Mental Capacity Act (2005) for England and Wales. If the person lacks any family or friends these questions must be discussed with an independent mental capacity advocate (IMCA) if it is deemed to be 'serious medical treatment', in accordance with the Mental Capacity Act (2005).

Box 2: Essential questions to help decide the most appropriate place of death

- Is cardiopulmonary resuscitation, ventilation or intensive care medicine appropriate?
- Would treatments with severe side effects be appropriate?
- Would complex surgical procedures (such as a major abdominal operation) be appropriate?
- Would hospital admission be appropriate for injuries such as fractures (generally 'yes')?
- Would hospital admission be appropriate for illness such as chest infections?
- If dehydration occurs and is causing the patient to suffer then would hospital admission be appropriate to treat?
- When dying is imminent and the patient is distressed we would expect that medication will be given to alleviate the distress that may occur during death.

Advance decisions to refuse treatment
Advance decisions to refuse treatment are legally binding in England, Wales and Scotland, but must be specific and valid. They offer the advantage of enabling those who lose mental capacity to continue to exercise control over their care after that capacity is lost. However, they also carry some risks and a binding decision may have unanticipated effects. They also suffer from the difficulty that some people who are ill may not make the same choices as when they are healthy. For example, some of the fears of dementia might lead someone to refuse care when in fact, once they have severe dementia they

can continue to enjoy a quality of life and ability to interact with others that they had not anticipated. It is for this reason that the Mental Capacity Act in England and Wales sets out stringent tests for validity so that an advanced refusal that is causing difficulties and is not specific to the treatment being offered can be rebutted and good care provided. A common scenario is an advance refusal for anything other than home-based care usually stated as 'never put me in a nursing home'. Although perhaps not strictly a medical treatment, this refusal must be weighed up at a time when nursing care is needed. If in fact, home care can be provided then the statement ought to strongly encourage that to happen. But if the patient will suffer alone at home and enjoy a better quality of life in a home, then the conclusion would be that a circumstance unanticipated by the patient has arisen and that therefore the statement is not valid. However, going against such statements ought never to be done lightly. A fuller discussion of the benefits, risks and way of dealing with advance statements and advance decisions to refuse treatment has been published by the Department of Health (2008c).

Lasting Powers of Attorney

The Mental Capacity Act in England and Wales and Adults with Incapacity Act in Scotland also allow the creation of powers whereby a person can appoint someone to manage their finances or health care decisions should they lose mental capacity to make decisions about these matters. In England and Wales these are known as Lasting Powers of Attorney (LPAs) and the person who is appointed to make decisions is the 'attorney' (in Scotland they are known as health care proxies) This generally works well and is a help, enabling complex decisions such as selling a house, spending money on care or consenting to treatment. Sometimes, of course, the attorney does not act in the best interests of the person who lacks capacity and financial abuse is not uncommon in those who manage finances on behalf of those with incapacity. Discussing the previous system of Enduring Powers of Attorney (that existed before the Mental Capacity Act) it was suggested to the House of Lords by Denzil Lush, the Master of the Court of Protection, that there was financial abuse in about one in eight existing Enduring Powers of Attorney (Hansard, 2005). However, there is currently some anxiety that the creation of LPAs is more complex and expensive. The documents as drafted, one for personal welfare and one for property and financial affairs are longer (25 pages vs. four pages for the EPA) and more complex than the EPA that people have been familiar with. The forms are subject to review at the time of writing (Ministry of Justice, 2008). So while these are very helpful and useful powers, care must also be exercised to protect the individual.

Key symptoms and problems in palliative care of dementia
Psychosocial

Poor care is a central and common issue in dementia care. There is a widespread and shocking history of poor training and poor conditions in nursing and residential care, and people with dementia are vulnerable and have difficulty in protecting themselves from such problems. Anyone who is abused will be distressed and may also try and fight back. If someone's resistance to inappropriate care is seen as symptoms of an illness and treated with medication, that is a tragic completion of a cycle of abuse. Thus we ought to insist upon the highest standards of care and quality care with regular inspections. The most widely used quality improvement tool is dementia care mapping (Bradford Dementia Group, 2009). Dementia care mapping (DCM) is a method designed to evaluate quality of care from the perspective of the person with dementia. It is used in formal care settings such as hospitals, care homes and day care. It is based on the philosophy of person-centred care, which promotes a holistic approach that upholds the personhood of the person with dementia. This has led to in-depth analyses and quality improvements in many settings. The central principle of patient-centred care stands out as a right and good concept that should drive all that we do for dementia. It is also a bulwark against the tendency of institutions to manage people in a way that will keep them quiet and make life easier for care staff.

Poor communication and understanding

Poor communication can be with both patient and also family or advocates. Advanced communication courses are a part of basic training for palliative care and the best communication skills are needed for dementia care. The distress of seeing a loved one deteriorate and die can be huge, and the fears and poor understanding of what is happening must be alleviated by professionals caring for the patients. More importantly still, good communication with a severely cognitively impaired individual is also required. If something is refused once, a different approach or a repeated approach may make it achievable – a low-key, gentle approach is almost always best.

On the other hand, sometimes things need to be done in the best interests of the patients, such as a bath or a dressing changed. The care needs to be provided, as otherwise the patient will suffer. This is discussed later under restraint and mental incapacity.

Sharing hospital letters with patients or key carers about patients with dementia has been shown to improve communication and also outcomes, in terms of carers understanding of the care plan for individual patients (Treloar & Adamis, 2005). We would recommend that whenever a letter is written about a patient with dementia, or treatment started or stopped (such as psychotropic or physical medicines) then next of kin or appropriate person is copied into a letter so that they know what is happening and can question it if they are concerned. We think that this significantly reduces the frequency of complaints. Very rarely, someone in early dementia will not want others to know and of course, in that circumstance confidentiality must be respected. Generally, by having a quick and routine discussion, agreement is reached easily as to who should be given the copy letter and information on care etc.

Isolation and boredom

Activities, visits and continuing the practice of faith or hobbies is a really important part of dignified and good dementia care. Many will report those who were artists or musicians still being able to paint or enjoy music at a late stage. Those who were frequent churchgoers may also show a real understanding of a church service at a late stage of the illness. Indeed the short moments when carers see the person's personality, smile or attitude coming through are hugely appreciated when they occur.

Specialist activities and activities accessible to those with dementia, including snoezellen techniques are therefore very important parts of the best dementia care. Snoezellen techniques are methods of providing simple multi-sensory stimuli that are interesting, understandable and comforting to patients. Many report success with the technique (Staal et al, 2007), though some have found them less helpful.

Hunger

All of us get pain and discomfort if we have not eaten for more than 12 hours and it is likely that starvation in dementia is a similarly unpleasant experience. People with dementia do lose weight naturally, and it is important not to end up force-feeding people. Such extreme efforts may be very distressing and of very little worth. But well presented food offered regularly, works well and sometimes patients will refuse to eat for a day or two and then eat well.

Spiritual issues

While prayer and religious observance are important, spiritual issues go a long way beyond this and must include the care of the patient and family in terms of saying goodbye etc. A recent example from our own professional practice involved a lady, dying with advanced dementia at home, who looked at her daughter and said 'God bless you' just minutes before she finally died. Another lady who had barely spoken for days, made a sign of the cross as prayers were said around her bed on the night she finally died. Similarly, hospices will often tell of the pain and distress being reduced when something that is a central concern to the patient (such as perhaps the pet dog, cat or an heirloom) is sorted out – interventions that may not seem important and relevant to doctors or nurses but which in fact go to the heart of our humanity.

Physical pain

Treating physical pain is very important. Elderly patients with dementia in pain are under-assessed and under-treated (Martin et al, 2005; Warden et al, 2003). Prevalence in US nursing home residents with physical pain is said to range from between 26–83% (Warden et al, 2003). Pain is not reported by the elderly who are cognitively intact as it is often attributed to 'natural ageing' and those with dementia are often unable to express their pain (Herr & Mobily, 1991). However, studies have demonstrated that patients with a diagnosis of dementia are less likely to receive analgesia (pain relief) compared to those without this diagnosis (Nygaard & Jarland, 2005). Also, patients with Alzheimer's dementia might experience a decrease in pain or might experience it differently compared to other types of dementia (Scherder et al, 2005). Untreated and unrecognised pain can manifest itself in other forms of distress such as aggression, vocalisations, insomnia and depression. It can thus increase disability and impact on quality of life (Herr & Mobily, 1991). The overwhelming evidence suggests that more training for carers and staff is necessary to improve their skills in recognising pain in dementia (Nygaard & Jarland, 2005; Martin et al, 2005).

Treatment of physical pain will include using simple analgesics, followed by codeine and then, if need be, opiates. Opiates given in patches that are placed upon the skin (patch formulations) can be very helpful. Analgesia does help agitation. Manfredi et al (2003) demonstrated that patients respond to long acting low dose opiates. This was a small study undertaken in the older (> 85 years) population, who had been previously unresponsive to antipsychotics. 20mg total dose of long-acting morphine (a low dose) was associated with reduction in agitation without sedation. Morphine is often considered the drug of choice as unlike non-steroidal anti-inflammatory drugs (NSAIDs) the dose can be increased further if it does not work enough. With NSAIDs there is a ceiling effect and the maximum dose may not end up working. Opiates are also good as they relieve all kinds of pain (Portenoy & Coyle, 1991). It must be borne in mind, however, that elderly patients are more sensitive to opiates and so lower doses may be needed (Kaiko, 1980, British National Formulary, 2009).

Mental pain

No less real or important than physical pain is mental pain and this must be assessed and minimised. One challenge of dementia is that mental pain especially fluctuates during the day and severe distress in the early morning or evening may then lead to periods of calm and much better quality life. When this is so, it may well be right to allow the distress to occur, with carer support etc. so that medication does not worsen the better times of the day. This, therefore, requires ongoing discussion and agreement with carers. Non-pharmacological responses to pain are also important, though as with physical pain, mental pain is not usually solely treated by non-pharmacological techniques.

Depression

Depression is a distressing experience. Depression is common in dementia and the treatments (newer or SSRI antidepressants) well tolerated with few side effects. They also appear to work. So it is worth having a low threshold for treating depression in dementia – if in doubt, treat. If 20mg of fluoxetine or citalopram does not work, and/or there is agitation, a more sedative antidepressant such as mirtazapine might be a good idea. There are few good reasons to stop an antidepressant in someone who is settled but suffering from dementia. Good palliative care demands that depression is treated (Lawrie & Edwards, 2006).

Psychosis

When psychosis is present this needs treatment and the treatment of choice is an antipsychotic. Antipsychotics have risks of stroke, falls, worsened confusion and death, and so the benefit (distress reduction) must be enough to justify the risk. However, conversely, to leave psychosis untreated with resulting ongoing mental pain and torment seems unethical in advanced dementia. It is important to use the minimum dose and review, stopping if possible. Given the difficulties associated with antipsychotics, merely being on an antipsychotic is probably a good reason why those with dementia ought to remain under specialist review.

Anxiety

Non-pharmacological measures such as anxiety management techniques (suitably modified), meditation and the use of touch (Kim, 1998) are first choice techniques. Medications can also be tried, though the frequency of use of benzodiazepines and other sedatives in dementia is probably best kept low. Benzodiazepines are sedating and increase the risk of falls. Newer antidepressants have fewer side effects and are of some efficacy.

Key challenges and solutions

Poor pain identification

Pain is a key issue and needs to be identified. Various scales have been used to identify pain and it is interesting that, in severe dementia both physical pain and mental pain are likely to be difficult to distinguish. Symptoms such as those listed in **box 3** may result from either physical or mental pain. But the imperative of not missing physical pain is heightened by the evidence presented that it is too often missed. Scales to identify pain have been developed (Regnard *et al*, 2007).

Box 3: Symptoms of distress may reflect physical or mental pain

- Anger/frustration
- Aggression/agitation
- Fear/anxiety
- Tearfulness/misery
- Pain when still
- Discomfort on moving
- Restlessness

Overuse of antipsychotics

The ongoing overuse of antipsychotic medicines in dementia has been a scandal with deep concern that those with dementia are merely sedated to keep them quiet. These concerns have led to parliamentary questions and enquiries (All Party Parliamentary Group on Dementia, 2008). The most recent enquiry strongly criticised the widespread tendency to prescribe antipsychotics for dementia and pointed out the harmful side effects that accrue from doing this. These include an increased risk of stroke, falls, confusion and also death. But the group also found that 'in specific circumstances the use of antipsychotic drugs can be appropriate. The Group recommends that the use of antipsychotics should always be a last resort, used at times of severe distress or for critical need. This fits well with the principles of palliative care set out above. If there is severe distress and that distress can be alleviated by using such medicines, then it may be right and proper to do so, notwithstanding the risks that come with the therapeutic benefit. The key in such circumstances is to have a clear discussion with the patient's advocate/next of kin to explain both the purpose of the treatment and the risks. Then an agreement can be reached as to whether or not to proceed with treatment.

Case study 1

John is 87 and in a nursing home. He has severe dementia and is agitated and distressed. Earlier on in his illness he was paranoid, thinking that his neighbours were trying to evict him and hallucinated, seeing people in the back garden who were not there. At that time he responded to a low dose of antipsychotic medication. Now, it is not possible to tell if he is psychotic, though he does seem fearful of staff and is very distressed, calling out for help. His antipsychotic medicine was stopped a few months ago while in hospital with a fractured hip as he was mobilising poorly. Now he is bed bound and frail. There does not appear to be a cause of physical pain.

His doctor feels that a small dose of antipsychotic medicine may be the best treatment and discusses the purpose and the risks with his wife and daughter. It is agreed that the distress is such that the risks must be accepted.

Review at two weeks shows a significant reduction in distress and the treatment is continued.

Covert medication – the need for a clear ethical framework

Another controversial issue is the administration of medicines within foodstuffs. Of course better trained staff, more person-centred care, good communication and better designed facilities etc. may reduce the need for such measures, which should only be a last resort. However, for those who lack capacity and will suffer harm otherwise, such practices may represent the least restrictive and best way to provide for either a restoration of health or a reduction of suffering. The majority of professionals conclude that, in exceptional circumstances such actions are appropriate and should be carried out as well as be recorded etc. Where covert medication is used, it is a form of restraint and would need, therefore, in England and Wales, to be justified under Sections 4–6 of the Mental Capacity Act as being in the person's best interests and a proportionate response to the prevention of harm (which can includes distress) in the patient (though the additional Deprivation of Liberty Safeguards might need to be invoked if medication is being used to detain someone lacking capacity in a hospital or care home because detention is deemed to be in their best interests). A further discussion as well as a policy statement from the Royal College of Psychiatrists will offer the reader more food for thought (Treloar, Philpot & Beats, 2001; Treloar, Beck & Paton, 2001; Royal College of Psychiatrists, 2004).

Case study 2

Jean is a 75-year-old woman with severe dementia and paranoia. She is very distressed – wandering the streets at night to avoid her 'persecutors'. Extensive efforts to find social and supportive solutions have been tried and failed. If her psychosis persists she will have to leave home and go into care. She has always refused to take medicines, despite best efforts to persuade her. Her daughter now visits each day and puts medication in her sandwiches. With the treatment she remains at home and has an improved quality of life.

Neglect and under-treatment of those who resist

The Mental Capacity Act (2005) set out for England and Wales the criteria by which those who lack mental capacity can be treated without their consent. Almost all those dying with advanced dementia lack capacity for the health care choices needed for them and are thus subject to this legislation (or the similar legislation that applies to their jurisdiction if they live in Scotland or Northern Ireland). Often enough, those with dementia merely accept the care they are offered and do not resist. In such cases, care must be taken to avoid abuse or over treatment.

At times, however, patients do resist the care offered. Patients will tell carers to leave, will refuse to be dressed or wash or they may refuse wound care etc. In normal circumstances, if a patient refuses such care their refusal must be respected. But in dementia, refusal may merely be due to the inability to understand the need for treatment.

In the **case study 3**, the right course of action is to use Sections 4–6 of the Mental Capacity Act (best interests, and acts in connection with care and treatment). This lady requires treatment to be imposed upon her or she will suffer harm. With treatment her comfort and dignity can be restored, while without it she will suffer neglect. The Act allows restraint to be used when providing care or treatment to a person who lacks capacity providing that it is proportionate to the risk of harm that the person would experience if the treatment was not provided.

Case study 3

A severely demented lady has leg ulcers which are becoming infected. She refuses any care to them and lacks mental capacity to make decisions about treatment, pushes away staff and hits them, says that what they are doing hurts. If you do not treat them, they are likely to become infected, she will be in severe pain, and although she may not die, she may need amputation, or may become much more confused and more distressed.

Do you:

■ allow her choice and do nothing?

■ treat the ulcers, using sedative medication if necessary?

Good end of life care

At home

The idea of looking after people at home with dementia until they die is a relatively new concept that has arisen from the demand of carers to provide a better standard of care and quality of life for those with dementia. Dementia is an illness where the likelihood of dying at home is especially low, and this is probably due to a number of factors.

■ Dementia is a complex condition that presents multiple challenges and the period of wandering and agitation that is common in dementia often leads to an irreversible move towards institutional care even when this might not be a necessary permanent need.

■ Services that provide care for those with dementia may develop an institutional belief that home care is not possible and thus recommend that people are placed in institutional care even when the family may want them to stay at home.

■ The skills equipment and support needed to care for advanced dementia at home are poorly understood by district nurses, GPs or specialist dementia services.

Providing the best care for dementia requires the following.

1. An understanding of how to provide equipment and support for those with advanced physical disability at home. Modern equipment, which has become much less expensive than hitherto, enables a hospital bed, pressure relieving mattress, hoists and toileting and washing equipment to be provided in the home, thus enabling the needs of those who are dying to be met. While hospices have become adept at doing this for those who have cancer, services for those with dementia need to import and use this knowledge from hospice at home services. The most useful equipment rated by our carers were incontinence equipment, hospital beds and hoists.

2. Good quality carers who are reliable and understand the issues of dementia and have good communication skills with both patient and relatives so that care can be provided even when there may be resistance and rejection. Adequate funding – this ought not to be a problem. The Hope for Home project demonstrated that it almost always saved money over the cost of residential or nursing care (National Audit Office, 2007). In the UK, the increasing use of NHS continuing care ought to provide a stimulus to such care, provided that funding can be adapted to meet need.

3. Adaptable care packages and adaptable carers are essential. Simply providing care that requires one particular task to be done is inadequate. It is not enough to visit to toilet a patient and then go if that is done. Carers need to meet needs at the time and to be able to vary what they do according to the variation in mental and physical state of the patient.

4. Ongoing specialist advice from dementia care is needed as the behaviour, disturbance and distress continue to be modifiable and require modification right through until death. As with conventional hospice care, we do not stop visiting just because someone is about to die. The converse is required.

5. Ongoing use of antipsychotic medication and analgesia. In our study (Treloar & Crugel, 2009) carefully titrated and reviewed antipsychotic medicines were the most valuable medicines according to carers.

6. For a fuller description of the Hope for Home service in Greenwich see below and Treloar *et al* (2009).

In care homes

Good dementia care in care homes requires that the best staff, with the best training on offer to them, are provided. Markers of better homes include stable staff group, the presence of a clear activities programme with an activities co-ordinator and also good inspection reports from statutory authorities (such as the former Commission for Social Care Inspection or the former Health Care Commission – that were merged into one, together with the Mental Health Act Commission, and relaunched as the Care Quality Commission in April 2009). An open management team who are willing to hear and deal with criticisms is very important as is the nature of ongoing medical support. It is not really enough to have a visiting GP who deals with coughs, colds and chest infections. Residents of care homes require ongoing review and adjustment of medicine as well as advance care planning (ACP). It is very sensible to discuss the possibility of trying to avoid hospital admission around the time of death and to decide what treatments are a good idea and which ones are less useful. ACP as described earlier in this chapter is feasible and advisable.

Given their harmful effects and the fact that the requirement for them may cease, antipsychotics should be subject to ongoing review and attempts to titrate the dose downwards and stop, with the proviso that the rationale for their use is distress reduction and if distress increases as a result of stopping them they ought to be continued. In consultation, some relatives will so fear the recurrence of distress that they ask that the antipsychotics are not stopped. This is a very reasonable thing to agree to.

Good practice examples

- The Croydon project delivered by St. Christopher's Hospice dementia project has been set up and takes referrals from primary care and nursing homes to provide advanced dementia with a specialist palliative care model. The project is successful and has identified some differences from conventional palliative care but huge similarities (Scott & Pace, 2009).

- The Disability Distress Assessment Tool (DisDAT) (Regnard et al, 2007) has been developed for use in learning disability and also evaluated for use in Alzheimer's dementia. Having identified a symptom or sign of distress, it monitors this sign and thus helps inform management.

- The Hope for Home project has developed specialist care at home for those with dementia, which aims to keep them at home until death. Of the first 50 cases, 30 died at home or very shortly after leaving home and the project has produced a wealth of information to improve the understanding of how this can be done. Carer feedback has been very positive and some carers have even set up a charity to promote this style of work (Hope for Home, www.hopeforhome.org.uk).

- The Lewisham and Southwark care homes team has provided dedicated specialist input to care homes from both geriatric and old age psychiatric care disciplines. The team focuses on providing reviews of care rather than merely approving funding streams and has been seen as a pioneer in terms of quality care in homes.

- The Joint Parkinson's Clinic in Greenwich is a joint venture shared by specialist neurology and community old age psychiatry, which has managed the most complex and advanced cases of Parkinson's disease. It had been observed that the majority of such patients are discharged from neurology when they become so frail that they cannot easily attend clinic, but that the need for ongoing specialist advice remains high. As the incidence of mental disability rises with disease progression to death, the team has been highly evaluated by carers for the work that it has done. For further information and a description of the service email (Kapila_ranasinghe@hotmail.com or Adrian.treloar@oxleas.nhs.uk).

■ The Supportive Care Pathway (www.birminghampalliativecare.com) (SCP) is a care pathway for patients admitted to hospital who have advanced life limiting illness. It has been developed to improve care for people moving towards the end of their life and to ensure that they have a comfortable and dignified death. Several groups of people have been identified who would benefit from a palliative approach to their care – those with advanced life limiting illnesses, those with advanced organ system failure, such as heart failure, those with advanced dementia and those who are extremely frail and debilitated (Main *et al*, 2006).

■ The Liverpool Care Pathway aims to guide and improve care during the last 72 hours of life (Marie Curie Palliative Care Institute, 2008). Designed initially for use in cancer patients it has been introduced more widely. But it has not yet been researched in dementia and difficulties around the diagnosis of dying as well as other issues give some cause for concern (Treloar, 2008).

Conclusion

Palliative care is a central concept in advanced dementia and in other neurological conditions that cause death. Most palliative treatments and decisions about the limitation of treatment will be made by those who are not working in specialist palliative care. Indeed, there is good reason to think that dementia services already provide a large amount of palliative care and that enabling them to better understand that this is what they do would provide significant quality improvements in the care of dementia.

Acknowledgements
With thanks to Lucy Sutton for comments upon earlier drafts of this chapter.

References
Abbey J (2006) *Palliative Care and Dementia. Discussion paper 7* [online]. Alzheimer's Australia. Available at: http://www.alzheimers.org.au/upload/PalliativeCare.pdf (accessed June 2009).

All Party Parliamentary Group on Dementia (2008) *Always a Last Resort. Inquiry into the prescription of antipsychotic drugs to people with dementia living in care homes* [online]. London: The Stationery Office. Available at: http://www.alzheimers.org.uk/downloads/ALZ_Society_APPG.pdf (accessed June 2009).

Bradford Dementia Group (2009) *Dementia Care Mapping* [online]. Available at: http://www.brad.ac.uk/health/dementia/dcm/ (accessed June 2009).

British National Formulary (2009) [online]. Available at: bnf.org.uk (accessed June 2009).

Brown S, Barraclough B & Inskip H (2000) Causes of the excess mortality of schizophrenia. *British Journal of Psychiatry* **177** 212–217.

Department of Health (2008a) *Transforming the Quality of Dementia Care: Consultation on National Dementia Strategy* [online]. London: Department of Health. Available at: http://www.dh.gov.uk/en/Consultations/Liveconsultations/DH_085570 (accessed June 2008).

Department of Health (2008b) *End of Life Care Strategy – Promoting high quality care for all adults at the end of life* [online]. London: Department of Health. Available at: http://www.dh.gov.uk/en/Publicationsandstatistics/Publications/PublicationsPolicyAndGuidance/DH_086277 (accessed June 2009).

Department of Health (2008c) *Advanced Decisions to Refuse Treatment: A guide for professionals*. London: Department of Health.

George R & Regnard C (2007) Lethal opioids or dangerous prescribers? *Palliative Medicine* **21** 77–80.

Gold Standards Framework (2009) Available at: http://www.goldstandardsframework.nhs.uk/ (accessed June 2009).

Herr KA & Mobily PR (1991) Complexities of pain assessment in the elderly. Clinical considerations. *Journal of Gerontological Nursing* **17** (4) 12–19.

Hansard (2005) Lord Christopher, *Parliamentary business* [online]. Available at: http://www.publications.parliament. uk/pa/ld200405/ldhansrd/vo050110/text/50110-15.htm (accessed June 2009).

Hughes JC, Robinson L & Volicer L (2005) Specialist palliative care in dementia. Specialised units with outreach and liaison are needed. *British Medical Journal* **330** 57–58.

Kaiko RF (1980) Age and morphine analgesia in cancer patients with post-operative pain. *Clinical Pharmacology Therapy* **28** (6) 823–826.

Kim EJ (1998) *The Effect of Physical Touch on Patients with Dementia*. Chicago: University of Illinois at Chicago, Health Sciences Center.

Lawrie I & Edwards A (2006) *Guidelines on the Use of Antidepressants in Palliative Care*. Leeds: Yorkshire Palliative Medicine Clinical Guidelines Group.

Main J, Whittle C, Treml J, Woolley J & Main A (2006) The development of an integrated care pathway for all patients with advanced life limiting illness – The Supportive Care Pathway. *Journal of Nursing Management* **14** 521–528.

Manfredi PL, Breuer B, Wallenstein S, Stegmann M, Bottomley G & Libow L (2003) Opioid treatment for agitation in patients with advanced dementia. *International Journal of Geriatric Psychiatry* **18** (8) 700–705.

Marie Curie Palliative Cure Institute Liverpool (2008) *The Liverpool Care Pathway for the Dying Patient*. Available at: http://www.mcpcil.org.uk/liverpool_care_pathway (accessed August 2009).

Martin R, Williams J, Hadjistavropoulos T, Hadjistavropoulos HD & MacLean M (2005) A qualitative investigation of seniors' and caregivers' views on pain assessment and management. *Canadian Journal of Nursing Research* **37** (2) 142–164.

Ministry of Justice (2008) *Reviewing the Mental Capacity Act 2005: Forms, supervision and fees*. London: Ministry of Justice.

Murray S, Kendall M, Boyd K & Sheikh A (2005) Illness trajectories and palliative care. *British Medical Journal* **330** 1007–1011.

National Audit Office (2007) *Improving Services and Support for People with Dementia*. London: NAO.

National Council for Palliative Care (2007) *Focus on Neurology – Addressing palliative care for people with neurological conditions*. London: NCPC.

NCPC & Alzheimer's Society (2006) *Exploring Palliative Care for People with Dementia – A discussion document*. London: NCPC and the Alzheimer's Society.

Newcomer JW & Hennekens CH (2007) Severe mental illness and risk of cardiovascular disease. *Journal of the American Medical Association* **298** (15) 1794–1796.

NHS National End of Life Care Programme (2008) *Preferred Priorities of Care* [online]. Available at: http://www. endoflifecareforadults.nhs.uk/eolc/ppc.htm (accessed June 2009).

Nygaard HA & Jarland M (2005) Are nursing home patients with dementia diagnosis at increased risk for inadequate pain treatment? *International Journal of Geriatric Psychiatry* **20** (8) 730–737.

Portenoy RK & Coyle N (1991) Controversies in the long-term management of analgesic therapy in patients with advanced cancer. *Journal of Palliative Care* **7** (2) 13–24.

Regnard C, Reynolds J, Watson B, Matthews D, Gibson L & Clarke C (2007) Understanding distress in people with severe communication difficulties: developing and assessing the Disability Distress Assessment Tool (DisDAT). *Journal of Intellectual Disability Research* **51** (4) 277–292.

Richmond C (2005) Dame Cicely Saunders. *British Medical Journal* **33** 238.

Royal College of Psychiatrists (2004) College Statement on Covert Medication. *Psychiatric Bulletin* **28** 385–386.

Scherder E, Oosterman J, Swaab D, Herr K, Ooms M, Ribbe M, Sergeant J, Pickering G & Benedetti F (2005) Recent developments in pain in dementia. *British Medical Journal* **330** (7489) 461–464.

Scott S & Pace V (2009) The first 50 patients: a brief report on the initial findings from the Palliative Care in Dementia Project. *Dementia* **8** (3) 435–441.

Staal J, Sacks A, Matheis R, Collier L, Calia T, Hanif H & Kofman ES (2007) The effects of Snoezelen (multi-sensory behavior therapy) and psychiatric care on agitation, apathy, and activities of daily living in dementia patients on a short-term geriatric psychiatric inpatient unit. *International Journal of Psychiatric Medicine* **37** (4) 357–370.

Treloar A (1998) Delirium: prevalence, prognosis and management. *Reviews in Clinical Gerontology* **8** (3) 241–249.

Treloar A (2008) Dutch research reflects problems with the Liverpool care pathway. *British Medical Journal* **336** 905.

Treloar A & Adamis D (2005) Sharing letters with patients and their carers: problems and outcomes in elderly and dementia care. *Psychiatric Bulletin* **29** (9) 330–333.

Treloar A, Beck S & Paton C (2001) Administering medications to patients with dementia and other organic cognitive syndromes. *Advances in Psychiatric Treatment* **7** 444–452.

Treloar A & Crugel M (2009) *Palliative and end-of-life care of dementia at home is feasible and rewarding: results from the Hope for Home study*. Accepted for Publication Journal of Dementia Care.

Treloar A, Crugel M & Adamis D (2009) Palliative and end of life care of dementia at home is feasible and rewarding: results from the 'Hope for Home' study. *Dementia* **8** (3) 335–347.

Treloar A, Philpot M & Beats B (2001) Concealing medication in patients' food. *Lancet* **357** 62–64.

Warden V, Hurley AC & Volicer L (2003) Development and psychometric evaluation of the Pain Assessment in Advanced Dementia (PAINAD) scale. *Journal of the American Medical Directors Association* **8** (6) 388–395.

Xie J, Brayne C & Matthews FE (2008) Survival times in people with dementia: analysis from population based cohort study with 14-year follow-up. *British Medical Journal* **10** January.